(Don't) Stop Me
If You've Heard This Before

and Other Essays on Writing Fiction

PETER TURCHI

TRINITY UNIVERSITY PRESS
San Antonio, Texas

Trinity University Press
San Antonio, Texas 78212

Copyright © 2023 by Peter Turchi

All rights reserved. No part of this book may be reproduced in any form or by any electronic or mechanical means, including information storage and retrieval systems, without permission in writing from the publisher.

Cover design by Derek Thornton / Notch Design
Book design by BookMatters
Cover art: iStock/Nastasic
Author photo by Reed Turchi

Rachel Cusk, excerpt from *Outline*. Copyright © 2014 by Rachel Cusk. Used by permission of Picador USA. All rights reserved.

E. L Doctorow, excerpts from *The March*. Copyright © 2005 by E. L. Doctorow. Used by permission of Random House, an imprint and division of Penguin Random House LLC. All rights reserved.

Toni Morrison, excerpts from *A Mercy*. Copyright © 2008 by Toni Morrison. Used by permission of Alfred A. Knopf, an imprint of the Knopf Doubleday Publishing Group, a division of Penguin Random House LLC. All rights reserved.

Katherine Anne Porter, excerpt from "Noon Wine" from *The Collected Stories of Katherine Anne Porter*. Copyright 1937 and renewed © 1965 by Katherine Anne Porter. Used by permission of HarperCollins Publishers.

ISBN 978-1-59534-976-7 paper
ISBN 978-1-59534-977-4 ebook

Trinity University Press strives to produce its books using methods and materials in an environmentally sensitive manner. We favor working with manufacturers that practice sustainable management of all natural resources, produce paper using recycled stock, and manage forests with the best possible practices for people, biodiversity, and sustainability. The press is a member of the Green Press Initiative, a nonprofit program dedicated to supporting publishers in their efforts to reduce their impacts on endangered forests, climate change, and forest-dependent communities.

The paper used in this publication meets the minimum requirements of the American National Standard for Information Sciences— Permanence of Paper for Printed Library Materials, ansi 39.48–1992.

CIP data on file at the Library of Congress
27 26 25 24 23 | 5 4 3 2 1

This book is for Laura and Reed

and for my students

CONTENTS

Introduction   1

Power Plays   7
  Toward More Dynamic Scenes

A Funny Thing Happened on the Way to the
Information Dump   26
  The Strategic Release of Information

I See What You're Saying   57
  Images and Motifs

The Roast Beef *Is* the Story   89
  Digression, Misdirection, and Asides

Don't Stand So Close to Me   123
  Narrative Distance in First-Person Fiction

Don't Stand So Close to Her, or Him, or Them, Either   158
  Narrative Distance in Third-Person Fiction

(Don't) Stop Me If You've Heard This Before   189
    Storytelling Characters

Archimedes's Lever   228
    Setting a Narrative World in Motion

Appendixes
    A. Out of the Workshop, into the Laboratory   251
    B. Annotations, or, Reading like a Writer   269
    C. Resources for Fiction Writers   283

Bibliography   289

Acknowledgments   295

Introduction

We took a keen interest in Swiftwater Rescue, after what happened at House Rock.

On day 2 of a sixteen-day trip, at the first of the notorious rapids, one of our rafts flipped, dumping three of us into the water, two of whom found themselves under the raft; another rower got smacked in the forehead with an oar, opening an impressive, bleeding wound. Once we got all of that sorted out, we took safety preparation more seriously. Which isn't to say our group wasn't already alert, attentive, and aware of the possible danger: but most of us had never rafted the Colorado through Grand Canyon before, and many of us had never been on an extended wilderness trip where we were entirely responsible for ourselves. There had been a lot to prepare for, a lot to anticipate.

Fortunately, Christian, the most experienced among us, was a calm and thorough teacher. We had all taken note of the throw bag on each raft—a bag of rope at the ready in case of an unintentional "swimmer," someone who needed help getting out of the water—and we all understood the basic concept (though that didn't prevent my brother-in-law, a very intelligent man and no stranger to back-country travel, from reacting in haste and throwing the entire bag—and so the entire rope—into the river). But after the House Rock excitement we paid close attention as Christian demonstrated: a right-handed man should stand on one end of the rope with his left foot, hold the rope firmly with his left hand, and use his right arm to throw the bag containing the rest of the rope to or past the swimmer. For most people, never mind any baseball heroics in the distant past, it's most effective, most accurate, to throw underhand.

The instruction continued: Once the swimmer grabbed hold of the rope (not the bag), he or she should roll onto their back and put the rope over their shoulder, so the act of being pulled toward the raft didn't pull their face underwater; and the person on the raft should pull the rope hand over hand, pinkie fingers toward the swimmer, as that provides the greatest strength. If the bag should fall short of the swimmer, there's a proper way to pull the rope in, a proper way to hold the bag in both hands, and a proper way to repack the rope into the bag both for speed and to make sure the rope doesn't get knotted.

All of that is too much to think about when your companion is unexpectedly dumped into cold, fast-moving water, which is exactly the point: it wasn't enough to understand the basic concept. We all needed to know in advance exactly what to do, and we had to practice, so that we would, if necessary, be ready to act.

Happily, the rest of our trip passed without any of us being put to the test. But the fact that we all had a better idea of what to do made us more confident, so made the rest of our time more enjoyable.

I DO NOT MEAN to suggest that studying the techniques and strategies of fiction writing will save your life—though writing can certainly be deeply important. And I don't mean to suggest that there is a right (or wrong) way to write any part of a story or novel. I do mean to suggest, though, that, if you take writing seriously, it isn't enough to know the general concept of any particular aspect of the work. There is value in thinking the process through, in examining every part of what we do. I have vivid memories from that Grand Canyon trip this past summer, many of which are similar to anyone else's memories of a similar trip. But that detail of pulling the rope hand over hand, pinkie fingers toward the swimmer, stands out, to me, as a reminder that it can be useful to examine even the smallest part of a process; and as a reminder that we can save time, and avoid mistakes, by learning from others who have dedicated their attention to what we're trying to do. Ideally, of course, we'll practice on our own, even make improvements. We adapt what we learn to our own abilities, needs, and interests.

In *Maps of the Imagination: The Writer as Cartographer* I considered mapmaking as a metaphor for writing, and particularly for the design of narrative. In *A Muse and a Maze: Writing as Puzzle, Mystery, and Magic* I considered particular elements of narrative as the strategic release of information, with an emphasis on what's provided to a reader, when, and what's withheld. In the essays that follow, I address specific aspects of fiction writing that have arisen in my work with developing writers—not the basic elements but the sorts of things that raise complicated challenges and provide greater opportunities. They include:

- Power dynamics. This is not only a question of characterization but a consideration of how people react and respond to one another, and how fiction can mirror the complex interactions we see in our lives.

- Exposition and other information. Although writers often worry about how it slows a story down, it can actually be used to create tension and momentum.

- Images. Poets shouldn't have all the fun. As they know, the effective use of imagery can help a piece of writing express more than it states.

- Digression. Uncontrolled, it can lead to tedium; harnessed, it can create surprise and open a reader to unanticipated possibilities.

- Narrative distance. A crucial aspect of point of view, one that often defines the work, yet one that is often insufficiently considered.

- Storytelling characters. Storytelling might be considered a particular sort of dialogue, but it can also be a dramatic event. Like us, characters tell stories for many reasons, in various ways.

- Setting a story in motion. This isn't about beginnings, exactly, but about how a carefully considered opening prepares the reader for everything to come—and allows the writer both to create expectations and to prepare for the unexpected.

I'VE USED A VARIETY of fiction to illustrate various points, and I discuss a few of the stories and novels from multiple perspectives:

the richest work benefits from that sort of attention. The writers referenced range from what used to be called the canon (Charles Dickens, Chekhov, Mark Twain) to notable voices of the late twentieth and early twenty-first centuries (Toni Morrison, Alice Munro, J. D. Salinger, E. L. Doctorow), to more contemporary writers (Jenny Erpenbeck, Adam Johnson, Mohsin Hamid, Jai Chakrabarti, Yoko Ogawa, Richard Powers, Deborah Eisenberg, Olga Tokarczuk, Rachel Cusk, Colson Whitehead). These are by no means the only writers whose work could illustrate these points. An interesting version of this book would have blank pages, so you could choose stories and novels you admire and look at them through these same lenses, and detail your own analyses. That's a book I encourage you to write, if only for yourself.

The essays are followed by three other pieces that I've been revising and adding to for years. The first contains some thoughts about effective workshops, which I hope will be helpful to any teacher, workshop participant, or group of writers meeting on their own. The second is about annotations, or a particular approach to reading like a writer that can help anyone learn more from the work they admire. Finally, I've included a list of some of the books on craft my students and I have found useful—companions for the work we do alone but not in isolation.

A question I sometimes hear—not from dedicated writers so much as from casual ones, or from readers who don't write fiction themselves—is whether examining a story or novel so closely takes the pleasure out of reading. My answer—with a new twist, after this summer—is that reading *without* looking closely is a little like floating down a river, wondering what that purplish-lined rock is, and hoping no one falls overboard. Plenty of people do just that.

But for some of us, there's a pleasure in recognizing the Bright Angel Shale, and in knowing that when the unexpected happens, we know just what to do.

Power Plays

Toward More Dynamic Scenes

When my wife and I lived in Arizona, she played in a community orchestra. Many of the people who attended the orchestra concerts were related to one of the musicians in some way, and the rest tended to be older folks. I am in no way a youngster, but as I shuffled past the frail, elderly couple seated at the end of my row one night, the sheer contrast made me feel like a teenager. I sat down and, like a teenager, began fiddling with my phone—checking email, sending texts, all the usual. The woman beside me, who might have been in her early eighties, said in a surprisingly strong voice, "Can you get the score on that?"

"Sure," I said, smiling like a minor god of technology. "Score of what?"

The woman gave me a look of something like surprise and pity. How could I be so young and virile and yet so ignorant? "Marquette-Syracuse," she said. "I'm pulling for Marquette, but Albert"—she gestured toward the man I assumed to be her husband, who was absorbed in the concert program—"says Syracuse is going to win."

I tapped my phone a few times and reported that Syracuse was up by two late in the first half. As I did, I noticed that the woman's left hand, wrinkled and discolored by liver spots, was freshly bandaged and badly bruised.

"I fell last night," she explained. "I got up in the middle of the night and tripped on the carpet, or something—I reached out for the dresser but missed, then fell on this hand. Hurt something awful." I made a vague sympathetic sound. "I was hoping it was bad enough that we couldn't fly tomorrow," she said. "We're supposed to go to Rochester, and I do *not* want to go to Rochester. I told Albert, 'Look—now we can't go.' And he was so angry with me. He gets angry. He accused me of falling on purpose."

As I was thinking of a way to ask what horror awaited them in Rochester, she continued. "He bandaged me up himself. He doesn't like for me to see the doctor." She turned toward me to say that part, and for the first time I noticed a bruise on her cheekbone. It looked older, less vivid than the bruise on her hand. At the same moment, Albert, without looking up from the program, reached over and rested his hand on his wife's knee. But "rested" isn't quite accurate. He put his hand on her knee and, spreading his thumb and forefinger, applied pressure to either side of her kneecap.

BEGINNING FICTION WRITERS USED to be—and perhaps still are—told that fiction is about conflict. Someone wants something and someone or something stands in the way. For a while, there seemed to be a proliferation of essays protesting that to discuss narrative in terms of conflict was to reduce narrative to a particularly male lens. This may be true. It might also be true that "power" is not the best word to describe the quality I want to discuss here. I considered "authority," but that conveys a certain self-awareness and agency that is not always present in the powerful, and someone can hold a position of authority without being particularly powerful (think Substitute Teacher). I considered "dominance" and "influence," but those terms seem too nebulous. One of my graduate students suggested the term "you know," as in, "When a character has, like, you know."

But "power" seems right, as does "authority" when a character is wielding same. This quality is by no means exclusively masculine, and we all know it when we feel it.

There are many forms of power, more than might be immediately apparent. Many are disguised as something else, including weakness. It's useful for writers to consider the different forms power can take, and the various ways power can be wielded, and how a narrative actively works to expose various types of power held by its characters. Why? Because when we get stuck in our attempts to develop certain characters, or when scenes or even stories begin to feel static, enabling characters to draw on their power reserves will make them more dynamic. More important, fiction that recognizes the different forms power can take more accurately mirrors the complexity of life. Anyone with a teenage son or daughter knows how quickly authority can evaporate, as when a young Stella McCartney reportedly told an interviewer that having a father who had been one of the Beatles was "embarrassing," or when a certain MacArthur recipient searched his kitchen for his car keys while his teenage daughter stood by the door saying, "Where'd you leave them, Genius?"

Power and authority are slippery, elusive, their sources sometimes hard to define.

Power is also constantly shifting. No matter what job we hold, no matter how much money we make, we're likely to find ourselves ceding authority, at some point, not just to someone wealthier or physically stronger but to a proctologist or plumber. A brilliant scholar can seem doddering in the presence of the twenty-year-old who knows how to solve his internet connection problems, and there is no end of professionals with the power to hire and fire employees but who are themselves answerable to company presidents and boards of directors, and dependent on underpaid assistants, not to mention their auto mechanics and personal trainers.

THAT ENCOUNTER AT THE orchestra concert provides a compact illustration of the shifting of power in a scene.

We have three characters, initially defined as Our Hero and Some Old Couple. The details of the dramatic context, or setting, are relatively inconsequential aside from the fact that they force our characters into close proximity—always a promising situation for drama.

As the scene begins, our hero has, or imagines he has, a certain narrowly defined superiority, based solely on the fact that he is less physically decrepit than the older couple.

Almost immediately, though, the woman scores what would be called, in wrestling, a reversal, as she is not only strong of voice but clearly more knowledgeable about March Madness than our hero.

The woman's authority is undercut somewhat when the story calls attention to her vulnerability, in the form of her injury; but because she is assertive, and doing nearly all the talking, dramatically, she retains power. She's at center stage, controlling the conversation; our hero has been relegated to listener, even been made the butt of a small joke. His assumed superiority has been exposed as pathetic, simple vanity.

Through all of this, the husband, Albert, has been inactive, dramatically neutral. But the combination of the woman's dialogue (what she says about Albert's anger, and the fact that he doesn't like her to go to doctors) and the disturbing physical evidence of the bruise on her face creates significant subtext. Albert's gesture— reaching out not as an act of love or companionship but to apply pressure to his wife's kneecap, quite possibly to silence her—suddenly makes him the most powerful figure in the scene: a dark, threatening force.

From this point, we might imagine the action unfolding in many ways. One would be for the woman to fall silent, intimidated; another would be for our hero to intervene in some way; yet another would be for the concert to begin, creating suspense, as the scene would need to continue without dialogue. All of those are promising scenarios.

WHAT ARE SOME OF the kinds and sources of power? We could start with the most primal: physical strength, which would quickly be followed by the possession of the means to do physical harm to others (bricks, bats, guns, matches, rolling pins). Also primal is sexual power, or the power of sexual attraction. A character can have power via possession of a desired object: in the film *Casablanca*, power belongs to the bearer of letters of transit that allow the holder to travel freely in the parts of Europe controlled by Germany; in *The Great Gatsby*, Tom Buchanan's power comes in large part from the fact that he has married Daisy, which is what Gatsby thinks he wants. A character can also have the power of possession of knowledge, or information. The power of enchantment can be related to or distinct from sexual attraction: think of Calypso's hold over Odysseus, and the Handsomest Drowned Man in the World's hold over the villagers in Gabriel García Márquez's short story. Intelligence or cleverness is a source of power at work in a great many folktales; wealth and control of resources are sources of power everywhere. Power can take the form of moral, emotional, or psychological dominance, and in all sorts of recognized authority, from store clerk to state senator, from classroom teacher to CEO, from parent to probation officer.

One reason power is in flux is that it is often contextual. When a policeman pulls a car over, he has authority granted by his job, supported by the law and by the pistol on his hip; when that same man calls a woman the next day and asks her to go out to dinner with him, that particular authority doesn't do him much good (see Jean Thompson's "Mercy"). When my wife taught high school English many years ago, she developed a habit of double-checking her appearance before running out to the store, as there was a good chance that at least one of her students would be bagging groceries. The authority she had worked so hard to earn in the classroom could be undercut by one dash for milk wearing sweatpants.

Thinking in broad terms of the powerful and the powerless—say, people who have a lot of money and people who don't—does not serve realistic fiction well. While a wealthy person may have access to better medical resources, he or she can still be relatively helpless when confronted with disease or a wayward child. Conversely, someone can be ill or bedridden or agoraphobic but nonetheless exert tremendous control over one or more people around them (see Ray, the wheelchair-bound father in *Billy Lynn's Long Halftime Walk*). Most of us can recall a moment when a poor person exerted some power over us, even if only enough to cause a momentary twinge of guilt. In Marisa Silver's *Mary Coin*, the title character, a migrant worker raising her children on her own, is powerful in her interactions with others despite her overall vulnerability and the near impossibility of her improving her socioeconomic status.

Power can be disguised, then, in many ways—even as its very opposite. In a key scene in Alice Munro's "Royal Beatings," Rose is physically punished by her father at the behest of her stepmother, Flo, in what we are given to understand is something of a family ritual. Flo has psychological power over her husband; she's able to get him to do something he is reluctant to do. He has obvious physical power, as well as the authority of the patriarch: in their world, it is his responsibility to discipline his child, and he hits her with his belt. But when Rose is sent to her room, presumably as further punishment, Munro exposes a darker truth: "[Rose] has passed into a state of calm, in which outrage is perceived as complete and final. In this state events and possibilities take on a lovely simplicity...She floats in curious comfort, beyond herself, beyond responsibility...in her pure superior state." For this brief period—in the aftermath following each beating, and despite her physical pain—Rose is "superior." And this is no delusion: Flo, responsible for initiating the beating, brings Rose her favorite foods, and fawns over her. Rose's role as victim is empowering.

I want to be very clear: Munro's story does not argue that to be beaten is to be powerful. Very often, to be beaten, or cheated, or betrayed confers no compensatory strength on the victim. But here, in this story, in the family Munro describes, having been beaten gives

Rose power, a moral superiority, due to the fact that her father and stepmother feel guilt about what they've done. And that's a critical point: power does not exist in a vacuum. To have a million dollars in cash is not much help if you're stranded alone in the desert without water; to be able to deadlift five hundred pounds is not much consolation if your heart is broken. In Ralph Ellison's "Battle Royal," the young Black boxers are physically strong, but that strength is no match for the power of the White businessmen who pit them against each other and humiliate them—in their world, race and class trump physical strength. In Munro's story, Rose might believe herself to be morally superior to Flo and her father no matter what they felt, but their guilt and shame are what give her power over them, temporary as that advantage might be.

THIS RAISES THE ISSUE of context, or the arena in which characters' powers are revealed or tested. Lesser fiction often suffers from one-dimensionality in this way. We see powerful people where they're powerful, weak people where they're weak. But interesting things tend to happen when characters are removed from the places where their power is most potent, like those boxers in "Battle Royal," or when the exercise of their power is directly linked to a weakness, as when Flo has Rose beaten only to feel immediate remorse. Once Toto pulls back the curtain concealing him, the Wizard of Oz is just another white-haired man with a hot air balloon.

Beginning writers' stories are often highly dramatic, heavy on plot and action. They also tend to focus on what we might call yes/no conflicts. This is the kind of story focused purely on someone who wants something and someone else who doesn't want him to have it. Stories of direct opposition. Often, instead of exploring characters or a situation, the writers of such stories hope high-stakes action will carry the day: hence violence. And who can blame those young writers, given that most of the fiction they know comes in the form of popular film and television, which favors dramatic confrontations between similar or complementary powers.

We see a simple illustration of those types of confrontations in sports. Two hitters engaged in a home-run-hitting contest are using similar powers. A pitcher and a hitter are using complementary powers. These kinds of conflicts are particularly common in action and adventure stories. In *The Princess Bride*, the Man in Black has to win a swordfight against Inigo Montoya, the master fencer, then he has to defeat the giant, Fezzik, using only his strength, and finally he has to beat the clever Vizzini in a battle of wits. It might seem obvious that the swordfighter who can beat the master fencer could just slice up Vizzini, but that's not how this game is played: all the conflicts are carried out using similar powers. In contrast, a typical superhero film might feature complementary powers: the villain of the day has a stockpile of Kryptonite, so he can hold Superman off—that sort of thing.

To encourage students to create stories that recognize dissimilar powers, I give them a simple exercise: write a scene with three characters in one room. At some point during the scene each character has to have authority over the other two. The power or authority that the characters assume cannot be physical—no guns or fighting. I even discourage violent arguments. No yelling. The final caveat: the characters must have different sources of power. They can't, for instance, each have information that the other two want.

The assignment has two common results. The writers invariably learn something new about their characters, just through the rotation of authority. And the scenes they revise in this way are nearly always the most dynamic scenes in their stories.

THE IDEA FOR THAT assignment came from Ernest Hemingway's "The Short Happy Life of Francis Macomber." In that story, Francis Macomber and his wife, Margot, are on safari in Africa, guided by the hunter Robert Wilson. While there are also Native helpers hired by Wilson, and a particularly thoughtful lion, Francis, Margot, and Wilson are our main characters. In terms of the safari, Wilson clearly holds the greatest power, as he is an experienced hunter and guide. He knows the country, he knows the tendencies of the animals they're hunting, and he is responsible both for his American clients and for the Natives who work for him. He speaks and acts with authority. In terms of the safari, Francis is the second most powerful, as he's paying for the trip, he's hunting, and he's a decent shot. Margot, along for the adventure, is not hunting, and Wilson doesn't bother to include her when he instructs Francis on how to kill the animals.

So that's one of the story's tiers of power: involvement in and mastery of hunting. No matter what you or I might think about shooting animals for sport, in the world of this story, knowing about hunting and being able to hunt well mean something. Wilson's power is contextual: in these circumstances, he has the greatest authority. If the three of them were, instead, playing tennis, Francis, the racquet sport champion, would have the most authority; if they were on a photo shoot, Margot, a professional model paid to endorse various products, would have the most authority. But the story takes place in Wilson's world: on the hunt.

Like many good stories, "The Short Happy Life" draws our attention to more than one tier of power. One of the others we might call sex appeal. In this realm, Margot is most powerful. Francis Macomber married her for her beauty, and Wilson admires her, in the way Hemingway's men admire women: "This was a very attractive one," he says. Margot's power arises from the fact that both men find her desirable, and she knows it. She also knows that although Francis is wealthy, he isn't good enough with women to trade up. If that sounds unromantic, well, the story isn't about love. In this story, sexual appeal is a kind of currency, albeit one with an expiration date.

A third tier of power in the story is one we might call honor. For much of the story honor is closely aligned with being a good hunter. There are other factors too, though: being afraid of a wild animal is not necessarily dishonorable, but being a coward is. Talking openly about your feelings can also be dishonorable. Because the story's honor code seems to be defined by Wilson, at the outset he is most powerful in this category. The cards seem stacked in his favor.

When Macomber, his wife, and Wilson set off on safari, Wilson ranked highest in hunting and honor, Margot in sex appeal—but those facts weren't consequential, because no pressure had yet been placed on the characters. If we imagine, for a moment, Francis and Margot going on safari with Wilson, Francis shooting his big five, the entire trip unfolding with no more drama than the usual exotic vacation, the fact that the characters were unequal in power or authority would be inconsequential. After all, Wilson, the guide, is *supposed* to be the best hunter. Margot, the former model, is *supposed* to be most sexually attractive. Characters can be unequal in power without any tension arising. If, for instance, a highway patrolman pulls a car over and gives the driver a ticket for speeding, power is exercised, but there is no surprise, no challenge. If, however, the driver resists the officer, or says that he's a local celebrity, or offers the officer a bribe, or if the highway patrolman tells the driver he'll tear up the ticket if the driver will take a suitcase to a nearby gas station for him, things get more interesting.

The writer's challenge, then, is to create a situation that destabilizes the characters in such a way that their powers—their potential strengths and weaknesses—can be exposed. If we were going to make a not particularly interesting Hollywood film based on Hemingway's characters, we might get them out into the wild and then have something endanger Wilson and his men, so that Margot and Francis would need to rise to the occasion or lose their lives. But that's a recipe for an adventure story. Hemingway does something similar but significantly different: he has something happen to Francis, something that reveals character.

When the story opens, one significant action has already occurred; the characters are under pressure. Wilson, Francis, Margot, and the rest of the hunting party have just returned to camp after a lion hunt, which has gone badly. While we don't immediately learn what happened, the tension is evident, and we're told Francis "had just shown himself, very publicly, to be a coward." Margot goes into her tent; the two men sit and drink. Then something curious happens, the importance of which isn't immediately evident. Wilson sees that the Native servants "all knew about it"—whatever happened on the hunt—and he snaps at one of the boys in Swahili.

"What were you telling him?" Macomber asked.

"Nothing. Told him to look alive or I'd see he got about fifteen of the best."

"What's that? Lashes?"

"It's quite illegal," Wilson said. "You're supposed to fine them."

We may not recognize it yet, but a chink in Wilson's armor has been exposed: his code of conduct is at variance with the law. Nothing more is made of that in the scene, but it prepares us for a more important moment that will come much later.

Then Macomber surprises Wilson. First, Francis apologizes for his poor behavior on the lion hunt. Then he says, "Maybe I can fix it up on buffalo." Francis is climbing his way back up on the tier of honor.

If this story were about hunting, which it is not, especially, or if it were merely a kind of coming-of-age story, which it is, partly, it would be enough to have Francis go out on a hunt, fail, then give it another shot and succeed. But Margot's presence—or rather, her active presence—changes everything. She returns from her tent no longer on the verge of tears.

"I've dropped the whole thing," she said, sitting down at the table.
"What importance is there to whether Francis is any good at killing lions? That's not his trade. That's Mr. Wilson's trade. Mr. Wilson is really very impressive killing anything. You do kill anything, don't you?"

In reply, Wilson thinks: "[American women] are the hardest in the world; the hardest, the cruelest, the most predatory and the most attractive."

Margot says she'll join them for the buffalo hunt: "I wouldn't miss something like today for anything." Her antagonism not only raises the stakes; it changes them. We understand how when finally, in a long flashback, we see the disastrous lion hunt from that morning. Francis shoots a lion in the gut, he suggests abandoning the wounded animal—a serious breach of a hunter's code of conduct—and, when they go into the tall grass to kill it, he runs in fear. Then, after Wilson kills the lion, Margot "reached forward and put her hand on Wilson's shoulder. He turned and she had leaned over the low seat and kissed him on the mouth. 'Oh, I say,' said Wilson, going redder than his natural baked color."

Here in Hemingway's animal kingdom, the female quickly transfers her attention to the stronger male. Up to this point, Francis's and Margot's strengths and weaknesses have balanced so that, Hemingway tells us, "they were known as a comparatively happily married couple…They had a sound basis for union. Margot was too beautiful for Macomber to divorce her and Macomber had too much money for Margot ever to leave him." Macomber reflects on all of this in his tent, unable to sleep—and realizes that the other cot is empty. When Margot returns, she says she was "out to get a breath of air." Francis grows furious, but Margot, all but purring, goes to sleep.

This scene is played almost comically, which is both entertaining and strategic. In the same way that the story is not about hunting, it is not primarily about a woman cheating on her husband. We can imagine Francis and Margot arguing late into the night, detailing each other's shortcomings, but the scene has another purpose. Something has to happen to turn cowardly Macomber into the man who will stand his ground against a buffalo. Because Margot is all sweetness and malice, drifting off to sleep, Francis has no one to argue with, no way to vent. He is left to simmer on his cot. When dawn comes, he directs his fury at Wilson: "Of all the many men he had hated, he hated Robert Wilson the most." Seething, Macomber says, "You're sure you wouldn't like to stay in camp with her yourself and let me go out and hunt buffalo?"

The tension increases through suppression: no one actually yells, no one punches anyone. A shared belief in decorum acts like the lid on a pot of boiling water, refusing to let pressure escape. Margot turns up the heat:

"If you make a scene I'll leave you, darling," Margot said quietly.

"No you won't."

"You can try it and see."

"You won't leave me."

"No," she said, "I won't leave you and you'll behave yourself."

"Behave myself. That's a way to talk. Behave myself."

"Yes. Behave yourself."

"Why don't *you* try behaving."

"I've tried it so long. So very long."

"I hate that red-faced swine," Macomber said. "I loathe the sight of him."

"He's really *very* nice."

"Oh, *shut up*," Macomber almost shouted.

That "almost" is key—Macomber is about to erupt, but instead the car pulls up, the gun bearers get out, and they all head off to hunt buffalo. Francis is "grim and furious," Margot is smiling, Wilson is hoping Macomber "doesn't take a notion to blow the back of [his] head off"—a bit of foreshadowing.

Out on the hunt, Wilson spots three old bull buffalo and instructs the driver to cut them off before they reach a swamp, which
involves a jarring ride across open country. Wilson and Macomber
both shoot well and are elated. Back in the car, Margot has gone
pale—possibly because of the fast, bumpy ride, possibly because she
slept with Wilson confident that wealthy Francis couldn't divorce
her. Now he appears fearless, and Margot realizes she may have
misplayed her hand. Her power over her husband is evaporating. In
the same way that Francis's anger at Margot turned first into anger
at Wilson, then into something like bravery on the hunt, Margot's
queasiness leads her to speak:

> "I didn't know you were allowed to shoot them from cars."
>
> "No one shot from cars," Wilson said coldly.
>
> "I mean chase them from cars."
>
> "Wouldn't ordinarily," Wilson says. "Seemed sporting enough…while
> we were doing it…Wouldn't mention it to anyone though. It's illegal
> if that's what you mean."

Margot, always eager to press her advantage, says, "What would
happen if they heard about it in Nairobi?" "I'd lose my license for
one thing," Wilson replies. "Other unpleasantness. I'd be out of
business." In response, Francis smiles "for the first time all day" and
says, "Now she has something on you."

For a brief moment, Wilson finds himself on the bottom of the
pile of this miserable little trio. Francis has proven his courage and
skill, and Margot has let Wilson know that she can cause him both
professional trouble and dishonor by reporting what just happened.

But once again, before the story can pursue that threat directly, before the pressure can be released, the narrative takes a turn.

Hemingway creates an explicit parallel to the lion-hunting fiasco: we're told that one of the big buffalo was only wounded. This time Francis embraces the challenge. He takes his place, the buffalo charges, and Francis holds his ground, fearless—at least, until his head explodes. Still sitting in the car, Margot has taken up one of the guns and shot. The story leaves open the question of whether she was trying to shoot the buffalo to save her husband or whether she saw the opportunity to "accidentally" kill him, but Wilson expresses no doubt: "He would have left you, too," Wilson tells her. And although he tells his men to record the details of the "accident," while it's clear he is not going to turn Margot in for murder, by asserting his understanding of her possible motivation and then protecting her, he has gained the upper hand.

At the end of the story, then, Francis is honorable, courageous, but dead; Margot has spent what power she has over Wilson, and lost honor; and Wilson is left with admiration for Francis and power over Margot.

Stories like this one remind us that to have power over someone else is to have the *potential* to act, as in the way Margot could report Wilson for hunting from the car, and the way Wilson could tell the authorities she shot her husband intentionally, and in the way Francis could leave his wife. They also remind us that to expend power is, often, to lose it. In "Royal Beatings," once Flo persuades her husband to beat Rose, and he does it, they have spent their power over her; once Rose yields to temptation and eats the food that Flo brings by way of apology, she loses the power of the moral high ground. When Margot threatens to leave Francis, he's scared; when she cheats on him, he decides he has nothing more to lose. Similarly, when Margot makes clear that she understands Wilson has illegally hunted from the car, he has something to fear; but when she kills her husband, she is vulnerable again.

Hemingway's story is dynamic not because it's full of action—animals and people being killed, a wife cheating on her husband—but because the ways in which the three characters are revealed and judged change, and no one's position in the hierarchy goes unchallenged. At the end, even Wilson has been sullied by the exposure of his ethical weaknesses.

IT'S WORTH POINTING OUT that the crucial scenes in "Royal Beatings" and "The Short Happy Life of Frances Macomber" feature three active characters. Two characters in opposition can be in only three positions: they can be equal, the first character can have the advantage, or the second can have the advantage. Three characters multiply the possibilities, especially when different kinds of power are involved.

I realize the stories I've discussed here feature dramatic violence—a young girl is abused and beaten, animals are hunted for sport, a man has his head blown off. All unpleasant. So I should reassure you that the woman I sat next to at that concert seemed to be doing just fine.

What actually happened was this: after the man put his hand on her knee, the woman used her good right hand to slap his. "Stop it," she said. "You *were* angry." And then: "That's our Jimmy playing cello. His real instrument is oboe, but he plays cello for fun." The woman went on to say that she didn't like to go to Phoenix Symphony concerts because she couldn't see well; that she didn't live in or go to school at Marquette but always rooted for the Big East; and that she had met Albert when, as a researcher at Bell Labs, he had been her summer intern "and we had a little fling, because that's what you did with your interns. Fifty years later, I guess I'm stuck with him."

The narrative I had imagined turned out not to be true—but several new possibilities had been revealed. And if my telling of the tale here seems manipulative, let that be a reminder of another power play: the power of the storyteller, always arranging information to suit his own ends.

A Funny Thing Happened on the Way to the Information Dump

The Strategic Release of Information

About halfway through the semester, I noticed something strange about the fiction my undergraduates were writing. I had noticed a similar tendency with previous students but hadn't thought much about it. This time, I just asked them.

We had read stories and novel excerpts, old anthology chestnuts by the usual suspects, contemporary work, all sorts of things. These were good students: ordinary-looking stories, strange-looking stories, they were game. And when I had them do exercises, things were fine. (Of course, their exercises were full of time travelers and warlords and identical twins with inexplicable powers, but that's a different discussion.) When they had free rein, though—when they got to submit a complete story of their own, with no constraints— not one of the drafts included an entire page without dialogue. Not even close. There were no extended expository passages, no descriptive passages, there was no extended narration. These stories were all scene—in fact, in many cases, they were almost entirely dialogue. Several could have passed as radio plays.

"What's the deal?" I finally asked them. "Every published story we've read has narration, often entire paragraphs of narration, and exposition. In your stories, it's all talk-talk-talk; no one stops to take a breath."

"That's just it," they said. "We don't want to be boring."

"Boring?" I said. "I can't tell if this conversation is taking place in a motel room or a submarine. Would it hurt to slow down long enough to establish the setting?"

They shook their heads sadly. They had a very disconcerting habit of acting as one.

And that's when they gave name to the evil they feared: an "information dump."

I told this to my graduate students, a particularly accomplished bunch, and they laughed and did a thing with their shoulders that meant: *undergraduates*.

But as we talked, they confessed that they, too, were wary of extended stretches of backstory, exposition, and narration—anything that smacked of *telling*. One of them said, "I mean, I don't want to be all *blah blah blah*." Most *tellingly*, they all agreed that it's imperative to minimize those narrative elements, to make sure they don't slow down "the story"—which, apparently, needs but doesn't really include information. They were, without saying as much, defining a story or novel entirely by its actions and events. Anything else was a necessary evil, and to be minimized.

I told them that back in one of my first graduate workshops at the University of Arizona, one of my classmates was struggling with a scene, a conversation at a restaurant, where he was trying to convey necessary information about his main character's past. It felt awkward to do this in dialogue, he said.

We were full of advice. We suggested he move his characters outside, to the patio, and at a convenient moment have a truck pass by—a truck painted with the words, "Talk about your mother." A few minutes later a plane could fly overhead, pulling a banner that said, "How'd you lose your job?"

My students laughed—they tolerate me. Then one of them said, "I want my stories to start like *Mission: Impossible*—like, 'Listen up, people!'"

He might have meant he wants his stories to have a memorable theme song; but I suspect he was referring to an arresting device the creators of that television show used to address a challenge of its premise. The challenge: in each show, information had to be conveyed regarding the nature and people involved in the next "impossible" mission both to the characters—or at least the group's leader, Mr. Phelps—and to the audience. The device: a manila envelope containing photographs and a self-destructing audiotape. The information could be heard once, and only once; that alone made it seem both essential and urgent.

We can find roots of that opening gambit in Arthur Conan Doyle's Sherlock Holmes stories. In the typical Holmes story, the detective and Dr. Watson are talking or puttering around 221B Baker Street when a visitor—that is to say, an information delivery device—arrives. In the scene that follows, the information provided by the visitor is animated by conversation and, famously, by Holmes's surprising deductions—from a glance at a woman's shoe, he knows she once dated a Scottish Anglican with a lisp.

There are some essential differences between a detective story and the stories most of us write that make our job if not more challenging, differently challenging. The most consequential difference is that the information we relay is not necessarily essential to plot; while it can be, the information in our stories and novels might also be related to character or setting or atmosphere, or even to theme or meaning. That is to say, the information might be necessary but not dramatic. So one question is how to animate it. Another is how to get the reader not just to read that information more or less patiently but to actually take interest.

I want to consider both of those questions, and I want to consider how the arrangement of information can transform a story, can play a crucial role in declaring or determining its nature, can even create opportunities for the writer. Then, as if on a dare, we will wade directly into the dreaded Information Dump.

A STANDARD PIECE OF advice for engaging a reader's attention in a story or novel is to start in scene. This advice is often given to first-time novelists who, concerned about introducing the world of his or her novel and the circumstances of its main characters, began the first draft with a dozen or so pages of turgid exposition. But even if a novel starts in scene, that contextual information has to be provided somewhere, somehow. So it's not unusual to see a second draft of a novel that begins in scene, only to continue with a dozen or so pages of turgid exposition. This mistake is perfectly understandable, even if it misses the point of the original advice. "When," the novelist might ask, "do I explain the hardships of living in nineteenth-century Nebraska? When do I get to tell the reader about my main character's tragic childhood? And what about her beloved grandfather, the clock-maker?"

As important as when to do this is how to do it.

A Sense of Purpose: Selection, Progression, and the Arc of Tension, or, You Need to Know This, and You Need to Know It Now

Colson Whitehead's *The Underground Railroad* offers a variation on a tragically familiar story: a young enslaved woman on a cotton plantation finds conditions so unendurable that she is willing to risk her life to run away. She's threatened by bounty hunters and by racists of all types; she finds assistance through a network of formerly enslaved people, free men and women, abolitionists, and other sympathizers. The original twists to the premise include the fact that the underground railroad in the novel is an actual subterranean railway; and the journey of Cora, the main character, is as much a journey through the history of slavery and oppression in this country as it is a geographical journey.

In the novel's opening chapter, Whitehead wants to establish his main character's situation, the context of her actions, and the novel's larger concerns. Like traditional biographies, and like novels of an earlier era, Whitehead's novel starts with his focal character's origins—in this case, that means beginning with her grandmother:

> Cora's grandmother had never seen the ocean before that bright afternoon in the port of Ouidah and the water dazzled after her time in the fort's dungeon. The dungeon stored them until the ships arrived. Dahomeyan raiders kidnapped the men first, then returned to her village the next moon for the women and children, marching them in chains to the sea two by two.

This encapsulated biography of Cora's grandmother, Ajarry, goes on for five pages, covering nearly her entire life, without a single word of dialogue. By my undergraduates' definition, it is an information dump. So how does Whitehead energize that information, and turn it into a compelling opening for his novel?

It helps that the information he wants to convey—Cora's grandmother's life story—takes the form of a dramatic narrative: we learn that her mother died when she was young, that her father died on the forced march to the slave ship, and that she was sold many times. Whitehead uses chronology, the biographer's friend; but within that temporal progression, he organizes the story of her life in three ways: by the times she's sold, the men she's married, and the children she's borne. He initially conveys Ajarry's story as a series of transactions, telling us who she's sold by, and to whom, and how her price changes. When she finally reaches Georgia, we're told she "took a husband three times," and the three husbands are described briefly, in sequence. Then we're told she bore five children, and a paragraph is devoted to them and their fates, ending with Cora's mother. Finally we read about Ajarry's death, and Whitehead summarizes her life in a way that suggests the novel's interests for the story to come: "Since the night she was kidnapped she had been appraised and reappraised, each day waking upon the pan of a new scale. Know your value and you know your place in the order. To escape the boundary of the plantation was to escape the fundamental principles of your existence: impossible."

("Waking upon the pan of a new scale" is a surprising metaphor, and it also suggests a pun: we might understandably think "pain of a new scale," and that's true, too. The phrase is also a reminder that one key to doing whatever you want in a story or novel is to write well.)

Chronology itself—the mere sequence of events that E. M. Forster called "story"—has limited inherent tension. "I woke up, I got dressed, I walked the dog, I came back in and made coffee." Whitehead doesn't rely on that to hold our interest. Instead, he omits much of Cora's grandmother's life, focusing on the elements that establish the novel's concerns: her history as a commodity, her married life, her children. (These last two are developed in the novel as the commitment of lovers, tests of those commitments, and the desire for family.) Each of those is presented in the form of an illustrated list, and in the cases of her husbands and children, Whitehead tells us how many there were, then offers specifics. It's a little like casting a line and reeling it in. "She took a husband three times," the narrator tells us, jumping ahead; then he steps back and tells us something notable about each man. It may seem like a small thing, but the emphasis on those lists creates expectation and, when we reach the end of each one, satisfaction. As readers, we understand that the narrator is purposeful, so he gains authority.

Cora's grandmother's life story is told in a way meant to lead us to a conclusion, and to make that conclusion persuasive: in her eyes, based on her experience, escape from slavery is impossible. Our understanding of that sense of futility and its sources are crucial to our appreciation of what follows.

Whitehead does two other things in those first five and a half pages that keep the information he needs to give us from feeling purely expository: he focuses on moments of Ajarry's life with the intensity and immediacy of scene, and while he maintains an omniscient third-person narration, he simultaneously moves us close to her thoughts, creating an intimacy with the character.

If you've read *The Great Gatsby* and found yourself thinking about one of its remarkable scenes—say, the one where Gatsby shows Daisy all of his beautiful shirts—and you've gone back to look at it and realized that the "scene" is really just a paragraph, you've recognized the power of scenic narration. An even better example is *One Hundred Years of Solitude*, a novel full of moments rendered so vividly that we remember them as if they were scenes—but in fact, they're rarely more than a few sentences. Like scene, this sort of narration focuses on a specific moment with vivid detail, but it's more concentrated, and often means for the moment to illustrate something larger. There are several examples in the opening chapter of *Underground Railroad*. We're told Ajarry was "sold a few times on the trek [from her village] to the fort"—a summary—but then we get this description of her journey to the boat that will take her from Africa to the United States:

> The *Nanny* was out of Liverpool and had made two previous stops along the Gold Coast. The captain staggered his purchases, rather than find himself with a cargo of singular culture and disposition. Who knew what brand of mutiny his captives might cook up if they shared a common tongue. This was the ship's final port of call before they crossed the Atlantic. Two yellow-haired sailors rowed Ajarry out to the ship, humming. White skin like bone. The noxious air of the hold, the gloom of confinement, and the screams of those shackled to her contrived to drive Ajarry to madness.

The narration shifts to the captain's thoughts, then to a precise moment—Ajarry's first view of white skin—before accelerating through time again.

Whitehead's omniscient narrator speaks to us directly, sometimes telling us things Ajarry can't possibly know, but he also slips into her point of view:

> When you are sold that many times, the world is teaching you to pay attention. She learned to quickly adjust to the new plantations, sorting the nigger breakers from the merely cruel, the layabouts from the hardworking, the informers from the secret-keepers… She knew that the white man's scientists peered beneath things to understand how they worked. The movement of stars across the night, the cooperation of humors in the blood… Ajarry made a science of her own black body and accumulated observations.

In addition to creating the foundation *content* for the story he means to tell, Whitehead is establishing his method for the novel as a whole. While Cora is the book's main character, the novel is highly populated, and Whitehead wants to be able to slip into the perspectives of a great many characters, briefly, just as he does here. By starting not with Cora but with someone who plays a more limited role, he essentially tells us: You're coming along with me, the narrator—not her. Get used to it.

But focusing on Cora's grandmother also poses a problem: If Whitehead simply began the novel with Ajarry's story, which ends in five and a half pages, he'd essentially be starting over again in the next chapter. One of the goals of the opening of a story or novel is to create momentum, to establish one or more engines that will drive the narrative forward. It's a little like pushing a car—once you get it rolling, you don't want the driver to hit the brakes. So Whitehead employs a strategy something like that self-destructing tape in *Mission: Impossible*. But he takes the device a step further: he creates an arc of tension that will span the entire chapter.

The first line of the novel is this: "The first time Caesar approached Cora about running north, she said no." The virtues of that opening line are several: It immediately introduces two characters and a conflict between them; it creates anticipation (we feel certain Caesar approaches Cora a second time, and possibly a third and fourth); and it suggests dramatic urgency—even before we know Caesar and Cora are enslaved, the verb "running" suggests escape, or transgression. (Think how much weaker, more passive, that sentence would be if it read, "The first time Caesar asked Cora to go north with him, she said no." It's not a horrible sentence, but it stands straight up; it's a car stuck in idle. Whitehead's version immediately creates forward movement.)

The second sentence is: "This was her grandmother talking." That sentence is intentionally jarring, even cryptic; it raises the question "How so?" Whitehead could provide the answer in a brief sentence; but by refusing to, he creates a minor mystery, and so a second arc of tension. What follows is the five-page biography of Cora's grandmother. After describing Ajarry's death, Whitehead ends the chapter by returning to those arcs of tension: "It was her grandmother talking that Sunday evening when Caesar approached Cora about the underground railroad, and she said no. Three weeks later she said yes. This time it was her mother talking." Whitehead reiterates the second sentence of the chapter, and now we understand: Ajarry, the African girl captured and enslaved, survived by believing, "Know your value and you know your place in the order. To escape the boundary of the plantation was to escape the fundamental principles of your existence: impossible." To some extent, that belief lives on in Cora, influences her.

When Whitehead tells us, "Three weeks later [Cora] said yes," he has deftly returned us to the present action—the game is afoot.

By telling us "This time it was her mother talking," he prepares us for another chunk of exposition; the attentive reader is prepared to turn the page to chapter 2 and read a similar biography of Cora's mother. But having established that expectation, Whitehead knows better than to satisfy it—not right away, at least.

IF A STORY OR novel you're writing begins by providing the reader pages of background information, or if it very quickly shifts to a long flashback, and it's not working, there's a good chance someone with your best interest in mind will tell you, Cut it. By which that person means: Start with scene, and continue with scene. Just slip the necessary information in, like the medicine in a spoonful of sugar. And that person might be right—but one can rely on scene to a fault. The opening of Whitehead's novel is one example of how necessary information can be made dynamic.

Tom Sawyer, Deprivation, and Making the Reader Want It

Sometimes we're so worried that the reader might be impatient with information we feel is necessary that we can forget one of our options, which is to make the reader eager for what we have to say. This is a little like Tom Sawyer's dilemma with that fence that needed to be whitewashed: he didn't want to do it, he knew no one else would want to do it—so he made it seem as if whitewashing a fence was just about the most fascinating thing in the world.

Toni Morrison's short novel *A Mercy*, which predates Whitehead's *Underground Railroad*, is also about the effects of and responses to slavery in this country; more specifically, it, too, is framed by the story of a young woman who feels betrayed and abandoned by her mother. In *Underground Railroad*, Cora believes that her

mother ran from the plantation where they lived to escape to freedom on her own. In *A Mercy*, Florens believes her mother coldly
offered her to an Anglo-Dutch trader, to repay her master's debt. At
the very end of both novels, we learn that the belief and attendant
resentment of both characters was the result of misunderstanding:
Cora's mother was exploring a path to freedom for both of them
when she was bitten by a deadly snake, and Florens's mother gave
her away because she believed, correctly, that the Dutch trader was
a kinder man than her current master, that her daughter would have
a chance for a better life if she sent her off. In other words, both
mothers made sacrifices, suffering in order to do what they thought
would be best for their daughters. The daughters never know this.
Whitehead and Morrison both suggest, then, that having partial
information not only limits but can dramatically distort our understanding of the past, as well as our understanding of other people,
even those closest to us. In these novels, they mean to give us, their
readers, access to the larger vision their characters lack.

Despite these similarities in theme and content, the books are
quite different. While Whitehead's narrator seems intent on giving
us information, on explaining things, Morrison seems intent on
withholding information, or restricting it. Her novel begins with
a deliberately disorienting monologue, one that makes any number
of unexplained assumptions: "Don't be afraid. My telling can't hurt
you in spite of what I have done and I promise to lie quietly in
the dark—weeping perhaps or occasionally seeing the blood once
more—but I will never again unfold my arms to rise up and bare
teeth." We understand that someone is addressing someone else,
and that the speaker assumes the intended audience has certain expectations. "Don't be afraid" implies that the listener might reason-

ably feel fear. "My telling can't hurt you despite what I have done" implies that the speaker has done dangerous, even harmful deeds, deeds we soon learn involved blood and bared teeth. "I promise to lie quietly...weeping perhaps" suggests that the listener might have reason to distrust the speaker—thus the promise—and that the speaker feels either remorse or loss. These opening lines create tension and expectation, but the dramatic context is unclear; the emphasis is on mood and emotion.

The bad writing workshop we all like to talk about—the one that does all the worst things we've seen or heard or imagined done in workshops—would be eager to tell Toni Morrison that her opening is confusing, that readers will be frustrated, that the editor who visited last week said your novel needs a clear hook, and while this is dramatic, sure, it's also kind of a mess, that is to say, unclear. Inevitably, someone in that bad workshop would ask, "Does anyone else want to know, like, who's talking? To whom? And what she's talking about?"

Of course we do; and Morrison is making use of our desire for that information. In the text, she gives the reader hope. The next line is promising—"I explain"—but our desire for explanation, for answers, is frustrated:

> I explain. You can think what I tell you a confession, if you like,
> but one full of curiosities familiar only in dreams and during those
> moments when a dog's profile plays in the steam of a kettle. Or when
> a corn-husk doll sitting on a shelf is soon splaying in the corner of
> a room and the wicked of how it got there is plain. Stranger things
> happen all the time anywhere. You know. I know you know. One
> question is who is responsible? Another is can you read?

We might find the speaker's promise to explain reassuring, even though not much is explained, for the same reason that "I know" and "I know you know" are both mystifying and reassuring: this speaker is aware of her audience, is trying to communicate something urgent, and we have faith—or at least, we have reason to hope—that this awareness and desire will ultimately lead to clarity. But before we get to that, we have the puzzle of a dog's profile in the steam of a kettle and the wickedness of the movement of a doll.

And here we see the author beginning to give us clues not quite despite but through the speaker. The "corn-husk doll" is a concrete detail that begins to suggest time and place. That detail is quickly followed by a perhaps surprising answer to the question "Can you read?" The speaker continues,

> If a pea hen refuses to brood I read it quickly and, sure enough, that night I see a minha mae standing hand in hand with her little boy, my shoes jamming the pocket of her apron. Other signs need more time to understand. Often there are too many signs, or a bright omen louds up too fast. I sort them and try to recall, yet I know I am missing much, like not reading the garden snake crawling up the door saddle to die. Let me start with what I know for certain.

That ends the first paragraph. While much is uncertain, explanations have begun. Our speaker reads signs. Things like the shape of steam from a kettle, a pea hen failing to brood, and the position of a dead garden snake have meaning for her—which is to say, she is constantly reading and interpreting the world according to a particular set of beliefs that are, most likely, different from our own. By emphasizing this in the first paragraph of her novel, Morrison is telling us how we will need to read this book. Some things will be clear—after all, we can read. But some signs "need more time to understand. Often there [will be] too many...[and we will suspect we are] missing much." In that way, as patient readers of fiction accustomed to the ways fiction makes sense, we are like the still-unnamed character who is speaking. And so despite all of our uncertainty, we feel a bond, a connection to that speaker.

A few sentences later we learn that the speaker's name is Florens and that the year is 1690. This basic information—identification of the character and setting—comes as a relief; but the withholding is key to the novel's strategy. If the book were to begin by telling us that the year is 1690, some of us would immediately feel a different sort of distance and be conscious of a particular kind of remoteness. We might lean back, figuratively speaking. As the beginning is written, we feel a different sort of remoteness, combined with intimacy: someone is trying to tell us something desperately important. Her urgency and the sense of danger draw us forward, collapsing the centuries between her and us—we lean in, wanting to hear more.

As anyone who has tried it knows, simply withholding information is no guarantee that the reader will continue patiently, or eagerly. Morrison uses the same basic strategy in *A Mercy* that she uses in other books: she engages the reader through a combination of mystery and clarity. Often she uses concrete details of setting, character, or scene to ground us, then slowly releases contextualizing information. This is yet another reminder that precision is necessary to effective mystery. Morrison's characters are often on a journey of understanding. Her novels are a journey of understanding for the reader, too, as she carefully controls what we see, and when, and how we perceive it.

A Mercy has a very simple plot: Florens is asked to summon a free African blacksmith her ailing mistress believes can heal her. But while the story of that journey and its result serves as a dramatic framework, Morrison is more interested in revealing and considering the plantation where Florens lives with an unlikely group: the Anglo-Dutch trader; his mail-order wife, who has escaped religious intolerance in England; a Native American woman whose tribe was nearly eradicated by smallpox; a girl born and raised at sea; and two gay men. The novel is largely discursive, drawing us into these characters' lives and perceptions; and in that way it is largely reliant on information. The challenge for Morrison is to engage the reader, to make us desire what she wants to give us. She uses dramatic contexts to keep the narrative leaning forward, and in this opening chapter, from Florens's point of view, she relies heavily on the carefully calibrated release of information to create tension and release from sentence to sentence, paragraph to paragraph. (The next section, which is in the third person but closely identified with the Dutch trader, is much more straightforward in its delivery of information.)

While I'm going to guess Toni Morrison didn't spend a lot of time with an Xbox controller in her hands, you could compare this narrative strategy to the strategy of many video games: it begins by placing us in a very narrowly confined space, without additional information or instructions. In order to understand what's going on, we need to explore, to consider the implications of the few things we can see. The writer's job, like the video game creator's, is to find the most effective balance of helpful information and provocative mystery.

E. L. Doctorow famously said that to write a novel you need to be able to see only what's just ahead, in the same way that you can drive across the country in the dark, only able to see what's illuminated by your headlights. A novel like *A Mercy* reminds us how little the reader needs to understand at any moment in order to be drawn forward. By the time clarifying information is offered, the reader is hungry for it.

Engineering, Reverse; and Deviation

When it comes to providing contextualizing information, Whitehead's and Morrison's opening chapters—one offering five pages of backstory, the other creating deliberate uncertainty—represent the range of the spectrum. The majority of drafts I see employ something akin to Whitehead's approach—they are eager to provide information, eager to be friendly to the reader. And there's nothing necessarily wrong with that. But if that's your default mode—if you tend to employ service-oriented narrators, narrators who aim to please—I encourage you to at least consider being a little more scheming, even a little devious. Mischievous. Yes, it's true, that means more work for the reader, and more work for you. But despite what we tell ourselves, readers—good readers, anyway, the kind we want—*like* to work. They like to be involved. And if you dislike the connotations attached to the words I'm using—"scheming," "devious"—and by "devious" I don't mean "unscrupulous," of course, but the other meaning, "indirect, deviating from the straightforward," like this sentence, but if you still don't like those words—I encourage you to be more strategic in giving your reader information—not to frustrate or annoy her but to enchant and delight her, and to deliberately create expectation, surprise, and the need for reevaluation.

SAY YOU'RE AWAY FROM home and you've had some car trouble. When you call to check in with your loved one, you might start your story this way: "I had a long night last night. Everything's fine—I'm fine, the car's fine. But sometime after midnight the back right tire blew out, and of course it was raining, and I had all my luggage in the trunk…." Out of consideration for your listener, you've given away the ending, tried to eliminate any suspense. Why? Because you're a thoughtful person. You might still try to get a good story out of your mishap, but you're going to need to get a lot of mileage out of the details.

You get the call to your loved one out of the way; now you call your best friend. This time you begin: "You know that long stretch of I-10 between Houston and New Orleans where that eighteen-mile bridge crosses the swamp? No exit ramps, not much of a shoulder, nothing? Where that guy on the History Channel saw a fifteen-foot alligator swallow a bobcat? Where the black bears are? That's where I was driving last night, all alone at two in the morning, in this torrential rain, when I feel this wobble, hear a *whump-whump-whump*, then the car lurched left, and I knew I was in trouble." Now we have suspense, drama. This conversation could go on for half an hour, and your friend would be grateful for the entertainment. By introducing the swamp and the fifteen-foot alligator, you aren't lying—you're just providing information you feel might interest your listener. Ditto the fact that the bridge is 18 miles long—18.2, actually. Might those details encourage your friend to imagine great peril? Let's hope so.

ADAM JOHNSON'S "HURRICANES ANONYMOUS" tells the story of Randall, also known as Nonc, a twenty-six-year-old UPS driver in Lake Charles, Louisiana, soon after Hurricanes Katrina and Rita. Randall has been evicted from the house he was renting; has had his truck stolen by his father, who drove it to California, where he is now in hospice and possibly dying; has had his wages garnished by his former girlfriend, who became pregnant by him and bore the child; has recently been forced to take responsibility for the child; and has a new girlfriend, Relle, who, thanks to the hurricanes, is living in a halfway house.

That's a lot of contextual information, and Johnson doles it out gradually, over the course of the opening pages, as he sets each aspect of Randall's life in motion. Like the writers of *Mission: Impossible*, Johnson creates an opening scene designed to facilitate the introduction of information: he has Randall stop at a restaurant that happens to be one of the few places he can get a strong cell phone signal. The fickle availability of cell phone messages takes the place of the self-destructing audiotape. Opening there allows Johnson to describe the state of the other hurricane refugees taking shelter at the restaurant, and having Randall check his messages allows Johnson to introduce Randall's current situation with his girlfriend, his job, and his father. As readers, we're distracted from the expository nature of the scene by Johnson's vivid descriptions and observations, by Randall's curious interactions with his son, and by Randall's resourcefulness: after procuring handfuls of plastic spoons and napkins, and checking his phone, he calls out to the crowd, asking if anyone has seen Marnie, his son's mother. In that opening scene, then, we receive introductory information establishing at least four plotlines.

The story's release of information seems straightforward. Here is the opening paragraph:

Nonc pulls up outside Chuck E. Cheese's and hits the hazards on his UPS van. The last working cell tower in Lake Charles, Louisiana, is not far away, so he stops here a couple times a day to check his messages. He turns to his son, who's strapped into a bouncy chair rigged from cargo hooks, and attempts to snag his cell from the boy, a two-and-a-half-year-old named Geronimo.

This narrator appears to be our friend. His sentences are clear and forthcoming. We have no reason to doubt or question him. What draws us forward isn't mystery or uncertainty so much as the vividness of the opening scene, the momentum of the sentences (Johnson's prose is full of active verbs), and a few curious, even comic details: we're outside a Chuck E. Cheese (an inherently tragicomic setting), a toddler's chair is suspended from cargo hooks in a delivery van, an adult has to pry his cell phone away from a child, and the kid's name is Geronimo. If the opening of Toni Morrison's novel is like entering a dark room wearing sunglasses, the opening of Johnson's story is like walking into a toy store at Christmas. There's plenty to attract our attention.

The surfaces of Johnson's stories are so energetic and interesting that he might easily rely on his eye for detail alone to draw us in. But the best of his stories work on another level, as he strategically manipulates information to create a variety of effects. In "Hurricanes Anonymous," he soon suggests that not all of the story's important information will be revealed so directly. The opening continues: "'Eyeball,' Geronimo says into the phone. 'Eyeball.' It's one of the boy's few words, and Nonc has no idea what it means."

In life we are surrounded by words, actions, events, and objects that have no meaning, or are inscrutable. By contrast, a short story or novel is a sense-making machine: if we're told on the first page that our main character has no idea what something his son says means, we expect either that he'll eventually learn what the boy means, or that his inability to decode his son's speech will in itself be meaningful—or both. This particular mystery—the meaning of "eyeball"—is a narrative poker card played faceup.

Randall is confronted with other cryptic messages and gestures in the story. We learn that he dated Geronimo's mother for only two months, and that, five weeks ago, he made a delivery, returned to his UPS van, and found his son "with a yellow boom box and a bag of clothes"—no note, no explanation, no instructions. He receives a text message from his father's doctor that reads, in full, "Your father is very ill and not expected." Later, in the middle of a conversation, Randall's girlfriend reaches out and sticks a cotton swab in his mouth. Only when Randall asks do we learn that she's gotten a kit from FEMA that will allow them to test his DNA, and that she hopes to learn Geronimo isn't Randall's son.

Even what should be routine conversations present challenges. When Randall calls the hospice in California, an orderly named Enrique answers.

"Enrique," Nonc says. "Can you help me talk to my father?"

"Hey," Enrique answers. "You the guy who had his girlfriend call? Because I heard about that. That business is cold-blooded."

"That was somebody else," Nonc says.

"Good, good," Enrique says, "cause your old man cracks me up. My dad, he was one crusty hombre, you know. Your dad reminds me of him."

"How's he doing?"

"He's dead," Enrique says.

"He's dead?"

"Yeah, died last year. Wait, are you talking about my dad or yours? I thought you were asking about my old man."

"You fucking with me?" Nonc asks.

Randall—Nonc—believes "the hurricane didn't change [his] life one bit. Neither will the death of his father." But nothing in his world seems entirely reliable; everything has to be tested for its true meaning.

Despite all of the challenges Randall faces in "Hurricanes Anonymous," the story's individual scenes are not especially momentous: he makes his deliveries, he talks with his girlfriend, he worries about his father, he tries to track down Geronimo's mother. Along the way, we learn a great many details about Randall's routines, and how he's coping with changes in his life that might be overwhelming, even paralyzing to others. In the place of high drama, Johnson creates and sustains momentum by keeping information coming to us in different directions, on different levels.

Near the middle of the story we learn that, because Randall has been evicted, and because Relle lives in a halfway house where Randall and Geronimo are not always welcome, the couple finds time to make love by going to AA meetings, which offer free childcare. This is a clever solution to the problem, and as information about Randall's life it would likely amuse the reader for a moment. But Johnson gets a lot more from it than a moment's amusement.

Earlier in the story, Randall went into a bar he and his former girlfriend, Geronimo's mother, used to frequent, to see if she's been in lately. She hasn't, but the bartender offers him a beer. He and

Relle, who joins him at the bar, both drink from it. A few pages later, back at the van, as they're talking about the child's mother—nearly arguing—they find that Geronimo has somehow loosened the lid to one of the shipping containers, and the UPS van is now filled with live crawfish. "We'll talk about it tonight," Randall says. Relle says, "At A.A.?" "Where the hell else," Randall answers, and busies himself corralling crawfish.

In all the commotion, it's easy to overlook that beer they both sipped. Depending on whether we remember it, we're likely to assume either that both Randall and Relle are recovering alcoholics or that both of them are unreformed alcoholics. Either way, there's no reason to suspect they're going to the AA meeting for any but the usual reasons.

A few pages later, when we get to the AA scene, all the narrator tells us is that Randall takes advantage of the free childcare to relax for a while. It's a deceptive partial truth, and it buys time—because Johnson has found another use for the situation he's created. Randall and Relle arrive at the meeting separately, and they sit across from one another. Relle wears tight track pants, and she slouches in her seat to pull them even tighter. The view creates, for Randall, a degree of erotic tension. Then, when the meeting starts, Relle starts talking about her "boyfriend," describing her situation with Randall in the third person. Others at the meeting—including Randall—offer her advice. Because Lake Charles isn't such a big town, the narrator tells us, and because Randall has made deliveries to the others at the meeting, they all know that Relle is talking about Randall, so they offer *him* advice, too—although because AA stands for Alcoholics *Anonymous*, they all address their advice to "the boyfriend," as if they don't know who Relle is talking about.

The scene is funny and disarming, and it gives unusual animation to what would otherwise be a fairly ordinary lovers' spat. More than that, it continues the pattern of ordinary-seeming conversations made complicated: Randall needs to decode the stories Relle tells everyone at the meeting to understand what she's trying to tell him. It's also consistent with his relationship with Relle, who is dramatic and manipulative (when she wanted to find evidence that Geronimo wasn't his son, she simply showed up and shoved that swab in Randall's mouth). She will continue to be manipulative throughout the story, and Randall will always be a step behind.

When the group conversation ends, Johnson plays his ace—at the break, Randall and Relle go to the van to make love, and we realize they aren't alcoholics at all.

Johnson had a fairly simple piece of information to deliver: Randall and Relle have figured out a way to have time together without the boy, and have sex, by going to AA meetings. Johnson could have told us that information from Randall's perspective—that they talked about ways to find time together, then hit on the idea of going to the AA meetings. That would be fine. A lot of perfectly satisfactory stories make do with that sort of Stage 1 invention. But Johnson reverses that information: first he tells us they go to AA meetings, and only later does he tell us why, creating surprise. And he can get away with that because Randall *knows* why they go to the meetings—he has no need to explain it, unless he wanted to explain something to the reader. That's a sort of knee-jerk exposition most of us provide in our stories without thinking, but Johnson resists. Then he plants an earlier clue, creating subtle tension by showing Randall and Relle sharing a beer before they mention the AA meeting, something Randall wouldn't give a moment's thought since he isn't an alcoholic. But the attentive reader wonders what's up, and Johnson has successfully aroused our curiosity—we look forward to the scene. Johnson also knows that for the AA meeting to be more than a simple joke, he should do more with it. And so we get Relle using the meeting to talk to Randall in front of other people, and another speech by a minor character, all of which leads in the most circuitous—I mean, the most devious—way to what Johnson needs us to understand: that despite his evident concern for his son, Randall falls short as a father. Also: that while Randall thinks he and Relle are scheming together, Relle has a larger vision, one that she isn't sharing.

Is there an easier way—a more direct way—for the narrator to tell us that Randall is not a particularly good father? Sure. But telling us isn't the point. The point is for us to see and believe that Randall is doing what he thinks is right, doing his best—and that he can't see how he's failing. It's critical for Johnson to emphasize that, because at the end of the story, Randall, whom we've come to like, is going to abandon his son. As readers, we're surprised, and disappointed in him, but because Johnson has carefully led us through Randall's story, we understand exactly how and why his decisions have led to this.

Just the Facts

I'll close by looking at an extreme case, the inclusion of a single large block of information, toward the end of a narrative, which would seem to be the very worst place to put a large block of information. In novels, in stories, in feature films, in the early episodes of series, the reader or viewer expects and wants a certain amount of contextualizing information, including information about setting and character and whatever seems necessary to an understanding of plot. To present a block of information late in the work could seem clumsy, and it might threaten to "break the spell," to frustrate the reader who has begun to feel close to the characters, caught up in the story.

An Iliad, by Lisa Peterson and Denis O'Hare, is essentially a one-man play based on the *Iliad* (there's also a nonspeaking role). A character called the Poet retells parts of the familiar story, largely based on Robert Fagles's translation, with additional commentary. The premise of the play is that the Poet witnessed the Trojan War, and he has been singing about it ever since. The burden of his singing, of his retellings, weighs on him; over time, his audiences have dwindled; he forgets some bits, and other parts he either can't or chooses not to revisit. In addition, the Poet knows that we—his current audience—don't know the people and places of ancient times; that is, he recognizes that most of the specific information important to his story is, well, Greek to us. What to do?

For one thing, while he begins by actually singing the poem in Greek, he soon stops, and begins speaking to the audience in contemporary American English.

For another, when he begins listing the hometowns of all the young men gathered on the dozens and dozens of ships—a list of Greek place-names—he stops himself:

> Ah, that's right, you don't know any of these places...but these
> names—these names mean something to me. And I knew these
> boys...The point is, on all these ships, are boys from every small town
> in Ohio, from farmlands, from fishing villages...the boys of Nebraska
> and South Dakota...the twangy boys of Memphis...the boys of San

Diego, Palo Alto, Berkeley, Antelope Valley...You can imagine, you can imagine...

He goes on to emphasize the differences among the young men:

You have soldiers from the Panhandle, with the snake charmers and evangelists, from the Okeechobee. You have soldiers from Miami who speak Spanish, Miami who speak French, Miami who speak English. You have Puerto Rican soldiers...you know what I mean?...You get the point.

In this way, in the first of its seven parts, the play enacts its true purpose: not simply to retell the story of the *Iliad* but to translate it for us, to help us understand its relevance not just in "modern times" but today, here, in the United States.

The play's most remarkable handling of information comes in the sixth of its seven parts. At the outset the Poet told us he's tired of this tale: "Every time I sing this song, I hope it's the last time." In part 6, he recounts Hector's fight with Achilles, which resolves with Achilles lashing Hector's feet to his chariot, leaving the head to drag, and then whipping his horses, driving them forward. Overwhelmed, the Poet says, "It's so...if you'd seen it, the—the waste... Just like—" and for a moment he tries to recall a specific moment in another battle, correcting himself:

I mean the conquest of Sargon—uh, the Persian War—no—

The Peloponnesian War

War of Alexander the Great

Punic War

Gallic War

Caesar's Invasion of Britain

Great Jewish Revolt

Yellow Turban War

He continues to recent conflicts in Afghanistan, Libya, and Syria.

In the script, the list of wars is five full pages—143 items long. There are no complete sentences, there is no contextualizing information or commentary, there is no action; in all three of the productions I've seen, the actor sat almost perfectly still through the recitation, at the end of which he slumped in his chair, silent. In each performance, the effect was crushing: the burden the singer of the *Iliad* has been carrying since ancient times is, at that moment, transferred to us: we feel the weight, and the waste, of a seemingly endless progression of wars.

The playwrights have taken a great risk. They could easily have made the list shorter, might easily have made the point—that wars have plagued us throughout mankind, and the destruction and loss are overwhelming—in much less time. But making the point—or rather, stating the idea—*isn't* the point. The notion itself is so familiar that it hardly seems worth saying. The goal, instead, is for the audience to *feel* this accumulation, this ongoing failure to transcend our worst selves.

And yet the Poet is simply reciting a list. In addition, the playwrights gave themselves the constraint of chronology, so once the Poet gets going, we only wonder how long he'll continue, how comprehensive he'll be. This moment could easily turn into what my undergraduates feared: the delivery of material sure to bore us. At the very least, it seems guaranteed to stop all the momentum the play has gained over the past hour. So why doesn't it?

The list's basic organizing principles become clear almost immediately: that clarity starts us on the journey. But while it begins as a list of named wars, it soon grows to include other types of mortal conflict: Caesar's Invasion of Britain, Great Jewish Revolt, Yellow Turban Rebellion, Fall of Rome. "Those aren't wars, exactly," we might say to ourselves, at the same time starting to consider what constitutes a war, and what else this list might include. Soon we get groups of related conflicts: Saxon Wars, Viking Raids across Europe, Wars of the Roses. Additionally, the syntax of the list's entries varies:

First Crusade

Second Crusade

Third Crusade

Fourth Crusade

Children's Crusade [and then simply]

Fifth

Sixth

Seventh

Eighth

Ninth Crusade

By the time we get to "First, Second, and Third English Civil Wars," they're included as one item.

While the list includes a great many historical events likely to be familiar to the audience in name, at least—the Spanish Conquest of Mexico, American Revolution—it also includes the Mugha Conquest of India, the Pequot War, First Opium War, and Honey War, which work to suggest all that isn't included, all the aggressions that even serious history students may not know about.

Finally, the last fifth of the list doesn't include the word "war" at all; instead, as if the Poet has reached the point of exhaustion, he gives us only locations: "Chechnya. Afghanistan. Kosovo. Iraq. Chechnya. Afghanistan. Rwanda."

The list offers pattern and variation; it satisfies our expectations by following chronology and including the major wars the audience is likely to know and anticipate, but it also surprises.

None of that fully explains the power of the list as part of the play, though. In fact, in the script, the list is not terribly compelling. As important as the construction of the list is its placement, its context. Coming when it does, immediately after the gruesome fight between Achilles and Hector, the list acts to compound the horror of the action and the fatigue of the audience. "Enough," we want to say; we *don't want* to see a corpse dragged in the dirt as a celebration of victory." We *don't want* to watch the scene being described; we don't want to listen anymore. We're at a point of emotional overload.

The transition to the list of wars offers, initially, an emotional escape. The list is pure information. We engage with it rationally, gradually understanding how it's working—and when we do, it summons our sense of horror again, except that instead of feeling repulsed by one man's celebration of killing another, we're repulsed by centuries of humankind's self-destruction.

If the same five-page list appeared in the opening minutes of the play, the audience would likely be restless; if it ended the play, it might still be powerful, but it might also seem reductive, as if the statement it illustrates were all the play was about. If the scene were more animated by the actor's gestures, if it were more emphatically performed, it could be clumsily overemphasized, the theatrical gesture interfering with the transmission of emotion from the Poet to the audience. Sometimes we need to trust the information. I spoke to someone involved in producing the play, and she said they considered showing images from historic battles during the recitation. That's the kind of thing we sometimes think will be necessary when we realize we're taking a risk. Imagine, for a moment, being that actor. Imagine sitting on a stage, not moving, reciting a 143-item list. It's a little like walking a highwire: once you start into it, there's nowhere else to go, no shortcut to the other side. But if you trust the power of the material—trust the fact that the length of the walk is necessary to the effect you mean to create—you commit to the compounding interest.

Those undergraduates I've been giving a hard time were right, of course: as writers we should be wary of the information dump. But that's not the same as being wary of information. Rather than rush to minimize it in our work, we should embrace the opportunities it affords, and make it as dynamic and compelling as possible.

I See What You're Saying

Images and Motifs

Music is a language that doesn't speak in particular words.
It speaks in emotions; if it's in the bones, it's in the bones.

—KEITH RICHARDS

My wife and I had the opportunity to spend several nights in a lodge on the Zambezi River, in Zambia. When I say "on the river," I mean that if our camera had fallen from the deck railing, it would have splashed. This was near the end of a two-week trip, so we had overcome jet lag and at least some of the excitement of being in what was, to us, a very exotic place, to the point that even the loud snurfles and snorts of the hippos in the dark water just beyond our door didn't keep us from sleeping. Still, sometime deep in our last night, I startled awake. There was no light in our room, and the moon had set, so no light shone through our curtains. I didn't hear a thing. Yet the hairs on my arms...I'm not going to tell you they stood on end, but they were on alert. Adrenaline had my arrector pili contracting.

I took my phone from the nightstand and first used its light to check the floor for snakes and scorpions. All clear. I got out of bed and parted the curtains covering the window just a few feet from our heads. Peering through the reflections on the glass, I made out what looked like the trunk of a tree. But there was no tree just outside our window. I was looking at part of a leg. A large, gray leg. If the window had been open, I could have reached out and rested my hand on it, which almost certainly would have been a bad idea.

Elephants walk on their toes, which are covered in large pads, which allows them to move silently. By that point in our trip, we had been surprised by elephants more than once. But we hadn't been this close to one. Suddenly the building we were in, a single room with a thatched roof, seemed awfully insubstantial.

When the elephant moved toward the river, my wife and I stood at the door. In three steps we could have crossed the landing and climbed onto the animal's back—another bad idea. But oh, the temptation to touch it! Instead, we listened to it drink—and realized there was a second elephant drinking in the dark, to our left. In the morning, looking at the prints in the mud, we saw that there had been three.

Everyone knows that elephants trumpet. It's an impressive sound, loud and brassy. Elephants also communicate through subsonic rumblings, imperceptible to human ears. Katy Payne, author of *Silent Thunder*, has determined that elephants communicate with sounds as low as 15 hertz from as much as six miles apart. (Human hearing ranges from about 20 to 20,000 hertz.) Imagine the deepest bass sound you've ever heard, how it feels in your chest. Now imagine a sound even deeper.

Of course, trumpeting can carry a good distance, too. But sometimes, if you're an elephant, you want to be able to talk to the rest of the herd privately—without alerting lions, for instance. Trumpeting is also exuberant; elephants standing along a waterhole, or in the midst of a seasonal migration of thousands of miles, are more likely to communicate through murmuring, or quiet—silent, to us—rumblings.

I could go on, but here's my point: that night on the river, I didn't hear those elephants in my sleep. I felt them.

MY ACTUAL TOPIC HERE is image and motif in fiction, but sound is a useful analogue. Sounds are, as you know, conveyed via waves, from the source to our bodies. Though we usually think of sound as something we hear, our ears and other parts of our bodies *feel* sonic vibrations. Sound is physical; we don't have to process it intellectually to feel it, or to be moved by it. Someone screams and we jump; someone laughs and we smile. We hear music and we move. We don't have to understand the source or intended meaning of sound to respond.

In *Making Waves*, a documentary about the various kinds of audio elements in film, supervising sound editor Cece Hall talks about her work creating the howl of fighter jets in *Top Gun*. And "creating" is the right word. She recorded actual fighter planes taking off, but she felt "they sounded kind of wimpy"; in an effort to give the planes more presence, to make them feel more powerful, she went to the zoo. There she recorded various predators, and screeching monkeys; back in the studio, she amplified the animal audio, played it backward, and blended it with the sound of the jets.

It's extremely unlikely that anyone unfamiliar with Cece Hall's process saw—or listened to—*Top Gun* and realized they were listening to reversed lion roars. And yet the sounds had their intended effects.

So it is—or can be—with images and motifs in fiction.

WHILE IMAGES SOMETIMES COMMAND our attention, they're also capable of doing their work in the background, without our being entirely aware of them. Of course, once we look more closely, more consciously, we begin to understand what's going on. As writers, like sound designers, our primary goal is to create effects for our readers. In the following examples, we'll see patterns of images, or motifs, used in a variety of ways—on different scales, with different degrees of subtlety, and toward different ends.

Motif as Harmonic Line

One possible function of a motif is to illustrate or underscore a scene's or a story's overall movement. That's how Jai Chakrabarti uses two relatively subtle motifs in "A Small Sacrifice for an Enormous Happiness," where repeated images directly reflect the changes in the story's central relationships.

"A Small Sacrifice" focuses on Nikhil, a wealthy landlord, and Sharma, his younger, handsome lover, who works in a foundry. The story takes place in Kolkata in 1979, and we're told that their relationship puts them in real danger: two other men who were seen together in another city had acid thrown in their faces. "Haunted by fear of discovery," for two years they met only once a week, on Thursday evenings, ostensibly to play backgammon. Finally, Nikhil had his servant find a wife for Sharma, a "marriage of convenience."

Another year of Thursday meetings followed. Like many stories, Chakrabarti's has a "one day..." that serves as a kind of hinge, a departure from routine. In this case, the story starts on a Thursday, as Nikhil nervously anticipates Sharma's arrival: he wants to propose something of great consequence. So while he has a servant, and we're led to understand that a great many things are done for him, Nikhil himself has prepared a special pyramid of sweets for Sharma's visit.

Soon after Sharma arrives, Nikhil reveals his plan: he wants them to have a child. Sharma doesn't reject the idea, but he doesn't commit either. Two weeks later, Nikhil, enthused to the point of fantasizing about the daughter he imagines having, buys a dress for the young girl. Then, in violation of one of the rules of their relationship, he visits Sharma at his workplace, the foundry, to show it to him. Sharma says, "Have you lost your soup?" and hurries him away. He skips their next meeting. The following Thursday Sharma appears but is clearly (to us) working to dissuade Nikhil. Nikhil decides to talk to Tripti, Sharma's wife. Tripti was very poor before the marriage, so Nikhil sees no reason she won't acquiesce—in his mind, she owes him.

But when Nikhil visits, Tripti says she has plans of her own— to become a teacher. Nikhil responds rudely, and she effectively throws him out of the house. It turns out he's missed the last train to Kolkata, and there are no hotels in this small town. So he returns to their home where, through the window, he sees Sharma and Tripti making dinner together, looking, if not like a happily married couple, like two equal partners.

That's the essential plot: One man wants to have a child, his lover does not, the first man pleads his case, is rejected, and the disagreement damages—quite possibly ends—the relationship. This is a lot of emotional ground to cover in relatively few pages, and Chakrabarti's decisions regarding point of view and where to begin and end the story are essential to its success. The story is also very attentive to staging, and to various sensory appeals, including smells. But here we'll focus solely on two motifs that convey the essence of the story in shorthand, as it were.

The first is the use of sweets—actual desserts, or tea snacks. Sweets appear surprisingly frequently in this brief story.

First: Nikhil prepares that "whole conical pile" of "delectable" sweets in anticipation of Sharma's arrival. The fact that he prepares them himself tells us something about the importance Nikhil places on this particular Thursday meeting. When he sees them, Sharma asks, "What's the special occasion?" and we're told that "his fingers became honey-glazed from the offering."

Next: We're told that while Nikhil paid for Sharma and Tripti's wedding, Tripti was "a little stubborn about the choice of sweets. She want[ed] the village kind." So we might say that, between Nikhil and Tripti, sweets have been a bun of contention.

As I mentioned, when Nikhil takes the dress to the foundry, Sharma is alarmed and unhappy, and skips their usual Thursday meeting. When they get together the following week, rather than eating at Nikhil's home, they go to Jimmy's Chinese Kitchen, and their awkward conversation—Sharma tries to reject the idea of a child, and Nikhil won't hear it—is accompanied by disappointing food: "chili noodles doused with sugary tomato sauce...along with stale pastries." The sweets have soured. In fact, we're told, "Nikhil ground away at the pastry in his mouth until the memory of sweetness dispersed."

When Nikhil takes the train to try to persuade Tripti to have the child, she offers homemade sweets—but Nikhil finds them "a little lumpy, only mildly flavorful." He grinds his teeth when Tripti refuses him, then "chewed another of Tripti's lumpy sweets. When properly masticated, it would have the consistency to be spat and to land right between Tripti's eyes... Soon he was all chewed out." This is, depending on your mood, the comic highlight of the story, the moment we see Nikhil at his very worst, or both. It's worth noting that Chakrabarti doesn't actually have Nikhil spit a lumpy sweet at Tripti's face—that would overwhelm the story, unbalance it, and compete with the bigger gestures about to come, as the story ends. Surely you've had moments like this in drafts—you've imagined allowing a character a bold action, then wondered if it's too much. Here Chakrabarti shows us you can have your cake and eat it, too.

There's one last food image that we'll get to in a minute, but that's the story in sweets: it begins with a "delectable" pile of them, lovingly made, that leave Sharma "honey-glazed," we learn that Nikhil and Tripti disagree about sweets, the sweets at the reconciliation dinner are stale, and when Nikhil visits Tripti, they all but do battle with sweets. None of those things changes the action or feeling of the story, but all of them complement it, reinforce it. If you consider these sweets an element of setting, a sort of prop, Chakrabarti has arranged them so that they reflect the tenor of the main action. The various sweets help to define the atmosphere of the scenes they appear in.

THE OTHER MOTIF I want to point out has to do with hands. Nearly everyone has them, and we tend to use them a lot, so the simple fact that hands are mentioned numerous times in the story isn't remarkable. What's significant is how they're mentioned, and what they're doing.

Again: in that opening scene, we're told Nikhil "had rolled [the sweets] by hand himself," which is significant for a man who has a servant not only to open his door but also to pluck his ear hair.

When Nikhil tells Sharma, "I desire to have a child with you," his hands are shaking, "but he took Sharma's anyway, gave it a squeeze." So Nikhil is using his hands, here and with the sweets, to try to draw Sharma close. But two weeks later, when he shows up at the foundry with the little girl's dress, Sharma's "hands [are] constricted by thick welding gloves, which excluded the possibility of even an accidental touch." You see what Chakrabarti has done—used an image to directly refute that offering of the hand-rolled sweets. The images are in conversation.

In a flashback to their very first meeting, we're told Nikhil "allowed his hand to linger on Sharma's wrist, pretending he was trying to see the hour." So a hand gesture was part of their initial flirtation. But after that unhappy meal at Jimmy's Chinese Kitchen, Nikhil senses "in the way that Sharma held his hands in his lap… that Tripti had wormed something rotten into him."

When Nikhil visits Tripti, he feels "his want for a child had become rooted in his body, in the bones of his hands and the ridge of his knee," and remembers a girl on the train "whose outstretched palm…had touched him." But Tripti will have none of it, Nikhil imagines spitting the sweet in her face, he leaves only to find he's missed the last train, he returns, he looks through the kitchen window—and this is what he sees

the two of them together in the kitchen. Sharma was slicing cucumbers and Tripti was stirring a pot. The way Sharma's knife passed over the counter seemed like an act of magic. Such grace and precision. Soon, he knew the lentils and rice would be combined, a pair of onions diced, ginger infused into the stew, the table set, the meal consumed. He watched, waiting for the first word to be spoken, but they were silent partners, unified by the rhythm of their hands.

Everything about those sentences works to convey the impression that Sharma and Tripti have something together—the sort of close relationship that Nikhil wants, and that comes not from buying everything for his lover, giving him presents and a wife and money for a house, but from true partnership, ultimately expressed by the image of their hands. They are literally "unified by…their hands."

Notice one other thing Chakrabarti has done in order to write that description while remaining close to Nikhil's point of view. He begins by telling us what Nikhil sees, then offers a figure ("like an act of magic"), then has Nikhil imagine what's going to happen, before returning to the hands. As a result, the final image blends in with the passage as a whole, even as it quietly draws the story toward a close.

There is one last hand reference. Earlier in the story, Nikhil gave Sharma a valuable necklace, a museum piece that once belonged to his mother. Sharma promised to wear it always. But when he and Tripti take their meal to the dining room, Nikhil moves closer to the open kitchen window and sees "his greatest gift" on the kitchen counter, next to the stained china. He snakes his hand through the window to reclaim the necklace, then runs off. When he turns back, "he thought he saw Sharma's hands in the window, making signs that reminded him of their first meeting, when in the darkness those dark fingers had beckoned. Nikhil almost called back, but too much distance lay between them. Whatever he said now couldn't be heard."

We understand that their relationship is over.

A GRAPHIC ARTIST OR filmmaker would be able to convey the emotional development of this story using those images. It would begin with the flirtatious touching of the wrist at their first meeting, move to Nikhil rolling the sweets by hand and offering them to his lover, then show his hands shaking as he reveals his desire. We'd see Sharma pull back from Nikhil, his hands covered by welding gloves, and later Sharma holding his hands in his lap. We'd see the outstretched palm of the young girl on the train, and after Nikhil leaves then returns to Sharma's house, Sharma's and Tripti's hands working together, as if from one body. Nikhil would grab the necklace from the counter, and finally we'd see Sharma's hand in the window, echoing their first touch. If the plot of a story is its melody, we might say that a motif like this one, that runs from the beginning of the story to its end, operates like a line of harmony.

I've said that Chakrabarti's use of these images is subtle. It might be more helpful to say that the images don't immediately attract every reader's attention because they are entirely realistic, presentational: the sweets are actual sweets that people are eating, the hands are actual hands that people are using the ways hands are typically used. And so as images they are nearly transparent, blending into the realism of the story. What makes them effective is repetition and placement, and the fact that they occur at emotionally and dramatically charged moments.

When we're drafting a story, we often don't know what images or objects, what memories or aspects of setting, will take on importance as the story develops. That's fine. In early drafts, we might not even notice that several of our scenes have two characters talking and eating—that's not so unusual—or even that they're usually eating sweets. And when we notice that we've got four or more references to sweets in a story, we might tell ourselves to stop writing when we're hungry, and change some of the references to avoid the repetition. But we might also recognize an opportunity. We might decide that instead of eliminating the sweets, we'll pare away some other details, maybe even put the sweets in more prominent places, to draw the reader's attention. Maybe we'll decide to start the story with a tower of homemade sweets and end it with a pile of dirty dishes. In revision we have the opportunity to filter, develop, and explore images, and by the final draft they can play an important role in guiding the reader's experience.

Narrating through Image

Sometimes we discover an effective image as we write. Other times, we consciously create images. And sometimes we're so intent on offering readers a fresh or vivid image that we don't think about whether it's consistent with or in the service of the rest of the story—or even if it serves the overall intention of a paragraph or scene. Some days, it can seem hard enough just to avoid tired expressions, or familiar images; we're pleased when we come up with something that feels fresh, interesting.

As a result, an early draft can contain a sort of grab bag of images, something like this:

> The full moon emerged like a half-remembered dream. Around
> it, clouds glittered like freshly split geodes. Stars shone like sparks
> risen from an eternal fire. A satellite crossed the sky, determined as a
> lawyer's closing argument.

It's certainly possible the night sky has never been described exactly that way, but originality is about all that passage has going for it. A dream, geodes, sparks, a lawyer's argument—the references are random. They don't create a composite image, and they don't reveal anything about who is doing the observing. The sentences call attention to themselves, but not in a good way.

When images, figures, or allusions are expressed by a character (in first-person narration or in dialogue), and even when they seem to be associated with a character by a third-person narrator, it can be helpful to draw from that character's world and associations. In "A Small Sacrifice," sweets take on significance not only because they're repeated but because they're something both Nikhil and Tripti care about; both have strong preferences about sweets, and they communicate through sweets, as when Nikhil hand rolls that assortment for Sharma and when Tripti takes a stand on the sweets for the wedding.

In her short novel *A Mercy*, Toni Morrison introduces a character this way:

> Fog, Atlantic and reeking of plant life, blanketed the bay and slowed him...He turned to wave to the sloopmen, but because the mast had disappeared in the fog he could not tell whether they remained anchored or risked sailing on...Unlike the English fogs he had known since he could walk, or those way north where he lived now, this one was sun fired, turning the world into thick, hot gold. Penetrating it was like struggling through a dream...It was only after he reached the live oak trees that the fog wavered and split. He moved faster then, more in control but missing, too, the blinding gold he had come through.

When we read those sentences, we don't know that this action is taking place in Virginia or that the year is 1682. We don't know the man is Jacob Vaark, that he's on a journey to collect a debt that will result in him taking Florens, a young enslaved girl, in partial payment, or that while Jacob is, compared to some, a good man, by the end of this section he will dedicate himself to accumulating wealth through the rum trade, profiting from slavery. But Morrison knows all of that, and in these sentences she tells us Jacob's story, or a thumbnail version of it, via the setting. He comes from the fog of England, and now he's struggling through a dream of (thick, hot) gold. Unlike Chakrabarti's story, here we immediately feel Morrison intentionally drawing our attention both to the images and their implications. While she begins the passage with what might feel like straightforward narration of the action—a man starts to walk through the fog, turns and waves—she shifts to comparing the present to "the English fogs he had known since he could walk, or those way north where he lived now"—still realistic details— then tells us "this [fog] was sun fired, turning the world into thick, hot gold. Penetrating it was like struggling through a dream." Here the figures transcend mere realistic description; for a moment, the language and images move into the foreground.

In retrospect, this imagery might seem heavy-handed; but since we don't know what's coming, we first read these lines only as an evocative depiction of setting. At the same time, we start to associate this man we're meeting with these images, which Morrison repeats and develops at the end of the section:

> Walking in the warm night air, he went as far as possible, until the
> alehouse lights were gem stones fighting darkness…He gazed at

the occasional dapple of starlight on the water, then bent down and placed his hands in it. Sand moved under his palms; infant waves died above his wrists, soaking the cuffs of his sleeves...As he walked back to the inn, nothing was in his way. There was the heat, of course, but no fog, gold or gray, impeded him...He fondled the idea of an even more satisfying enterprise. And the plan was as sweet as the sugar on which it was based. And there was a profound difference between the intimacy of slave bodies at Jublio and a remote labor force in Barbados. Right? Right, he thought, looking at a sky vulgar with stars...The silver that glittered there was not at all unreachable...His dreams were of a grand house of many rooms rising on a hill above the fog.

Roughly twenty-five pages separate those two passages—enough that the repetition of images doesn't seem overdone, but not so many that we've forgotten the dreamlike golden fog. Here Morrison adds gemstones and silver; and in case we have any doubt that Jacob is dedicating himself to a bad idea, "the sky is vulgar with stars." We've probably never seen the night sky described exactly that way, but Morrison is doing more than offering us an unexpected image; she's showing us how Jacob's vision is corrupting his view of the world around him. Jacob's dreams are "rising on a hill above the fog" because now he knows how to get what he wants. And while we don't know it yet, even those "infant waves [that] died above his wrist" are telling us something: Jacob and his wife lose a young child.

Morrison uses imagery here to serve both an immediate purpose, as evocative description, and deeper, long-term purposes. She uses imagery (among other things) to direct our attention. The images describe the present, but they also act as supplemental characterization and as foreshadowing. These two passages are also part of one of the novel's larger goals: distinguishing each of the main characters while simultaneously depicting their relationship to the setting.

Three: Image through the Eyes of Character

Most of Morrison's novel is in the third person, and while she draws us close to Jacob's perspective in that section of the book, she does not say that Jacob thought of the fog as golden, or that he believed the sky was vulgar—she associates the character with those images without claiming they emanate from his consciousness. But it can be helpful, at times, to move even closer to character, to draw both images and the language used to describe them from the character's voice and experience, even her immediate emotions and attitude.

IN OPERA, MOST FAMOUSLY in Wagnerian opera, a leitmotif is a melody or musical passage identified with a particular character or element. If, like me, you don't listen to as much opera as your doctor recommends, you still might have encountered a popular example in Sergei Prokofiev's *Peter and the Wolf*. If not, you're still in luck; film composers also use motifs. You might recall Obi-Wan's theme or Yoda's theme, among many others, from *Star Wars*, or the notorious alternating F and F-sharp which, played menacingly on the tuba, summon the shark from *Jaws*.

Richard Powers does something similar with motifs in his long novel *The Overstory*. I mention the length because a longer or more complex work can employ a prominent use of recognizable motifs as part of its apparent structure, part of the architecture that shapes the whole.

Like *A Mercy*, *The Overstory* has an omniscient narrator and multiple point-of-view characters. Powers could distinguish those characters simply by their names, their appearances, their jobs, speech, attitudes, and desires—the way we typically define characters—but he goes further, to help us remember what matters most to them, and to show us how their concerns overlap.

In the second section of the novel we meet Winston Ma, who leaves China for the United States. He marries and has three daughters—of whom Mimi will be one of the novel's main characters. An engineer, Winston enjoys fishing. When he fishes, Powers tells us, "He maps the sandbars, measures the speed of the water, reads the bottom, watches for hatch—those simultaneous equations in multiple unknowns that one must solve to think like a fish." Winston maps, measures, solves equations. In other words, he fishes like an engineer. Here and elsewhere, the information we're given about Winston's background and interests is both reinforced and persuasively embodied in his thoughts.

In contrast, Neelay Mehta, a computer programmer, sees the world through the lens of logic and coding. At one point he thinks his father's body "is so riddled with rogue programs and syntax errors he won't make it to this world's opening day." No other character in the book would think about illness in exactly that way. The image of an ailing body "riddled with…syntax errors" is intimately associated with Neelay.

Ray Brinkman is an intellectual property lawyer; when Dorothy, a woman he's attracted to, says she wants to pick the venue for their first date, "He signs off on the deal, never imagining the hidden clauses." Dorothy thinks of him as "criminally responsible." When they're in Rome and succumb to the ritual of throwing coins into

Trevi Fountain, Ray thinks, "They probably owe someone royalties." Powers knows better than to give each character a single frame of reference; that could quickly become reductive. Together, Dorothy and Ray act in community theater; their romantic relationship is off and on. The narrator tells us, "Their average run is five months," applying the language of theater, their hobby, to their relationship. And so on.

The result of all this is that each significant character in *The Overstory* has his or her own constellation of references, one that is kept in the foreground through repetition and developed through variation. In isolation, these examples might seem a bit crude, exaggerated. But *The Overstory* is more than five hundred pages long and has many dozens of named characters, so Powers can afford to—he *needs* to—use bold strokes. The basic technique is one that can be applied to any length work. (Using images, figures, and allusions this way is akin to free indirect discourse, where the narrative takes on aspects of a point-of-view character's voice, their diction and syntax. There are examples of that throughout *The Overstory*, too, as in the section introducing Olivia Vandergriff. Olivia is a free-spirited young woman enjoying the indulgences afforded by being in college, and the narrator's language reflects that in describing "the nest of crap by her bed," by telling us Olivia's claim that her mother was a writer "was pretty much bullshit," that she'll head west "where all good fuck-ups always head," and that rereading the music she writes in her notebook when she's stoned is "like copping a contact buzz." This colloquial language is interwoven with the narrator's more formal language.)

In addition to creating individual frames of reference for each character, Powers draws them together through overlapping interests and references. For instance, the first play Ray and Dorothy act in is *Macbeth*; we're told that, for the audition, they "screw their courage to the sticking place" (a line delivered in the play by Lady Macbeth). Ray gets cast as Macduff, an appropriate role for many reasons, among them the fact that Macduff is one of the men who, disguised as part of Birnham Wood, fulfills one of the witches' prophecies. Rather than allude to that subtly, Powers makes sure we know ("he had to play a man who had to play a tree"), and he develops what could be a sort of coincidence, a one-dimensional reference, into something more revealing. During rehearsals, Ray thinks, "Something is happening to me. Something heavy, huge, and slow, coming from far outside, that I do not understand," thus aligning him with Macbeth in that regard, and suggesting that having Ray act in Shakespeare's play is more than an idle detail. One of the things "happening to" Ray is Dorothy, who will become a central figure in his life; another, much later, will be the discovery of the importance of trees. The references to *MacBeth* continue throughout the sections including Ray and Dorothy. They also subtly overlap Mimi's world, as her father is an opera buff, and in an early scene she and her sisters sit in a mulberry tree while their parents make love, the sounds of which are drowned out by Verdi's *Macbeth*.

The *Overstory* is ultimately interested in trees; but Powers knows that people want to read about people, and his purpose in writing about trees is to get us to look at trees differently, to think about them, and to take action to save them. To make that argument to a variety of readers, it's crucial to his project that his characters are led to appreciate trees in a variety of ways. Powers takes this further: in the opening eight sections of the book, each of the main characters is associated with a tree, or in some cases a group of trees; the book is divided into sections titled "Roots," "Trunk," "Crown," and "Seeds"; and the novel's imagery often references roots, seeds, branching, and so on.

Winston Ma plants that mulberry tree in his backyard, the tree his daughters sit in while listening to him and his wife listen to Verdi's *Macbeth*; he leaves each daughter a ring with the image of a tree, and of course Mimi chooses the mulberry, the tree of renewal. At age eleven, Neelay falls from an oak tree and is partially paralyzed. He goes on to develop a series of computer games; he calls his company *Sempervirens*, for the coast redwoods around him in California. Even when Powers wants to include a character who, initially, pays no attention to trees, he draws our attention to that: "She has lived under the tree for a whole semester and doesn't know it's there."

Unlike the repeated appearance of sweets in "A Small Sacrifice for an Enormous Happiness" or Toni Morrison's reference to those "infant waves" dying above Jacob Vaark's wrist, the motifs in *The Overstory* aren't subtle: they don't do their work deep in the background, and they don't require the reader to read the novel a second time to notice them (though if you do read the novel a second time, you notice a lot more of them). But that's OK; images and motifs don't *need* to do their work only in the reader's subconscious. Hawthorne titled his book *The Scarlet Letter*. Charles Dickens starts *Bleak House* with nearly a thousand words about fog; does any reader mistake that for a weather report? He might as well have titled the opening chapter "A Metaphor." John Williams has said that the first time he played that two-note shark theme for Steven Spielberg, Spielberg laughed; he assumed Williams was joking.

Years later, Spielberg said those notes were probably responsible for at least half of the movie's success. If you saw *Jaws*, you remember the shark theme; if you saw *Psycho*, you remember the shrieking strings from the shower scene.

Sometimes, in some misguided devotion to "realism," we tell ourselves that turns of phrase, or descriptions, or images, shouldn't stand out, that nothing should interrupt a reader's attention to character and story. But readers read for the pleasures of reading, which are many. Sometimes an aspect of fiction that normally does its job in the background is more effective in the foreground. In *The Overstory*, recognizing the interlocking motifs and watching them develop is part of the pleasure.

Like Music to Our Eyes: Lyricism

A year or so ago, my wife and I watched the television series called, simply, *Chernobyl*, about the catastrophic failure of the nuclear reactor and the immediate aftereffects in 1986. While we knew the essence of the story, the somewhat fictionalized, dramatized account was still, due to the depiction of the emotional and physical suffering involved, agonizing. As a story of mechanical failures caused and amplified by human failures, it was also enthralling, as captivating as any well-told tragedy.

My wife is not squeamish, or sentimental; while she won't watch horror films, and prefers not to watch movies that depict bloody violence, she watched all of *Chernobyl* with open eyes. Even so, at the end of each episode, as the credits ran, she said, "Turn it down! Mute it! Good lord."

What she found unbearable—or just barely bearable, until the credits—was the score. Icelandic cellist Hildur Guðnadóttir won an Emmy for the soundtrack. The defining elements of the tracks—which have titles like "Bridge of Death" and "Dealing with Destruction"—came from field recordings she made at the decommissioned power plant in Lithuania where the film was shot. At one point she uses the high-pitched squeal of the door to a pump room to evoke radioactivity, which is, to human ears—like the subsonic rumblings of elephants—silent. At other times she slowed sounds down, or distorted them to convey what she called "invisible, oppressive danger and fear."

My wife and I didn't know any of that while we were watching. We only knew that we felt exhausted, wrung out, by each episode, and while a lot of that had to do with the events being depicted by the actors—and the sets, and the lighting—a large part of it had to do with what we were hearing.

I doubt many viewers of *Chernobyl* failed to notice the soundtrack—even if, like us, they didn't know the sources and components of those sounds. But often the sound in films and television shows have their effect on us more subtly.

The NPR show *Science Friday* once dedicated a Halloween episode to "Monster Music" and, more specifically, "Why Some Tunes Scare Us." In that episode, neuroscientist Daniel Levitin says that the discomfort we feel in response to some music is caused in part by a bit of tissue in our brain known as Brodmann Area 47. (We actually have two Brodmann Area 47s, one just beyond each temple.) BA47, as it's known, is part of our brain that attempts to detect shapes, predict patterns, find order and resolution. "The brain likes order," Levitin says. When BA47 is confused, or defeated, as by dissonance or unresolved chords, we feel anxious, unsettled. We feel it without necessarily thinking about it in words, any more than most of us know that we *have* a Brodmann Area 47. It does its job without our knowing.

BA47 is also important to language processing and comprehension, both finding order and identifying significant distinctions. Our brains are wired to find patterns.

IN "A SMALL SACRIFICE for an Enormous Happiness" and *A Mercy* I've argued that images play a supporting role, essentially illustrating what is happening to the characters internally, or what will happen to them. But while those images are largely visual, to say they "illustrate" the narrative seems reductive; like a film soundtrack, patterns of images often play a tonal and emotional role as well. In *Beyond Words: What Animals Think and Feel*, Carl Safina writes,

> [Human] music is—obviously—in the range of human hearing, usually at tempos corresponding to human heartbeats or footbeats, and with patterns and intonations comparable to qualities of human speech. These qualities of sound, tempo, and tone are technically called "paralinguistic features," and they all come under the umbrella term "prosody." Prosody refers to the sound qualities of human speech. Prosody is why, for instance, listeners can distinguish lullabies from yelling in any language. It's why a piano, violin, saxophone, or guitar solo can sound mysteriously like a person telling a story, though it is devoid of words.
>
> Sound sometimes carries emotion across species. Dogs understand when people are arguing. And we understand a growl as a warning... A human just prior to coming into the world has been hearing the beat of its mother's heart, the tonalities of her voice, the pace and

pattern of her steps. The capacity to perceive meaning in a mother's tone of voice is present at birth. (Many birds begin vocalizing to their chicks as soon as the chick has chiseled a tiny hole in its eggshell.) ...

Music, in a sense, abstracts the tone and rhythm of our lives and hands it back to us as an aural package of pure emotion-triggering stimulation.

LITERARY IMAGES, DESPITE BEING conveyed in words, can speak to us beyond words; and in doing so, they can convey something I'll call meaning, though that meaning might be more emotional than rational, more felt than neatly paraphrased. Ellen Bryant Voigt puts it this way in her essay "Image":

> The power of an image, in a literary work, derives largely from its own essential paradox—a "picture in words" articulates a nondiscursive apperception through the discursive systems of language—which reflects the paradox of human consciousness: the fact that mind is body, whether sense organs or cerebrum. The most effective images, then, may be those in which the two opposing poles, the two ends of that mind/body spectrum, are collapsed in on themselves. Such images ... [deliver] simultaneously the concrete and the abstract, the empirical and the assumed, the representational and the expressive.

In the final story I'd like to discuss, images aren't simply background support, or elaboration of what's being conveyed in other ways; the images tell us things the plot and narration don't, and they are central to both our emotional response and our understanding of the story.

Guy Vanderhaeghe's "The Jimi Hendrix Experience" is, on its surface, a familiar-looking coming-of-age tale. The narrator recalls a summer when he was in his teens, the summer his family moved from Winnipeg "to a new city." In need of companions, he falls in with Conrad and Finty, whom he does not consider friends: "With school out for the summer I lack opportunities to widen my circle of acquaintances. Beggars can't be choosers." While "there's not much wrong with Finty," Conrad is a troublemaker, a sniffer of glue and gasoline. Troy, the narrator, recognizes that to keep Conrad occupied and out of serious trouble he needs a sense of structure and purpose. So Troy devises a prank: the boys knock on the doors of strangers and say they've come in response to the ad the stranger has placed, offering the sale of a Jimi Hendrix album. Of course, there was no ad, so whoever opens the door is confused; the boys grow indignant. That's it. Harassing strangers amuses these guys, for a while.

Like "A Small Sacrifice," this story has its "one day" hinge, a departure from the norm. Once the characters and the ritual are established, Troy tells us about the day they knock on a stranger's door, tell the old man who answers that they "came to inquire about the album," and the old man says, "Come in. I've been expecting you." They (and we) are surprised, but in they go. The man invites them to have a seat, then leaves the room. He returns holding a rifle. He points it first at Finty, then at Conrad. He talks about JFK, Bobby Kennedy, and others who, he says, have too much copper in their system. "Too much copper," he tells the boys, "attracts the lightning bolt. Don't blame me. I'm not responsible." To demonstrate his immunity, the old man swallows a penny.

The boys are, understandably, uneasy. The tables have been turned, and they aren't happy about it. In an effort to get back to their prank, Conrad reminds the old man that they came about "the

album." Here the story hinges on a coincidence. The old man pulls
out "a bulging photograph album." Every photo in the album is in
black-and-white; every photo depicts a road under construction;
in none of the photos are there any people. "In a former life," the
old man explains, "I was a highway contractor. Unrecognized for
my excellence." He then asks the boys to identify the person in the
pictures. To antagonize him, Conrad says he sees Jimi Hendrix.
Finty doesn't answer. Troy sees "the old man's finger guiding [him]
to the pale gray froth on the horizon...the phantom light crowning
his nail."

"Light," Troy says.

"The aura," the old man says.

"The aura," Troy repeats.

Now even more unnerved, Conrad kicks the album away; he and
Finty leave. Troy and the old man sit quietly for a moment, "with
bowed heads." Then the old man says, "I knew you were the one to
tell the truth. I knew it at the back door when I saw all the generous
light..." He pauses, touches Troy's head—and Troy bolts from the
house. The story ends,

> Here I am, running through the late afternoon stillness of an empty
> suburban street, sucked down it faster than my legs can carry me, this
> hollow, throaty roar of fire in my head, that tiny point on the horizon
> drawing me to where the sun is either coming up or going down.
>
> Which?

"THE JIMI HENDRIX EXPERIENCE" is a typical coming-of-age
story not because it involves a sexual initiation (it doesn't) or be-

cause the main character, at the end, is sadder but wiser (he isn't, necessarily), but because a teenager has lost a kind of innocence. Troy has been introduced to something so disturbing that he literally can't stand it—he has to run away. And rather than have a moment of insight, an epiphany, he's haunted by a question—one that, on its surface, might not be immediately clear.

This is a job for BA47. We want to detect shape. And while the narrative, or the chronological recounting of the event from the past, is complete, something essential remains unresolved. Why was young Troy so disturbed? And why is the older Troy telling us this? We know that a story's intention is often defined by where it begins and where it ends, so our questions at the ending lead us back to the opening lines:

> It's the summer of 1970 and I've got one lovely ambition. I want to
> have been born in Seattle, to be black, to be Jimi Hendrix. I want
> a burst of Afro ablaze in a bank of stage lights, to own a corona of
> genius…I'm fourteen and I want to be one of the chosen, one of the
> possessed. To soak a guitar in lighter fluid, burn baby burn, to smash
> it to bits to the howl of thousands. I want to be a crazy man like Jimi
> Hendrix.

In retrospect, we see that the story is shaped not only by plot but also, and ultimately more meaningfully, by image. In the anthology where it first appeared, "The Jimi Hendrix Experience" is not quite eleven pages along. Over the course of those eleven pages, there are, by my count, over thirty images related to fire, to that corona of genius, to Jimi Hendrix's haze and the old man's aura.

A bit excessive, you might think. But while those images are bold enough and numerous enough to attract our attention, they aren't easily deciphered, or reduced to paraphraseable meaning. In order to make my point, though, I'm going to attempt to explain how they contribute to meaning. If we slow the story down, and listen carefully, we might just hear the lion's roar.

AT THE OUTSET, TROY wants "a burst of Afro ablaze in…stage lights" and "to soak a guitar in lighter fluid, burn baby burn." This establishes the story's dominant motif, but it doesn't draw unusual attention because the references work on a literal level: Jimi Hendrix wore his hair in an Afro, he was illuminated by stage lights when he played, and he did, famously, set his guitar on fire at the Monterey Pop Festival in 1967. It's also worth noting that in the story's first paragraph Hendrix is referred to both as a genius and as "a crazy man."

The imagery takes on another dimension when Troy tells us, "What I didn't know then is that before my man Jimi flamed his guitar at Monterey, he warned the cameraman to be sure to load plenty of film." Again, this reads as biographical fact, and the narrator doesn't tell us why he finds the information significant—but it's the story's only leap forward in time until the last page, one of only two references to what the adult Troy knows that his younger self didn't. We understand that while young Troy believed Hendrix acted impulsively, the older narrator learned the act was deliberate, part of a calculated performance.

It is not accidental that Conrad sets fires to garbage cans and heaves them onto garage roofs, that he flicks lighted matches at someone's dog. He, too, is associated with fire, but not with genius. In contrast to Jimi Hendrix, Conrad is impulsive, unpredictable, and scary. Troy says the glue produces "dangerous vapours in Conrad's skull."

The story is set in the summer, so we take no particular notice when Troy tells us they could "feel the heat coming off the asphalt"—but in retrospect, this connects directly to the old man's photographs of roads under construction disappearing into "a haze of pale light."

In the old man's house, Troy detects a "strange odour," "a weird, gloomy smell" that he associates at first with the glue on Conrad's breath; later he recognizes that "it's coming from him"—the old man. So the smell connects impulsive Conrad with the threatening man who appears holding a rifle. And it's the old man who says, "Chemistry is destiny. Too much copper...attracts the lightning bolt." The lightning connects indirectly, almost imperceptibly, to the fire initially associated with Jimi Hendrix, the "genius." Here in the middle of the story, the talk of copper, auras, and the haze of the rising and setting sun in the photographs is attached to a potentially crazy stranger—but the "phantom light crowning" the old man's fingernail is a clear echo of the "burst of Afro ablaze" and "corona of genius" Troy earlier assigned to Hendrix. So while two people could hardly seem more different than one of the world's most famous rock guitarists and this strange, lonely man wearing a yellow cardigan, they—and Conrad—are bound together by the story's imagery.

The story assigns Troy his own variation on these images. Soon after the old man enters the room holding the rifle, Troy provides a strange aside:

> Some nights I turn on the tv at four in the morning when all the
> stations have signed off the air. I like how the television fizzles in my
> ears, how my brain drifts over with electric blue and grey snow, how
> the phantom sparkles of light are blips on a radar screen tracking

spaceships from distant planets. Similar things are happening in my head right now, but they feel bad instead of good.

On the surface, this seems like a gratuitous digression, an indulgence; it's irrelevant to the narrative. We know very little about Troy's daily life, and there's no other talk of his late nights up alone. Again, the images provide all the connection: "the television fizzles in [his] ears," his "brain drifts over with electric blue and grey snow," he sees "phantom sparkles of light." In a few minutes, a man who believes he could see "John and Bobby giving off copper right through the television screen" will ask the boys to identify the person "evident" in the photographs of roads under construction: "So tell me, who else is in the photograph?"

In response, Troy thinks: "It's no different from staring into a blank television screen. The snow shifting, forming the faces of famous people locked in the circuitry from old programs. The hiss of static turning into favourite songs, guitar chords whining and dying." The indirect allusion to Jimi Hendrix again connects him, via imagery, to the old man. And so Troy knows who is "evident" in the photographs:

I hold my breath, and then I say it: "You."

"Yes," says the old man.

THIS—NOT THE MAN'S WIELDING of the rifle, or the penny swallowing—is what propels Conrad and Finty to the door. And it's Troy's disturbing realization that he understands this stranger—who says, "I knew you were the one to tell the truth. I knew it at the back door when I saw all the generous light," and touches his head—that sends him flying.

YOU REMEMBER THAT AFRO ablaze and the corona of genius from the opening paragraph because I've slowed the story down, drawn attention to them. But even the most attentive reader is unlikely to make all these connections while reading the story for the first time. So, similar to the way Jai Chakrabarti featured the tower of sweets at the start of his story and unified hands at the end, and Toni Morrison places those meaningful images of fog, gold, and gems at the beginning and end of the section of *A Mercy* focused on Jacob Vaark, Vanderhaeghe concentrates a cluster of images toward the very end of the story, making the connections more explicit.

> I'm running, my scalp prickling with tiny flames. I feel them, the flames creeping down the nape of my neck, licking at my collar, breathing hotly in my ears.
>
> And Jimi, two months from being dead, is out there in front of me, stage lights snared in his hair, a burning bush. And a young road builder is standing alone on a blank, unfinished road, his head blooming with a pale grey fire.
>
> And here I am, running through the late afternoon stillness of an empty suburban street, sucked down it faster than my legs can carry me, this hollow, throaty roar of fire in my head, that tiny point on the horizon drawing me to where the sun is either coming up or going down.
>
> Which?

THE STORY DOESN'T ANSWER the question; and of course the question itself is metaphorical, not about sunrise or sunset but, we now understand, about some combination of genius and cra-

ziness. We don't know anything about Troy the adult, so we have
no idea what he's become. What we do know is that as a teenager
he had a naive notion of genius, of passionate engagement and
dedication to a livelihood, and that it was challenged by a chance
encounter with a retired road contractor who feels he was "unrecognized for [his] excellence." We know Troy is terrified by what
he's just beginning to recognize. That terror and confusion isn't
described or explained; instead, it's evoked through the orches-
tration of images. We don't process Troy's fear in words so much
as we sense it. I suppose you could say Troy has felt the elephant
in the room.

As in *The Overstory*, each character is assigned a variation on the
central motif: Jimi Hendrix has the flaming guitar and the corona
of genius; Conrad has flaming trashcans and the fumes of glue and
gasoline; the old man has the aura of copper, lightning bolts, and
the haze at the end of incomplete roads; and Troy has the "electric
blue and grey snow" and "phantom sparkles" of light on the television. These distinctions, as well as the overlapping images, allow us
to see the characters not on a spectrum (the story would be much
less interesting if it encouraged us to see the characters illustrating
a line from genius to madness) but in a constellation. Vanderhaeghe
leaves it to us to find the meaning in the pattern.

IN HER ESSAY ON image, Ellen Bryant Voigt says of Sylvia Plath,
"In poem after poem it is the image that tries to mediate between
poet and page, between page and reader, to articulate the interior landscape … [Her figures] are the weight-bearing walls of
the lyric structure." The essential narrative of "The Jimi Hendrix
Experience" is a simple anecdote: *The summer my family moved*

from Winnipeg, two other guys and I played a prank on people, and one day something crazy happened. In lesser hands, that would be the story. The import of the anecdote—the key to what made it terrifying to teenage Troy and makes it memorable to the adult Troy—is conveyed almost entirely through image. To put it another way: the narrative of "Jimi Hendrix" is a vehicle for the lyric moment the older narrator wants to convey.

SOME WRITERS BEGIN WITH images; others recognize or develop them over the course of multiple drafts. "It was like treasure hunting," Hildur Guðnadóttir said about visiting the Lithuanian power plant used for *Chernobyl*. "You go in there with completely open ears and you just listen." When she was approached for the project she began wondering "what the soundworld would be" in a radioactive power plant. "What does that danger *sound* like?" she wondered. "It's an element that we don't see, but it's an element that we *feel* very strongly." Similarly, we might think of the "image world" of a character, a scene, a story. What are the sensory elements of the characters' lives, or of the setting, that might complement what's being said about them, or even express more than a character can, or more than a narrator chooses to, put into words? And if those images aren't already present in our draft, how might we reimagine a scene or setting through the lens of all we know about our story?

The Roast Beef *Is* the Story

Digression, Misdirection, and Asides

A movie poster in my office shows five men in tuxedos sitting at and standing near a banquet table. The flowers in the foreground suggest a wedding reception; the fact that one of the young men is wearing his bowtie untied, hanging from his neck, suggests that the reception is, if not over, well under way. The tagline reads, "Suddenly life was more than french fries, gravy, and girls."

The movie is called *Diner*, and I initially saw it with great reluctance. Set and filmed in Baltimore, where I grew up, its cast includes a disc jockey my sister listened to, who mentioned several times on the radio that he had a small part in the film. On top of that, the film's titular setting is based on an actual diner that our mother had frequented when she was a teenager. But what had my sister most excited was the rumor that the movie, set in 1959, was essentially a sequel to *Grease*. I could not have been less interested—but my sister couldn't find anyone else who would go to the movie with her on opening weekend, so I made an uncharacteristic sacrifice, grudgingly. I might even have taken a book.

Within five minutes, I was enchanted. My sister, who kept wait-ing for the characters to burst into song, was hugely disappointed.

If my students at the University of Houston are any indication, whatever popularity *Diner* once had seems to have faded. The mov-ie's poster has been hanging on the wall of my office for five years; for five years, students who come in for conferences have asked me what it's about.

In case you're like them: released in 1982, *Diner* was written and directed by Barry Levinson, who somehow assembled a cast featuring a young Mickey Rourke, Kevin Bacon, Steve Guttenberg, Daniel Stern, the comedian Paul Reiser, and Ellen Barkin. Set in Baltimore in the final week of 1959, the film focuses on a group of young men spending time together for the few days before one of them, Eddie, is due to get married. I am not spoiling anything for you by revealing that the film's final scene is at the wedding reception, at which nothing much happens (unless you count a memorably awful rendition of "Blue Moon").

People who enjoy the movie—and not all of us are from Balti-more—find it highly quotable; but lines like "She'll *be* twelve" and "You ever get the feeling there's something going on that we don't know about?" and "Details: shit," don't convey much to the uniniti-ated. Fans of the movie will refer to the football trivia quiz, to Big Earl consuming the entire left-hand side of the menu, and, most often, to the roast beef sandwich scene.

If you're curious, you can go to YouTube and search "roast beef sandwich scene"—no need to identify the movie. But here's what happens: the guys get together at the diner. Modell asks Eddie if he's going to finish eating his sandwich; a debate ensues; Shrevie ends up eating the sandwich.

It loses something in the retelling.

While it may be the most famous scene in the movie, the roast beef sandwich scene could be cut, and the characters' fates would not be affected in the least. For that matter, you could arguably cut the entire football trivia quiz sequence. Nothing at all hinges on the fact that Big Earl eats everything on the left-hand side of the menu; for that matter, Big Earl doesn't say or do anything of consequence. If we were given the assignment to edit the film, and operated under the assumption that we should keep only what's essential to the plot—the same way writers are often encouraged to approach their stories and novels—we could probably find reason to cut just about everything. This has to have been the realization that led MGM to decide not to release the film. Happily, *New Yorker* reviewer Pauline Kael screened it, loved it, wrote a rave review, and the movie found its audience. Perhaps more important, filmmakers—directors and editors—now see it as one of the most influential American films of the past four decades. Some say it's the film that made *Seinfeld*— the TV show that was, famously, "about nothing"—possible.

Diner is organized not so much by plot as by an internal clock, the ticking down to the wedding. It accumulates thematically, as we see the various ways these overgrown boys are, grudgingly, dragged into adulthood. Through dialogue and anecdote, through detail and atmosphere, *Diner* evokes a time and a place, and it illustrates the bonds of friendship that hold the characters together, without ever making the mistake of trying to put that into words. Almost everything in *Diner* seems beside the point; yet every moment contributes to the final effect. (It even includes what we might call visual asides, as when the camera cuts away from a conversation to focus on all of the diner's ketchup bottles set out on the lunch counter, half of them right side up, the rest upside down, draining into them. The image has nothing to do with plot; it has everything to do with atmosphere.)

According to an article in *Vanity Fair* on the movie's lasting influence, "During postproduction, an MGM executive complained to Levinson" about the roast beef sandwich scene. The executive "wanted it cut because it didn't advance the story. 'You don't understand,' Levinson explained…between the lines about roast beef lies all you need to know about the characters' fear, their competitiveness, their friendship. The roast beef *is* the story."

In other words: if we edited the film to remove everything inessential to its plot, we would, paradoxically, lose its essence.

WILLIAM TREVOR FAMOUSLY DESCRIBED the short story as "the art of the glimpse," and compression is generally a virtue. But the most engaging and compelling short stories and novels are not necessarily the shortest or most direct. Clarity and directness appeal to our rational selves. But fiction has an emotional component, one that often requires sidestepping the rational, disguising "the point" or the path to it. Humor and suspense depend on indirection, on the calibration of expectation and surprise, and they aren't the only effects best achieved by taking an unexpected path. In extreme cases such as *Diner*, the meander is everything. By the time we get to the wedding, it serves not so much as a matter of plot or character but as a reminder that one stage of those young men's lives has come to an end.

When I recognized that a lot of the fiction I admire has a digressive quality, I thought I would write in defense of strategic misdirection. Appropriately, I suppose, pursuing that idea led me someplace unexpected.

Digression

While our focus here is on fiction, I'll offer two examples from political discourse. Successful politicians learn to master the art of sidestepping questions they don't want to answer and finding ways to answer virtually any question with what they want to say, sometimes on an unrelated topic. It's a curious sort of discourse. When it works, listeners don't notice what's happening; when it doesn't, listeners are likely to say, "Politicians! They're all the same." To avoid muddying the waters with any hint of political allegiance, I'll quote two Republican presidents.

Here's one's response to the question, "Would you like to start?"

No, other than to say, we're working hard, I think we're all in the same business of trying to make our country better, a better place, so we have something in common. I've been treated very, very badly by the *Washington Post*, but, you know, I guess—and I'm your neighbor, I'm your neighbor right down the road, in fact we're actually giving a press conference there in a little while, I think your people are going to be there. And by the way, Bob Costa is an excellent reporter, I've found him to be just an excellent reporter. I should tell you, because I have to give you the good and the bad. Not that he does me any favors, because he doesn't, but he's a real professional.

So we're having a news conference today in the new building that's going up, and the building is very much ahead of schedule, because it was supposed to open two years from September, and we're going to open it in September. We could open it actually sooner but we're going to break it in a little bit, so we're going to open it in September, and it's under budget, even though we've increased the quality of the finishes substantially, marble finishes, very high quality of marble, so we're under budget and ahead of schedule. And I'm, you know, I am that way when I build, I know how to build, I know how to get things done.

A reminder: the question was, "Would you like to start?"

While you and I may disagree about politics, I think we can agree that this is not an artfully contrived digression; this is the real thing, as seen in the wild. If digression is a potential virtue, or even simply a tool, the desirable form is *harnessed* digression—or what I'm calling strategic digression.

IN CHAPTER 53 OF *Roughing It*, Mark Twain tells us that while he was in Nevada, men he knew urged him to get Jim Blaine to tell the story of his grandfather's old ram—but to wait until he was "comfortably and socially drunk." Finally, the night comes. Blaine sits on a powder keg smoking a clay pipe, surrounded by his audience, and begins:

> I don't reckon them times will ever come again. There never was a more bullier old ram than what he was. Grandfather fetched him from Illinois—got him of a man by the name of Yates—Bill Yates— maybe you might have heard of him; his father was a deacon— Baptist—and he was a rustler, too; a man had to get up ruther early to get the start of old Thankful Yates; it was him that put the Greens up to jining teams with my grandfather when he moved west. Seth Green was prob'ly the pick of the flock; he married a Wilkerson— Sarah Wilkerson—good cretur, she was—one of the likeliest heifers that was ever raised in old Stoddard, everybody said that knowed her. She could heft a bar'l of flour as easy as I can flirt a flapjack. And spin? Don't mention it! Independent? Humph! When Sile Hawkins come a browsing around her, she let him know that for all his tin he

couldn't trot in harness alongside of *her*. You see, Sile Hawkins was—
no, it warn't Sile Hawkins, after all—it was a galoot by the name of
Filkins—I disremember his first name; but he *was* a stump—come
into pra'r meeting drunk, one night, hooraying for Nixon, becuz he
thought it was a primary; and old deacon Ferguson up and scooted
him through the window and he lit on old Miss Jefferson's head, poor
old filly. She was a good soul—had a glass eye and used to lend it to
old Miss Wagner, that hadn't any, to receive company in; it warn't big
enough, and when Miss Wagner warn't noticing, it would get twisted
around in the socket, and look up, maybe, or out to one side, and
every which way, while t'other one was looking as straight ahead as a
spy-glass. Grown people didn't mind it, but it most always made the
children cry, it was so sort of scary. She tried packing it in raw cotton,
but it wouldn't work, somehow—the cotton would get loose and stick
out and look so kind of awful that the children couldn't stand it no
way. She was always dropping it out, and turning up her old dead-
light on the company empty, and making them oncomfortable, becuz
she never could tell when it hopped out, being blind on that side, you
see. So somebody would have to hunch her and say, "Your game eye
has fetched loose, Miss Wagner dear"—and then all of them would
have to sit and wait till she jammed it in again.

Blaine goes on to say that Mrs. Wagner would also borrow Miss
Higgins's wooden leg, which was too short, and Miss Jacop's wig;
that Jacop was married to a coffin salesman; and that the coffin
salesman stalked old man Robbins, who he kept thinking was on
the verge of death. From there we get to a story of a missionary
couple eaten by cannibals, and the cooking method the cannibals
used, and eventually to the story of a Mr. Wheeler, who died when

he was sucked into the machinery of a carpet factory, and whose widow bought all fourteen yards and planted him full length.

A reminder: Blaine set out to tell the story of the old ram.

Unable to restrict himself to the relevant elements of the tale he set out to tell, Jim Blaine wanders from this to that to something entirely different, for no other reason than one thing reminds him of another. He has no sense of audience, no real sense of purpose. He's rambling.

Mark Twain, however, is not rambling. His story is carefully framed by a first-person narrator who, he tells us, is the butt of the joke. His new friends watch Blaine tell his tale—or not tell his tale—and take no small pleasure in the narrator's confusion. But the story works on yet another level, as Jim Blaine's supposed ramblings are in fact carefully curated by Twain to create comic effects for the reader. While Jim Blaine may be losing track of his story, Mark Twain is in full control of his, carefully attending to choices in diction, repetition, and transitions, as well as the escalating absurdity.

DIGRESSION IS DEFINED AS a turning away or wandering from the main path of a journey. One could argue that *The Canterbury Tales* consists almost entirely of digressions, if one sees the main path as the journey of Chaucer's characters from London to the shrine of Saint Thomas Becket at the Canterbury Cathedral. To pass the time, they agree to a storytelling contest. If these were properly devout pilgrims, their conversation along the way should be incidental. But Chaucer makes the incidental the substance. At the same time, because the narrative spine is the progression of the journey, he can do whatever he wants with the ribs. The traveler's tales are varied and, at least potentially, unpredictable, with no obligation to build on or respond to one another. *The Canterbury Tales*, like "The Story of the Old Ram," is an example of curated digression. Chaucer's pilgrims get sidetracked in all sorts of ways, but Chaucer knows where he wants to take us, what he wants to show us not only in the individual tales, but in what they reveal about their tellers, and in how other characters respond.

CATCHER IN THE RYE is a short novel that uses digression in its form, in its first-person narration and, in one scene, as its subject.

In chapter 24, Holden Caulfield goes to visit Mr. Antolini, his former English teacher. After inquiring about Holden's sudden departure from Pencey Prep, Mr. Antolini, asks, "How'd you do in English?"

> "Oh, I passed English, all right...I flunked Oral Expression, though. They had this course you had to take, Oral Expression. *That* I flunked."
>
> "Why?"
>
> "Oh, I don't know." I didn't feel much like going into it. I was still feeling sort of dizzy or something, and I had a helluva headache all of a sudden. I really did. But you could tell he was interested, so I told him a little bit about it. "It's this course where each boy in class has to get up in class and make a speech. You know. Spontaneous and all. And if the boy digresses at all, you're supposed to yell 'Digression!' at him as fast as you can. It just about drove me crazy. I got an F in it."
>
> "Why?"

"Oh, I don't know. That digression business got on my nerves. I don't know. The trouble with me is, I *like* it when somebody digresses. It's more *inter*esting and all."

Mr. Antolini goes on to ask Holden if he doesn't like it when somebody sticks to the point, and Holden acknowledges that those who did got the best marks in class; but he felt bad for a classmate who began a story about his father's farm, then went on to tell about his uncle, who had polio:

It's nice when somebody tells you about their uncle. I mean it's dirty to keep yelling "Digression" at him when he's all nice and excited…I don't know. It's hard to explain." I didn't feel too much like trying, either. For one thing, I had this terrific headache all of a sudden. I wished to God old Mrs. Antolini would come in with the coffee. That's something that annoys the hell out of me—I mean if somebody *says* the coffee's all ready, and it isn't.

"Holden…One short, faintly stuffy, pedagogical question. Don't you think there's a time and place for everything? Don't you think if someone starts out to tell you about his father's farm, he should stick to his guns, *then* get around to telling you about his uncle's brace? *Or,* if his uncle's brace is such a provocative subject, shouldn't he have selected it in the first place as his subject? Not the farm?"

I didn't feel much like thinking and answering and all. I had a headache and I felt lousy. I even had sort of a stomach-ache, if you want to know the truth. "Yes—I don't know. I guess he should. I mean I guess he should've picked his uncle as a subject, instead of the farm, if that interested him most. But what I mean is, lots of time you don't *know* what interests you most till you start talking about something that *doesn't* interest you most. I mean you can't help it sometimes. What I think is, you're supposed to leave somebody alone if he's at least being interesting and he's getting all excited about something. I like it when somebody gets excited about something."

Again, a reminder: the question was, "How did you do in English?"

Holden answers that in a little more than one sentence. What he goes on at length about is another class, Oral Expression. Why? Because he flunked it, and Mr. Antolini's other concern is how Holden did in his classes. But Holden doesn't then go on to talk about his own speeches in that class; instead he makes an impassioned argument against the practice of criticizing someone for digressing, especially if they're excited about what they're talking about; and to explain that, Holden feels he needs an example, and he uses Richard Kinsella's story about his uncle's farm. From one perspective, then, Holden's speech is a well-organized argument, one with a thesis, a compelling example, or evidence, and a conclusion that restates the thesis in a new way: "Lots of time you don't *know* what interests you most till you start talking about something that *doesn't* interest you most."

So again: while Holden the character is digressing, Salinger the author is not. Where Mark Twain used pauses in his performances, we see Salinger punctuating Holden's articulate defense of digression with a smokescreen of inarticulateness, including the repetition of "I don't know," "I mean," "I admit it," and even the references to his headache.

Holden digresses because what really matters to him is hard to express, and he knows it isn't what the authorities want to hear.

The entire short novel is framed as a refusal to speak to the assigned topic: "If you really want to hear about it, the first thing you'll probably want to know is where I was born, and what my lousy childhood was like, and how my parents were occupied and all before they had me, and all that David Copperfield kind of crap, but I don't feel like going into it, if you want to know the truth." With that, Holden launches into his narrative, one in which present events are much less significant than perspective and understanding. The three days Holden ends up recounting are ultimately a frame arranged to allow him to—compel him to—tell us what's most important to him.

Asides

Asides are essentially shorter digressions—as short as a word or a phrase, as long as a paragraph. While a digression might lead the reader to wonder when or even if we'll return to the apparent path of our narrative journey, an aside is more of a pause, or momentary diversion. Asides tend to take on a strategic function if and when they accumulate. As we'll see, their function can be tonal and rhythmic, they can amplify one or more aspects of the narrative voice, they can characterize, and they can even serve to underscore a story's central movement.

J. D. SALINGER MOVED from a relatively undistinguished narration in his earliest published stories—the ones he never collected—to the voice we recognize from his books. While his stories have different narrators, those narrators tend to share certain characteristics. Their prose is defined by contrasting high and low diction, bold use of sentence rhythm, idiosyncratic use of italics, and asides. While all of these techniques work in concert, the asides play a particularly important role in establishing intimacy with the reader and in defining the character of the narrator.

"The Laughing Man" is a retrospective first-person story about one spring in the (unnamed) narrator's youth. The narrator was a member of something called the Comanche Club, a sort of do-it-yourself Cub Scout troop with an emphasis on sports. A young man they call the Chief serves as their bus driver and leader. The Chief also passes the time by telling installments of a serial adventure story about the Laughing Man, a kind of Robin Hood–meets-Tarzan hero who, because of a hideous deformity, always wears a poppy petal mask.

The season the narrator tells us about is notable because the Chief invites a young woman, Mary Hudson, onto the bus and, soon enough, into their games. She becomes a subject of fascination for the narrator's younger self. It's clear she's the Chief's girlfriend, and it's just as clear, later in the story, that she breaks off their relationship. When she does, the Chief gets back in the bus and, in that final installment of his story, the Laughing Man dies. Salinger's story ends: "A few minutes later, when I stepped out of the Chief's bus, the first thing I chanced to see was a piece of red tissue paper flapping in the wind against the base of a lamppost. It looked like someone's poppy-petal mask. I arrived home with my teeth chattering uncontrollably and was told to go right straight to bed."

THE THREE NARRATIVE LINES—THE story of the idyllic days of the narrator's youth, the story of the Chief and Mary Hudson, and the story of the Laughing Man—all end with a strong sense of loss. But the reasons the narrator was so shaken as a boy, what he sensed or believed about the Chief's relationship to Mary Hudson—what he felt he lost when they broke up—and the reason the adult narrator is moved to tell this story now all go unspoken. As voluble as our narrator may be, his author knows what not to let him say.

And yet the presence of this older narrator is critical. The story isn't told in a nine-year-old's language or with a nine-year-old's understanding.

The narrator's asides vary in length and presentation. Most take the form of parentheticals; others, set aside by em dashes, are grammatically equivalent to parentheticals. Others aren't set off by punctuation at all.

The content of the asides is varied as well. Some are explanatory:

We then pushed and punched our way into the Chief's reconverted and commercial bus, and he drove us (according to his financial arrangement with our parents) over to Central Park.

(It took the Chief a couple of months to get that far into the story. From there on in, he got more and more high-handed with his installments, entirely to the satisfaction of the Comanches.)

Some offer persuasive illustration:

If our Comanche hearts were set on camping, we went over to the Palisades and roughed it. (I remember getting lost one Saturday somewhere on that tricky stretch of terrain between the Linit sign and the site of the western end of the George Washington Bridge.

I kept my head, though. I just sat down in the majestic shadow of a giant billboard and, however tearfully, opened my lunchbox for business, semi-confident that the Chief would find me. The Chief always found us.)

Some serve to add or modify details:

The rest of the afternoon, weather permitting, we played football or soccer or baseball, depending (very loosely) on the season.

The story ended there, of course. (Never to be revived.)

Sometimes she talked a blue streak in the bus, sometimes she just sat and smoked her Herbert Tareyton cigarettes (cork-tipped).

One could reasonably ask why this information is being presented parenthetically—why it's being presented in the form of asides. In that last case, Salinger might just as easily have written, "Sometimes she just sat and smoked her cork-tipped Herbert Tareyton cigarettes," and his place in American letters would not be significantly impacted. But perhaps you can sense the difference—changes in rhythm and emphasis. The version of the sentence that ends "smoked her cork-tipped Herbert Tareyton cigarettes" fizzles out. What's she smoking? Cigarettes, of course. The sentence has detail but no clear emphasis. Salinger's version lands firmly on "(cork-tipped)." Of course, it doesn't matter that the cigarettes are cork-tipped—what matters is the emphasis on the narrator's attention to detail, and his authority. The sentence emphasizes the parenthetical, the additional information, the commentary. (There's also a wonderful sonic emphasis in the hard consonants of "cork-tipped." Salinger's prose offers a lot of aural pleasure.)

This editorial aspect of the narration is even more evident in asides such as

> but he refused to kill them. (There was a compassionate side to the Laughing Man that just about drove me crazy.)

and

> I'm not saying I will, but I could go on for hours escorting the reader—forcibly, if necessary—back and forth across the Paris-Chinese border.

and

> In the best faith in the world, the Laughing Man agreed to these terms. (Some of the minor mechanics of his genius were often subject to mysterious little breakdowns.)

It's as if the narrator is annotating his own story—as if he had written a fairly straightforward version, then gone back and edited it, with an attitude.

> In consequence, where the Laughing Man breathed, the hideous, mirthless gap below his nose dilated and contracted like (as I *see* it) some sort of monstrous vacuole. (The Chief demonstrated, rather than explained, the Laughing Man's respiration method.)

"THE LAUGHING MAN" EMPLOYS what is often called a framing narrative—the frame being the narrator's time in the Comanche Club—which leads us to this particular spring, when the Chief meets and loses Mary, and the Laughing Man meets his end. But in fact the frames and things being framed are more numerous.

The final installment of the Laughing Man is framed by an over-view of the entire series, which the narrator provides. And this entire story is framed by the presence, the voice, of the retrospec-tive narrator.

We learn nothing about the narrator's current life. We don't know where he is, what he does, or what has moved him to tell this story. Virtually everything we know about him we know through his voice, his knowledge, and his selection and emphasis of details—which is to say, his attitude and sensibility. Salinger's best work transports readers by means of a sensibility that seems simultaneously accessible and exotic. That sensibility is conveyed in several ways, including choices in diction, but perhaps most uniquely by means of asides.

> Offhand, I can remember seeing just three girls in my life who struck me as having unclassifiably great beauty at first sight. One was a thin girl in a black bathing suit who was having a lot of trouble putting up an orange umbrella at Jones Beach, circa 1936. The second was a girl aboard a Caribbean cruise ship in 1939, who threw her cigarette lighter at a porpoise. And the third was the Chief's girl, Mary Hudson.

The story is set in 1928; the narrator is referring, in two cases, to women he saw nearly a decade later. This is the only specific ref-erence to his life since the events of 1928. The content of the aside is entirely unnecessary to the plot: those two women aren't men-tioned again; they don't factor into the narrative in any way, and neither does the narrator's love life. The sole function of the aside is to tell us something about the worldly experience of the man telling us this story, to remind us that he knows a great deal more than he's telling. And while it appears to add information of a sort, the aside simultaneously underscores the narrator's inclination toward omission and highly idiosyncratic selection. How were these women beautiful? One struggled with an umbrella, one threw a lighter at a porpoise. To this narrator, gesture is everything. We had better watch carefully.

WHILE A STORY'S NARRATOR is most often the source of asides— as in Jane Austen, Henry Fielding, Jorge Luis Borges, and David Foster Wallace—they can also be a function of character.

In "Some Other, Better Otto" Deborah Eisenberg uses asides, initially, for comic effect. Otto is an attorney specializing in intellectual property rights. The particular nature and tone of Otto's nitpicking establish aspects of his character. As soon as we meet him, on the story's first page, Otto complains about an impending Thanksgiving dinner he's agreed to attend. His partner, William, responds indirectly: "I was reading a remarkable article in the paper this morning about holiday depression...Should I clip it for you? The statistics were amazing." Otto responds by attacking William's word choices: "The statistics cannot have been amazing, the article cannot have been remarkable, and I am not 'depressed.'"

A few pages later, repetition encourages us to see Otto's focus on diction as a habitual defensive strategy. He and William are discussing the need to visit Otto's sister Sharon and make an effort to persuade her to go to the dinner.

> "We could just go have a plain old visit, though. I don't know. Urging her to go to Corinne's—I'm not really comfortable with that."
>
> "Oof. William, phrase, please, jargon."

"Why is that jargon?"

"Why? How should I know why? Because it is. You can say, 'I'm uncomfortable *about* that,' or 'That makes me uncomfortable.' But 'I'm uncomfortable *with* that' is simply jargon."

THE ASIDE MAY OR may not distract us from the fact that Otto fails to acknowledge his own mixed feelings about Sharon, who he believes is both brilliant and possibly insane, or at least deeply troubled. What Otto doesn't say—but we understand—is that he, too, is deeply uncomfortable about approaching Sharon to attend the dinner.

Later, when William suggests that "the desire for children is hardwired," Otto goes off on another antisemantic rant:

"Hardwired." You know, that's a term I've really come to loathe! It explains nothing, it justifies anything; you might as well say, "Humans have children because the Great Moth in the Sky wants them to." Or "Humans have children because humans have children." "Hardwired," please! It's lazy, it's specious, it's perfunctory, and it's utterly without depth.

Only later do we learn that William has wanted a child, but Otto does not.

There are other examples of this particular sort of aside, William's aggressively refusing to discuss the content of a remark by debating its phrasing. They culminate in the final scene, when Otto and William are back home after the Thanksgiving dinner and Otto has managed to apologize passive-aggressively. William tries to calm him by saying, "Can it wait until tomorrow? I'm very tired, and you're obviously very tired as well. Try and get some sleep, please." Otto replies,

> "Try *and* get some sleep?" "Try *and* get some sleep?" This is unbearable! I've spent the best years of my life with a man who doesn't know how to use the word "and"! "And" is not part of the infinitive! "And" means "*in addition to.*" It's not "Try *and* get some sleep," it's "Try *to* get some sleep." *To! To! To! To! To! To! To! Please try to get some sleep!*

And with that he sits down at the kitchen table and begins to sob.

The semantic asides function initially as comedy, and in a lesser story they might serve purely as entertainment, a bit of cleverness attributed to character that allows the writer to go on about the sorts of abuses of language writers like to go on about. Here, though, the asides ultimately serve not just to illustrate Otto's difficulty in engaging with others, his repressed sorrow, and his eventual breakdown; they also illustrate how, like Sharon, Otto lives on the brink of careful attention to the world and what the world defines as unsociable behavior.

The asides are varied—they aren't all about specific words—and they intensify, until at the end of the story what had seemed to serve as a secondary character trait becomes the most dramatic evidence of Otto's internal struggle.

AS FOR THAT OTHER Republican president:

> Four score and seven years ago our fathers brought forth on this continent, a new nation, conceived in Liberty, and dedicated to the proposition that all men are created equal.

Now we are engaged in a great civil war, testing whether that nation, or any nation so conceived and so dedicated, can long endure. We are met on a great battle-field of that war. We have come to dedicate a portion of that field, as a final resting place for those who here gave their lives that that nation might live. It is altogether fitting and proper that we should do this.

But, in a larger sense, we can not dedicate—we can not consecrate—we can not hallow—this ground. The brave men, living and dead, who struggled here, have consecrated it, far above our poor power to add or detract. The world will little note, nor long remember what we say here, but it can never forget what they did here. It is for us the living, rather, to be dedicated here to the unfinished work which they who fought here have thus far so nobly advanced. It is rather for us to be here dedicated to the great task remaining before us—that from these honored dead we take increased devotion to that cause for which they gave the last full measure of devotion—that we here highly resolve that these dead shall not have died in vain—that this nation, under God, shall have a new birth of freedom—and that government of the people, by the people, for the people, shall not perish from the earth.

ABRAHAM LINCOLN WORKED HARD on his prose. He studied Greek oratory, he memorized and recited Shakespeare, and he greatly admired the finest speakers of his day. He was interested in philology as well as in logic, which led to his criticizing Stephen Douglas, during their first debate, as the sort of man who through "a specious arrangement of words" would attempt to prove "a horse chestnut to be a chestnut horse." (It's the sort of wordplay that encourages Garry Wills to compare Lincoln to Mark Twain, who wrote that "the difference between the almost-right word and the right word is the difference between the light-ning bug and the lightning.")

Lincoln's best prose is far from digressive—it's notoriously eco-nomical. Edward Everett, the featured speaker on November 19, 1863, spoke for approximately two hours; Lincoln's speech took less than three minutes.

But Lincoln was famous for responding to requests and argu-ments indirectly, with anecdotes, apocryphal tales, and jokes, nearly all of them intended as answers or rebuttals by analogy. He was, in that sense, a master of indirection. He knew his audience—the person asking him for something, or arguing with him—was pre-pared for a direct rejection, or disagreement; so he took a slantwise course. And Garry Wills argues that, in his address at Gettysburg, Lincoln executed one of the great left turns in American history, essentially reinterpreting the Constitution. On the smaller scale, we see one of Lincoln's favorite devices in the sentence: "Now we are engaged in a great civil war, testing whether that nation, or any nation so conceived and so dedicated, can long endure." The phrase "any nation so conceived and so dedicated" is an aside, and a significant one. Even on an occasion so specific to the nation as the recognition of the dead at Gettysburg, Lincoln considers the democratic experiment on a larger scale.

The part of the speech that many scholars consider a curious digression—one that, because of its brevity, I'm calling an aside—is the beginning of this sentence: "The world will little note, nor long remember what we say here, but it can never forget what they did here."

"The world will little note, nor long remember what we say here" would, in a lesser writer, seem like unnecessary throat clearing.

One can see it as evidence of modesty; but one can also see it as a politician, a speechmaker who understands his role as dignitary, honoring the men who gave their lives. "Nor long remember," and "any nation so conceived and so dedicated" are examples of what Wills calls "parenthetic enriching" of a phrase.

A study of Lincoln's asides shows that he consistently used them to refine, reiterate, and elaborate on the central meaning of his assertions, simultaneously using them as rhythmic elements. "The world will never forget what they did here" is a perfectly functional sentence. "The world will little note, nor long remember what we say here, but it can never forget what they did here," is a memorable one.

Misdirection

Writers are often reminded of the need to guide the reader's attention, to make certain things clear, to do away with distracting uncertainties. This is all good advice, but it can be interpreted to mean that stories, novels, and poems should be designed for maximum ease of use. A key element of both poetry and fiction is surprise. Most readers are looking for something like John Barth's funhouse—a story or poem in which we're carefully guided, in which our attention is focused but in which, for long stretches, we may have no idea where we're going. As writers, we need to be willing to provide our readers periods of anxiety, uncertainty, or misapprehension.

Misdirection can take many forms, and can be used on both the large and small scale. Poets know it as one of the possible uses of enjambment, and any writer can misdirect the reader by employing a familiar form. In a classic blues verse, the singer tells us,

I ain't never loved
But three people in my life:
That's my mother, my sister
and the woman who wrecked my life.

The lyricist trusts the listener both to understand the logical progression of mother, sister, _____, and to be familiar with the blues verse form, so anticipate the rhyme. That combination gets us to hear the unspoken word "wife"—and so tells us that the singer's wife is the one who wrecked his life—without ever saying any such thing.

ONE SEMESTER NOT LONG ago, in an undergraduate fiction course, we discussed Andre Dubus's "The Intruder." The students were a particularly lively and engaged group, great fun to talk to, so when I got to class I asked which of the three stories assigned for that day they'd like to start with. Some called for one story; some called for the other. None called for the Dubus. Out of curiosity, I asked, "But not 'The Intruder'? Why not?" They looked around, somewhat sheepish.

Finally Corey, one of those eager students who sits in the front and always seems to be leaning forward, said, "Maybe because it's not so good?"

"Not so good?" I said. When you plan these things, they never turn out this well. "Why not so good?"

"Well," Corey began. "It seems a little…obvious."

The rest of the students, relieved that one of their own had dared step forward, began nodding. It was clear they felt sorry for me.

"Obvious?" I said. "Is that right? Obvious how?"

Corey then summarized the story. On the first page thirteen-year-old Kenneth Girard, the main character, is in the woods, fantasizing about the kinds of things certain boys fantasize about: hitting a grand slam, leading soldiers on a daring attack, and saving a beautiful girl. When he heads back to the hunting camp his family is staying at, Dubus tells us that Kenneth's sister, Connie, is "the most beautiful girl he knew." Their parents are going out for the night, and he's looking forward to being alone with her. Kenneth is dismayed to learn that her boyfriend, Douglas, a football player, is coming over; nervous, he begins cleaning his rifle. Kenneth is no good at football, we're told; he's good at hunting.

Connie and Douglas clearly want to be alone; intuiting this, Kenneth refuses to go to bed. Connie argues with him, but Kenneth still refuses. Soon Douglas whispers to Connie and says goodnight; as soon as he leaves, Connie says she's going to bed, and asks if Kenneth is. A little while later, lying in bed, Kenneth hears a twig crack outside, the rustle of leaves; he gets up and sees a prowler making his way toward Connie's window.

"So," Corey concluded, "it's not exactly a surprise."

"Not a surprise?" I said. "What's not a surprise?"

Corey winced. You could see that it pained him to have to explain it to me. "That Kenneth shoots and kills the boyfriend."

"Well, no," I said. "I shouldn't think so. But what about the last two pages?"

"That?" Corey said. "I have no idea. That came out of nowhere."

WHEN KENNETH FIRES HIS rifle, his sister screams, then runs outside yelling "Douglas! Douglas! Douglas!" The story resumes after the parents have returned home, after the doctor and sheriff have come and gone, after the body has been carried away. It's almost sunrise. Kenneth's father gives him a pill and a glass of water. Kenneth takes the pill and says, "I thought it was a prowler." What happens next is what my students found—and any other reasonable reader of the story should find—surprising.

"It was, son. A prowler. We've told you that."

"But Connie went out there and she stayed all that time and she kept saying 'Douglas' over and over; I heard her—"

"She wasn't out there with *him*. She was just out in the yard. She was in shock. She meant she wanted Douglas to be there with her. To help."

"No, *no*. It was *him*."

"It was a prowler. You did right. There's no telling what he might have done."

Kenneth looked away.

"He was going in her room," he said. "That's why she went to bed early. So I'd go to bed."

"It was a prowler," his father said.

Now Kenneth was sleepy. He closed his eyes and the night ran together in his mind and he remembered the rifle in the corner and thought: *I'll throw it in the creek tomorrow. I never want to see it again.* He would be asleep soon. He saw himself standing on the hill and throwing his rifle into the creek; then the creek became an ocean, and he stood on a high cliff and for a moment he was a mighty angel, throwing all guns and cruelty and sex and tears into the sea.

The narrator never intervenes, not even to describe the father in any way that would influence our understanding of his speech. We're confronted with the fact that, despite our certainty that Kenneth has in fact killed his sister's boyfriend, his father insists that he did not. Having led us directly to the event we anticipated from the beginning of the story—having delivered on that old Chekhovian gun-above-the-mantle business—Dubus continues past it into a hairpin turn.

In "The Intruder," Dubus telegraphs the dramatic action in the manner of the best Hitchcock films: he strongly suggests what's going to happen, then leads us through an almost painfully suspenseful sequence before it finally does. Along the way, there are bits of humor and pathos: when the children's parents leave the cabin, their father tells Kenneth, "Hold down the fort, son," a line so pointed we wince, or laugh, or do both. When Kenneth looks at a picture in a magazine of a young woman in a bikini, he puts it away and forces himself to do pushups, which tells us plenty about his age, his morality, and his confusion. Kenneth and his family are god-fearing people; at the same time, Kenneth is tempted by those pictures of scantily clad women, his mother enjoys a beer before going out, and Connie, his beloved sister, has not only started smoking but has also kept her new habit a secret from him. Kenneth, his mother, and his sister each have their secret; as a family, and as characters in a story, they are perfectly established so that Dubus can introduce an event that will call their private actions and their professed morality into conflict.

Still: if the story ended with Kenneth killing his sister's boyfriend, it would be a good bit worse than the not-very-good story my students took it to be. When Dubus takes us past the event we anticipated, he surprises us; and he leaves us with questions. Why is the father protecting his son this way? How long will he be able to maintain this fiction? How is he going to respond to his grief-stricken, traumatized daughter? And given the family's morality, is it possible the father actually believes his son did the right thing? Suddenly a story that seemed almost painfully predictable has left us with a great deal to wonder about.

THERE'S A SIMILAR SORT of turn, executed differently, in Jim Shepard's "Krakatau"—one that suggests how we might address a particular problem in the process of drafting and revising.

Shepard's story is told by a man who has an older brother who is not mentally well. The brother, Donnie, is angry and frustrated. The narrator and his parents worry about what Donnie might do. The narrator, writing in retrospect, expresses a sense of guilt, or at least responsibility, for not doing more to help his brother, and so his parents. Alice Munro has written a variation of this "two brothers" story in "Monsieur Les Deux Chapeau," James Baldwin gave us "Sonny's Blues," and more recently Jamel Brinkley gave us "Everything the Mouth Eats." All of them are excellent stories, but of course the premise alone is no guarantee.

So let's say we find ourselves writing yet another observer-narrator-feels-remorse story. To give it a little texture, a little depth, and to see what might happen, we decide to introduce a metaphor: the narrator's volatile brother was like a volcano. Well, maybe, maybe not. Some days that's the best we can do. Maybe we stare at it a while, think, "Iceberg?" But no, then our reader will start thinking about Hemingway, and besides, it doesn't make sense, volatile like an iceberg.

So we've got our metaphor, and of course we want it to be subtle and clever and perfect, we want the reader to see the comparison at just the right time…but volatile like a volcano? How are we going to hide that? Our ideal reader isn't that dense.

So instead you give yourself a challenge. You make the brother volatile like a volcano—and you make the narrator a guy who studies volcanoes. For that matter, you call the story "Volcano!" (Later you'll think better of it, and drop the exclamation mark.) In the great tradition of Nathaniel Hawthorne and "The Birthmark," John Steinbeck and "The Harness," you're going to make it impossible for your reader to miss this volcano metaphor.

And once you commit to that, the challenge is to push the story beyond the obvious, beyond what the thoughtful reader might anticipate—to use the metaphor not to clarify something for the reader but to explore what you already understand about the story you're trying to tell.

Here's how Jim Shepard does it:

The focus of the story is Donnie, the volatile, explosive, physically violent brother. The narrator is a volcanologist whose graduate work focused on the causes of the eruption of Krakatau in 1883, but his specific interest is in eyewitness accounts. Most important, for our purposes, is that Shepard allows the narrator to be aware that he's enacting a metaphor. He tells us: "My father's theory was that explosions could be avoided if everyone did their utmost to work around him. My theory was that something cyclical and inexorable was going on, and that one way or another, sooner or later, he had to go off."

There's no pretense. But in case there is a reader of English who doesn't yet get it, roughly midway through the story the narrator tells us about a meeting with his thesis advisor: "What is it with you and Krakatoa, anyway? ... You can talk to someone like me now or talk to a shrink later." Donnie sends the narrator a book about Krakatau:

> Even my brother, in other words, had seen through the schematic of my private metaphor and knew the answer to my advisor's question. Why is he obsessed with volcanoes? Because they go off, regardless of what anyone can do. And because, when they do go off, it's no one's fault. Volcanology: the science of standing around and cataloguing the devastation.

The story has started to change terms, to shift focus. We're still keeping an eye on Donnie, but we realize the narrator's stance is unstable. He's telling us that he somehow thought other people wouldn't understand why he's so interested in volcanoes; and he's telling us that he sees himself as distant from Donnie, a cool observer.

Over the years, Donnie's outbursts have grown increasingly violent. As a teenager, he threw the narrator down the stairs; around the same time he threw a footstool through the television and, when his parents called the police, said that as soon as the police left he would kill all three of them. In his thirties, he slaps their mother, knocking her to the floor. The narrator describes a visit from his brother when Donnie is forty-two, then tells us, "I warned my parents. Which, I thought to myself, would help my conscience later." And he asks, "Why didn't I help?"

All of that is to say, everything the narrator tells us suggests that the big explosion is coming—or, since this is a retrospective narrative, that the explosion has happened, that Donnie has killed their parents, possibly even himself, and what we are reading is, in effect, an eyewitness account of the events leading to the eruption. Like "The Intruder," the story has all but promised us a horrific act, a scene of devastation.

And that's where Shepard makes his boldest move.

Donnie is never mentioned again. Neither are the brothers' parents.

Instead, the narrator turns inward: "Volcanoes, volcanoes, volcanoes. In a crucial way he didn't resemble volcanoes at all. Most volcanoes look like oceans. Because they're *under* oceans. Nothing happening for hundreds of years. Something destructive surfacing only very very rarely; who did that *really* sound like?" The narrator shifts our attention, applying the metaphor to himself; he's the one who provokes Donnie, intentionally or unintentionally, every time they're together. The eruption, then, is not just Donnie's expression of anger but the result of the narrator's provocation.

The final two pages consist of eyewitness accounts of the eruption of Krakatau, from the narrator's collection. They describe the rising and falling of the sea, "a blinding rain," "darkness...spread across the sky," "a cliff of water, trees, and houses disappearing," and then this, from a Dutch boat pilot:

> The moment of greatest anguish was not the actual destruction of the wave. The worst part by far was afterwards, when I knew I was saved, and the receding flood carried back past me the bodies of friends and neighbors and family. And I remember clawing past other arms and legs as you might fight through a bramble. And I thought, "The world is our relentless adversary, rarely outwitted, never tiring." And I thought, "I would give all these people's lives, once more, to see something so beautiful again."

We thought we were heading toward murder, or suicide, or something equally and predictably awful: but instead we're led to the narrator's darkest secret, his most revealing, albeit indirect, confession. In the same way that old blues lyric makes us hear "wife" in "the woman who wrecked my life," we understand that Shepard's narrator is telling us he would sacrifice his family in order to see something as beautiful as Donnie's eruptions.

As beautiful as his brother's violence.

As *beautiful*.

As readers, we anticipate everything about the progression of the story until we're completely surprised.

IN "KRAKATAU," SHEPARD'S BLATANT deployment of the titular metaphor encourages the reader to look beyond the surface events and to anticipate the nature of the final explosion, its causes, and what could have prevented it. In changing the terms of the story—in shifting our attention from the volatile brother to the narrator, who takes a sordid pleasure in eruptions—he surprises us, not for the sake of surprise alone but to expose a dark truth, one we are likely to resist. But the odds are good that the reader is the sort of person who has slowed down to take in the scene of a car wreck, or gone out to the sidewalk to stand and watch, at a safe distance, when a neighbor's house burned, or sat enthralled by television coverage of the devastation caused by a hundred-year flood. There is, Shepard suggests, not only a horror but also a fascination to these scenes, one we might deny but would be better off forcing ourselves to acknowledge.

"Krakatau" and "The Intruder" serve as reminders to embrace and then work to transcend what we understand about our stories, refusing to give the reader a surprise that's simply clever or prepos-terous. Instead we have to search until we find the unexpected thing that feels true.

ONE OF THE OLDEST ploys of magicians—and their cousins, con men—is to explain how the trick is done. Or, rather, to explain how a simpler version of the effect they're about to execute is done. Then, having prepared us to see one thing, they show us something transcendent. This is how Dubus and Shepard lure us in—not by avoiding the familiar or predictable, hoping to come up with a way to tell a story that we've never seen before, but to embrace the familiar or predictable, and to write past it.

While I've been using *misdirection*, I've come to believe that's not the most accurate term to use to describe what this fiction is doing. When nonmagicians talk about what magicians do, they often use that word; but magicians are divided over it, much as they're divided over the word *trick*. Misdirection sounds like a mistake, or willful confusion; it sounds as if the goal is solely to distract the viewer (or reader). In magic, it often is. But in his essay "Getting the Mis Out of Misdirection," the Dutch magician who performed and wrote as Tommy Wonder says, "Misdirection must be attention directed *toward* something, not away from something." So while digressions, asides, and related techniques sometimes serve as intentional distractions, in the work I've been discussing they have a larger purpose. Watching *Diner*, we might feel the film is taking a very leisurely path to the impending wedding, when in fact it's everything we see and hear along the way—the late-night conversations, the pranks, the friendly antagonism and the idle hours at the diner, and what all of those things reveal about the main characters—that are the heart of the film.

Digressions and asides are in fact a form of direction: used effectively, they focus our attention on what we would otherwise overlook.

Don't Stand So Close to Me

Narrative Distance in First-Person Fiction

Uncle Mac and Aunt Vera had done well, my wife's family felt: they had left small-town Iowa and gotten themselves a nice place in Florida, on the water, and a boat; they were members of a musical society; they drank martinis; and they owned a bowling alley back in Burlington, Iowa. Mac died before I joined the family, but now Vera was gone, and everyone wanted to know, among other things, what would happen to her famous collection of miniature pitchers.

I don't remember what month the funeral was held. I remember it was outside and it was uncomfortable, but of course funerals are always uncomfortable. We were all dressed formally and doing our best to look appropriately mournful, as members of the family, even though my wife and her brother and sister hadn't seen Mac and Vera all that often, and we spouses barely knew anything about them. Before the service started, there was some bad feeling about the fact that remarks would be made not by a member of the family but by Paul, the manager of the bowling alley.

When he spoke, though, we learned that Paul had a moving story to tell. Mac had hired him when he was a young man, and

gradually took him under his wing. Mac had been quite a successful businessman, twice: once before the Great Depression, when
he lost nearly everything, and again after, when, having learned his
lesson, he conducted all of his business in cash, never taking a loan,
never using a credit card. He and Vera had no children, and Paul
became their project. Over time he was promoted, and treated less
like an employee than an adopted son. For this, Paul told us, he
was deeply grateful. In addition to running the bowling alley, he
had helped Vera when Mac died, and more recently, he had been
actively involved in arranging for her medical care.

So far, so good. Now we understood why Paul had been chosen
to give the eulogy.

Like many people, Paul was at his best when talking about his
own experience. The trouble came, that day, when he had to turn
his attention to others. He understandably felt obliged to recognize
various people in attendance. And while he had notes, Paul did, it
soon became clear that they consisted solely of a list of names and
relationships (cousin, niece, neighbor, fellow martini drinker, member of the musical society, etc.). He had not, apparently, thought
through what he would say about each person, and I'm afraid the
man was not a gifted spontaneous orator. At first it was perfectly
fine that cousin Judy was special to Vera; and no one objected to the
notion that Vera and Sandy always had a special relationship. But
the word seemed to get stuck on his lips. After that, every person
he mentioned was either "special" to Vera, "very special," or "very,
very special." The six of us—my wife and I, her brother and sister,
their spouses—were sitting together, and about the tenth time Paul
the bowling alley manager said someone was special, we made the
mistake of exchanging glances. From that moment on, "special" was
the only word we heard.

But redundancy was only part of the problem. I don't know that Paul had what should properly be called a speech impediment; it may just have been a regional accent. Whatever the cause, he pronounced the word "spatial." Ralph was spatial; Marie was very spatial. It got to the point that we waited for it; when it came, we all mouthed the word together. My lovely and goodhearted wife had tears streaming down her cheeks, but not from the loss of poor Vera; my brother-in-law struggled mightily to study his shoes, but the twenty-third "spatial" had him keeling forward, even as his wife ground her heel into his foot.

When the service was finally over, we ran to the black limousine waiting for us; finally, when we slammed the doors, we could scream with laughter. I can only hope that we looked delirious from grief.

I HAD MET VERA once, a few months before she died. She suffered from dementia, and had been brought from Florida to a modest nursing facility in Burlington, the small town she had been so eager to escape. She didn't have many remaining relatives, and not everyone felt compelled to visit, given the progression of her disease. She believed Mac was still alive, and that they would be returning to their home in Florida any day. My wife and I lived in the western suburbs of Chicago then, and my wife truly is a good person, so one morning we made the three-and-a-half-hour drive to Burlington.

That day, Vera didn't understand who my wife was, much less follow Laura's explanation of who I was; and after we had absorbed the few simple decorations in the room, and the supposedly cheerful sign straight out of a kindergarten classroom meant to remind Vera of the month and date, there wasn't much to do.

A small television showed an automobile race. None of us paid attention, though occasionally Vera seemed to be trying to say something about it. Her statements were either incomplete or without context. Vera had trouble forming sentences, much less stringing them together. At first, we tried to converse; then, defeated, we sat.

If you've known someone in the final stages of dementia, you know how sad it is. But—and I know this sounds hard-hearted—after a while, the sadness has time to settle in, and give way to something like restlessness, even boredom. Not for her caretakers, of course, but for visitors. Or maybe it's just me; I'll admit it, I started checking the time.

After an hour or so of keeping Vera company, we said goodbye, and that we were sure the people at the facility would take good care of her, and we were glad she was comfortable—the sort of nonsense you say when the truth is unspeakable. Vera looked at us as we took her hand, but once again she couldn't get any words out.

It wasn't until we were halfway to the door that she began to speak.

"I—" she said. And again, "I—." Who could walk out on a dying woman attempting to form a sentence? Not us.

We waited.

Finally—slowly—Vera said, as clearly as we had spoken to her, "I'm losing my mind, you know."

THERE IS OFTEN A difference between what someone says and what we comprehend; the difference between what someone means to communicate, or thinks he or she is communicating, and what actually gets the listener's attention. If we want to put a craft label on it, we could identify this as the narrative distance in first-person narratives.

If, for instance, we think of Paul the bowling alley manager as a first-person narrator, and the gathered mourners as his audience, that audience was perfectly happy to accept his authority, to accept his tale without question, until we noticed unintentional repetition; that unintentional repetition gradually took on meaning, of a sort, until Paul lost virtually all authority, all control over his story; instead of attending to what he hoped to tell us, we, his listeners, were focused elsewhere.

Now you might say, "Pete, that's because you're a terrible person, the kind of person who scrutinizes someone's speech even at a funeral. And the rest of your in-laws, they're apparently unpleasant people as well." And maybe you're right. But if you're now thinking about me and my perspective on the story I've told, you're also illustrating my point—you're studying the speaker as well as what's spoken.

There are certainly times when people tell us stories and our focus remains largely if not entirely on what they're telling us—and we accept what they say. But there are all sorts of situations, every day, when we find ourselves evaluating the teller as well as the tale.

If we think of Vera as a first-person narrator that day my wife and I visited her, we see nearly the opposite of what happened with Paul: the story she tried to tell was so cryptic, so obscure, so fragmented, as to verge on nonsense; we could only guess what she was trying to say. Instead, we focused on her appearance and surroundings, essentially creating our own stories. Then, as we left, she said something that forced us to reconsider—our distance from her was collapsed, our entire experience transformed. Initially, as a narrator, she had no authority at all; but in her final statement, she spoke to us with terrifying urgency, and heartbreaking self-awareness.

The Primitive First Person (How Can There Be Any Sin in Sincere?)

For three consecutive years, I was asked to serve as the final judge of a short story contest. Other readers reduced the entries to what they believed to be the best five, which I then had to rank. The stories were perfectly fine; what got my attention was that, each year, at least four of the five finalists were stories told in the first person, and all of those first-person narrators were, or were meant to be, clever, amusing, and entertaining, as well as insightful and, depending on the story, proud, regretful, or sadder but wiser. Whatever the narrator might be talking about—some sort of escapade or relationship—the focus was always on the events and what the narrator thought about them. I came to think of this point of view as the Sincere First Person. The sincerity had nothing to do with the tone or emotional register of the story, only with the fact that we, the readers, were never meant to doubt or question or criticize the first-person narrator, except to the extent that the narrator doubted or criticized herself. If we did find ourselves disagreeing with the narrator, we were also disagreeing with the author.

In other words: There was no apparent difference between the author's view of the story and the narrator's view of the story.

I've come to feel it might be more accurate to call this the Primitive First Person: not in a derogatory way, but in the sense that this stance is primal; it comes first. If we imagine our early ancestors sitting in the flickering light of the fire, we imagine them focused purely on content. The teller of the various creation myths and folktales handed down to us is transparent, invisible. (This transparency is one reason many readers—and a dismaying number of interviewers—assume a first-person story or novel is more or less autobiographical.)

That apparent difference, or the lack of it, gives us one way to test the perspective of a story in the first person: We can ask, What does the *narrator* believe this story is about, or reveals? And then, What does the *author* seem to believe this story reveals? If the answers are the same, the story is written in the Primitive First Person.

Of course, the next question should be: Is that the right choice? Or has that stance been used by default?

EVEN BEFORE READING THOSE contest finalists, like most of us who have taught for a while, I had read thousands—literally, thousands—of MFA application manuscripts. And over time, I came to recognize that colloquial first-person narratives of this type were some of the trickiest to evaluate. It was often hard to tell if the writer could do anything else. Even Paul, the bowling alley manager, could tell an engaging story about himself.

Again: there is nothing wrong with the Primitive First Person. But one of the potential shortcomings is that the first-person narrator can be a voice describing events, rather than a fully considered character, one with the same sorts of strengths and weaknesses, biases and blind spots as any other fully developed character. We might ask ourselves: Over the course of the story, does no other character question the narrator's account, or point out his or her misperceptions, or reveal something to the reader that the narrator has omitted or failed to see? If so, the character of the narrator may not be fully considered.

Retrospection

Frederick Reiken has written a very useful essay on what he calls "the A-N-C merge." He points out that in first-person novels based closely on autobiography, writers often fail to recognize the necessary or useful distinctions among author, narrator, and character. Even in first-person novels that aren't autobiographical, the failure to recognize the potential differences between the main character as they take action and the main character as they recount that action results in Primitive First Person by default.

One of the most common strategies to expose the character of a first-person narrator is retrospection. *Great Expectations* is told in the retrospective first person by Pip, at some unknown amount of time after the events he recounts took place. When he treats his loving brother-in-law, Jo, brusquely, or spends money recklessly, we're critical of his speech and actions—but the older Pip, our narrator, is always quick to rush in and tell us he acted badly, that he was being thoughtless or foolish. That older Pip, our narrator, is intended to be authoritative; if we have any disagreement with him, we're also in disagreement with his creator. The advantage of the retrospective narrator is that it allows for a distinction between the narrator and the character, the teller and his actions.

In "Araby," James Joyce's adult narrator perceives and shapes the meaning of a childhood incident his younger self understood much differently; in *The Great Gatsby*, Nick Carraway is writing fairly soon after the events he describes took place, but his psychic distance from them is great enough that he's contemplated them, rearranged them, found significance in them. In the *Paris Review*, Ralph Ellison said the narrator of *Invisible Man* moves from "purpose to passion to perception…The maximum insight on the hero's part isn't reached until the final section." But while the main character might achieve "maximum insight" only in the epilogue, his understanding filters his retelling of past events: his younger self may act out of ignorance, innocence, or naïveté, but we see those actions from the distance of the older, insightful man.

Another advantage to the distance provided by retrospection is that it frees the character to be more of a writer, for the telling to be more considered. Without it, the immediacy of the Primitive First Person—which is sometimes compounded by the use of present tense—often comes at the expense of contemplation, reflection, and self-examination.

Irony

The opposite of sincerity might seem to be irony. Edgar Allan Poe's "The Tell-Tale Heart" begins like this:

> True!—nervous—very, very dreadfully nervous I had been and am; but why will you say that I am mad? The disease had sharpened my senses—not destroyed—not dulled them. Above all was the sense of hearing acute. I heard all things in the heaven and in the earth. I heard many things in hell. How, then, am I mad? Hearken! and observe how healthily—how calmly I can tell you the whole story.

Yes; well. That quickly, we are convinced that our narrator is not to be trusted, and nothing he goes on to tell us changes our opinion of him. "The Tell-Tale Heart" is a horror story, and much of the horror comes from Poe's demonstration of misapplied reason. While the action—killing an old man so as to keep his eye from disturbing the narrator—is unpleasant, Poe's real interest was in the rational mind gone wrong, and to demonstrate that, he has us board the crazy train in the first paragraph, and never lets us off.

Crucial to the success of this choice is conveying that the reader isn't to take the narrator's claims and assertions at face value. Here Poe achieves that in the first paragraph through extreme repetition, overemphasis, insistence, and highly dubious claims. This narrator doth protest too much.

While our relationship to an Ironic First-Person Narrator is certainly different than our relationship to the Sincere or Primitive Narrator, in both cases that relationship is (or can be) static: our essential understanding of and attitude toward the character doesn't change. But in practice it's relatively rare for us to feel distant—or, rather, at a single distance—from an ironic first-person narrator. And shifting narrative distance leads to some interesting options.

Shifting Distance

My particular interest is in first-person narrators with whom readers have a dynamic relationship—which is truest to the sort of relationship we have with storytellers in life. No matter whether we're listening to our parents or our children, our spouse or lovers, our friends or strangers, sometimes we find ourselves agreeing, sometimes disagreeing; sometimes we're moved by the speaker's insight and understanding, other times we feel certain she's missing something essential.

Yet there's an excellent reason to avoid creating this sort of first-person narrator in stories and novels: the risk of being misunderstood.

You may have seen this: the writer meant for the narrator's actions to be bold, but readers find that action distasteful; the writer means for the narrator to be witty, but readers find the character annoying; the writer meant for a character's action to be detestable, but readers find the action forgivable—and so on. In other words, it seems difficult enough to keep the reader on board, to use the Primitive First Person effectively. Why make our job any harder?

Those moments when the reader finds herself at odds with the writer's apparent intention are failures of narrative control—breakdowns in the writer's attempt to guide the reader's perspective on the character or event. (Of course, not all readers will agree with any writer; we all have differences in taste, sensibility, morality, and politics, as well as in what we find clever, what we find moving, etc.; but as writers we're generally trying to communicate a perspective on people and events, as well as the events themselves.) When a moment like those is written well—when we disagree with the first-person narrator but understand that the author disagrees too—the story or novel actually gains authority. While we might feel a momentary distance from the character, we feel a greater intimacy with the work.

THE ADVENTURES OF HUCKLEBERRY FINN is, for long stretches, a master class in the delicate balance of sincerity and irony. One famous moment illustrates Mark Twain's narrative control.

The passage appears in chapter 31, when Huck is faced with a dilemma. Jim, his enslaved companion, has been turned in by the Duke and Dauphin. Huck has two apparent options: not to intervene, and let Jim be sold; or to write to the Widow and Miss Watson, the "owners" Jim is escaping, so they can claim him. The novel is set two decades before the Civil War. Huck is a boy. In his world, enslaved people are valuable property, and the Bible is often invoked not to condemn but to justify slavery. Huck was given such religious training by the Widow and Miss Watson. Society, the law, and religion as he's been guided in it all tell Huck that the right thing to do is to help return Jim. So he writes a letter to the Widow and Miss Watson to let them know where Jim is, and how to claim him. He tries to pray. But Huck is in turmoil: while he knows what's "right"—what society, law, and religion say he should do—he can't ignore his own experience, and Jim has been kind to him. The most famous line of the passage is the climax of Huck's decision-making, when he says, "All right, then, I'll *go* to hell"—by which he means he won't send the letter but will instead try to free Jim.

Of course, we believe that's the right thing to do. But the pressures acting on Huck lead him to believe he is doing something terrible, something unforgivable:

> It was awful thoughts and awful words, but they was said. And I let them stay said; and never thought no more about reforming. I shoved the whole thing out of my head, and said I would take up wickedness again, which was in my line, being brung up to it, and the other warn't. And for a starter I would go to work and steal Jim out of slavery again; and if I could think up anything worse, I would do that, too; because as long as I was in, and in for good, I might as well go the whole hog.

Here's the magic of that moment: when Huck says, "All right, then, I'll *go* to hell," the reader knows that exactly the opposite is true—that Huck has taken the moral high road. More than that, the reader knows that Mark Twain, the author, believes Huck is doing the right thing. No character tells Huck or us that he's made the right choice; and of course, since the novel is in first person, no other narrator tells us Huck is doing the right thing. We simply understand, at this point in the novel, that we're to believe exactly the opposite of what we're being told.

That moment alone is an example of ironic distance: while Poe used irony to show us the perspective of a madman, Twain uses it to show us the perspective of a naive boy—and he often uses that distance for comic effect. But to take on the moral issues that concerned him, Twain needed to be able to collapse that distance at times. And so while Huck is naive, he can be surprisingly observant, even insightful; he can also be honest, serious, and compassionate. As early as chapter 2, when he is still playing with Tom Sawyer and other boys, Huck tells us, "When Tom and me got to the edge of the hill-top, we looked away down into the village and could see three or four lights twinkling, where there was sick folks, may be; and the stars over us was sparkling ever so fine; and down by the village was the river, a whole mile broad, and awful still and grand."

There's no irony in that description, and Huck's surprising consideration that the lights in houses late at night might indicate someone is sick introduces a compassionate imagination. These moments increase in intensity through the novel, building to passages such as the one when Huck feels shame for lying to Jim about being lost in the fog, and apologizes. Tom Quirk writes, "The most poetic and memorable passages in *Huckleberry Finn* are those when Huck's (and sometimes Jim's) subjective consciousness permeates the world…In *Huckleberry Finn*, the author sometimes yields entirely to the voice and sensibility of its young narrator, and when that happens there is magic in the book."

The question before us is, How does Twain do it? How does he establish a first-person narrator who we are to take at face value one minute and understand from a significant ironic distance the next?

Most stories and novels that shift narrative distance offer significant clues to the reader at the outset. While the common saying is that every good story or novel teaches us how to read it, it might be more helpful for us, as writers, to recognize that when we write a story or novel that eventually leads the reader to a place of surprise or complication—not just in terms of plot but in terms of technique, or strategy—as in this case, when the writer wants to signal a complex and dynamic relationship to the narrator—we need to make sure to establish the possibility, or the plausibility, of that effect before it happens. Otherwise, the reader is likely to feel cheated, or confused in a way that doesn't serve the work but instead undermines it.

Twain conceived of the novel as a companion to his enormously popular *The Adventures of Tom Sawyer*, but Huck Finn is a different sort of character, with a different perspective. To announce that, Twain started the novel like this:

> You don't know about me without you have read a book by the name of *The Adventures of Tom Sawyer*; but that ain't no matter. That book was made by Mr. Mark Twain, and he told the truth, mainly. There was things which he stretched, but mainly he told the truth. That is nothing. I never seen anybody but lied one time or another, without it was Aunt Polly, or the widow, or maybe Mary. Aunt Polly—Tom's Aunt Polly, she is—and Mary, and the Widow Douglas is all told about in that book, which is mostly a true book, with some stretchers, as I said before.

Tom Sawyer was told in the third person, narrated by a witty and nostalgic man. *Huckleberry Finn* is not only in the first person, but begins with what might seem like a startling bit of premodernist postmodernism—though in fact it's in the tradition of certain eighteenth-century novels. Huck, a character, is passing judgment on his author, Mark Twain. The initial effect is comic. But this opening also establishes the grounds for Huck's authority, which is to correct and continue the previous book, written by Mark Twain—which serves notice to the reader that this will be a different sort of book. And of course, the reader understands that this criticism of Mark Twain's storytelling comes, through Huck, from Mark Twain himself. And so from this opening paragraph, we're reading two books at once: the one Huck is narrating, and the one Mark Twain is suggesting, or implying. It's as if the author is standing directly behind his character, and chooses at times to stretch out his arms, or lean one way or another, to get our attention—then draws in again and disappears.

Twain made a career, or most of one, out of manipulating distance toward comic ends; and he could have very easily continued in the vein of the opening paragraph to make *Huckleberry Finn* merely a comic novel. But by that point in his life, Twain had seen the steamboat era end, he had seen towns destroyed by the Civil War and its aftermath, his brother had been killed, and he was more critical than sentimental toward what he had come to see as small-town small-mindedness, particularly in the South. The challenge he confronted, then, was to make Huck more than a comic figure, to use Huck's outsider status as the motherless son of the town drunk to provide a very different perspective than Twain had in *Tom Sawyer*.

On the book's second page, Twain introduces Huck as social critic:

> Pretty soon I wanted to smoke, and asked the widow to let me. But she wouldn't. She said it was a mean practice and wasn't clean, and I must try to not do it any more. That is just the way with some people. They get down on a thing when they don't know nothing about it. Here she was a-bothering about Moses, which was no kin to her, and no use to anybody, being gone, you see, yet finding a power of fault with me for doing a thing that had some good in it. And she took snuff, too; of course that was all right, because she done it herself.

Are we laughing *at* Huck, or *with* Huck? Both, possibly.

This is one of the most challenging elements in work in any point of view that shifts narrative distance: there are, necessarily, transitional passages, moments that rest somewhere on the border between two more distinct effects. Look closely at virtually any story written in the close third person by Alice Munro, Chekhov, Katherine Anne Porter, or Mavis Gallant, among others, and you'll find sentences that aren't clearly representing the character's thoughts or clearly coming from the narrator. This is not a mistake; on the contrary, it's a sign of mastery. A story isn't a paint-by-number, with clear borders between colors; there are mixtures and combinations of colors, moments of intentional blurring, moments of transition. In *Huckleberry Finn*, Twain uses these passages to lead us from high irony to sincerity.

Soon Huck's irritation turns to melancholy and fear:

> Then everybody was off to bed. I went up to my room with a piece of candle, and put it on the table. Then I set down in a chair by the

window and tried to think of something cheerful, but it warn't no use. I felt so lonesome I most wished I was dead. The stars were shining, and the leaves rustled in the woods ever so mournful; and I heard an owl, away off, who-whooing about somebody that was dead, and a whippowill and a dog crying about somebody that was going to die; and the wind was trying to whisper something to me, and I couldn't make out what it was, and so it made the cold shivers run over me. Then away out in the woods I heard that kind of a sound that a ghost makes when it wants to tell about something that's on its mind and can't make itself understood, and so can't rest easy in its grave, and has to go about that way every night grieving. I got so down-hearted and scared I did wish I had some company.

That quickly, Twain has broadened the novel's tonal and emotional range. The satire yields to sincerity; the narrative distance has collapsed.

Tom Quirk writes that "Mark Twain often submerged himself in and submitted to the voices of his created characters, the lowliest of the low, a 'community of misfortune' as he later called the pair, and let them speak for themselves. In other words, *Huckleberry Finn* is the supremely democratic novel, at least it is when Twain stays out of the way." But this is misleading. Huck Finn is Mark Twain's creation. To the extent that Twain "stayed out of the way" at times, he was allowing himself to access another part of his own nature. Like a lot of humorists, Twain—Samuel Clemens—had a dark side. As a young man, he once came close to committing suicide; as an old man, he was frequently depressed. Perhaps more to the point, when Twain wrote *Huck Finn* he was a different man, a different writer, than the one who had written *Tom Sawyer*. He wanted to do more than entertain, and his social satire was increasingly cutting. What we see in Huck that we don't see in Tom is a complex person, one as full of doubt and shame and regret and sympathy as bold assertion, naïveté, and ignorance. Far from "staying out of the way" in *Huckleberry Finn*, Twain dared to reveal more of himself, to surrender, at least for moments, his well-polished comic stance.

THE MOVEMENT FROM SINCERITY to irony and back, over and over, helps to establish Huck as a compelling character, one capable of surprising us, and capable of change; and it requires the reader to be actively engaged, not simply listening to Huck but considering how we're meant to respond to him at any given moment. That's the real difference between the novels *Tom Sawyer* and *Huckleberry Finn*: the first was an entertainment, a performance piece, one that allowed, even encouraged, the reader to be a passive recipient. *Huckleberry Finn* was meant to *animate* the reader—not simply to amuse us and to arouse our sympathy for the main character but to engage us in his moral dilemma. When Huck says, "All right then, I'll go to hell," and we think, "Oh no, you're doing the right thing," Twain has succeeded in leading us to participate in the narrative.

You might recall that famous letter of Chekhov's, when he wrote to a writer in response to her manuscript and said, "The trouble is, when you want your reader to cry, you cry. Be cold." Twain knew from long experience that his dry delivery encouraged his audience to laugh; but in *Huckleberry Finn* he discovered how to combine sincerity and irony in order to move the reader to a much larger range of emotions.

Putting the Reader to Work, Part 1: Unlikability and Deliberate Provocation

Few if any readers will doubt that the narrator of "The Tell-Tale Heart" is a madman; few if any readers will misunderstand when Mark Twain intends for Huckleberry Finn to be sincere and when he intends for us to see Huck through the lens of comic irony. But there are a great many works that offer the reader a more complex relationship with a first-person narrator, works that choose not to give us broad, clear signals but instead, intentionally, lead us into dimly lit alleys, in suspect company.

Perhaps the most notorious of these is Vladimir Nabokov's *Lolita*. Humbert Humbert is no Primitive Narrator. He's as far from transparent as he could be, and we're certainly not meant to take him at face value—Nabokov begins his novel with an introduction by a fictitious psychiatrist to tell us as much. But neither do we stand at one clear distance from Humbert, something Nabokov makes impossible with those memorable opening lines:

> Lolita, light of my life, fire of my loins. My sin, my soul. Lo-lee-ta: the tip of the tongue taking a trip of three steps down the palate to tap, at three, on the teeth. Lo. Lee. Ta.

> She was Lo, plain Lo, in the morning, standing four feet ten in one sock; she was Lola in slacks. She was Dolly at school. She was Dolores on the dotted line. But in my arms she was always Lolita.

Humbert Humbert is introduced as a poet, a lover, and a wit. He is maniacal, he's obsessed, and he's smarter than we are—something he reminds us when he offers passages in French, without translation, and when he confronts us with elaborate puzzles. He's arrogant. He makes us laugh despite ourselves. And he is detestable. The novel asserts all of this at the outset: in the foreword, fictitious John Ray Jr. tells us Humbert is "horrible," "a shining example of moral leprosy" guilty of "sins of diabolical cunning. He is abnormal. He is not a gentleman"; but he also has a "desperate honesty" and "makes us entranced with the book while abhorring its author." By asserting and then demonstrating all of these readings, Nabokov forces us beyond them. The novel would be something much less if it didn't make us so uncomfortable, if Humbert were as easy to judge as Poe's madman, or Huck.

To be clear: the larger issue here isn't whether a first-person narrator is likeable or unlikeable; it's creating a fully developed, complex narrator—not for the sake of difficulty but to replicate our actual experience with complex human beings. To paraphrase Chekhov, if we want readers to engage seriously with our narrator, we need to create a narrator that requires serious engagement. We can be briefly persuaded by Humbert Humbert about one thing or another—say, for instance, his descriptions of the American West, or of small motels, or even his own monstrosity—even as we disagree with him about quite a lot.

Typically, narrative distance is used to describe our intimacy with or distance from a character's thoughts. You could argue that we're as intimate with the thoughts of the narrator of "The Tell-Tale Heart" as we are with the narrators of John Updike's "A&P" or Eudora Welty's "Why I Live at the P.O." In first-person narratives, we always have some degree of intimacy with the narrator, if only because we have constant access to that narrator's language, and way of making meaning. The distance we feel from Poe's narrator arises not from a lack of access to his thinking but from a difference between what he tells us and what we understand to be true. That distinction is successfully controlled by Poe.

Similarly, in *Adventures of Huckleberry Finn*, we always have access to the narrator's thoughts, doubts, suspicions, and so on. Sometimes we're in agreement with them, sometimes we're not, sometimes we laugh, sometimes we're saddened, but we feel confident that we know when the author wants us to accept the character at face value, and when we're meant to question him. What shifts is our affiliation with the narrator, our agreement with his expressions and assertions. But while our relationship with the narrator is dynamic, our relationship to the book's greater authority is steady. (Except: Roughly three-quarters of the way through *Huckleberry Finn*, as many readers have noted, things fall apart.)

Lolita creates a more complicated relationship between author, narrator, and reader. Nabokov often seems to be just out of sight, as elusive as Claire Quilty. What does he really think of Humbert Humbert? How does he mean for us to react to him? At times, it's clear that Nabokov wants us to be outraged, even as he wants us to be amused, and moved, at others. If the novel succeeds, we can't simply dismiss Humbert any more than we can simply embrace him. If the novel succeeds, Nabokov leads us into a contemplation of art, artist, and bad behavior as complex as any we're likely to experience in life. There is no question about what we should think of Humbert's actions: he's a serial rapist and pedophile. There are serious questions about what we should make of his narrative, and what we should make of Nabokov's novel. In complicating our relationship to Humbert Humbert, Nabokov employs an approach more daring than Twain's and Poe's, more dangerous.

These days, when it seems that offending or possibly offending any reader might lead to the equivalent of being locked in the stocks of social media, many writers feel obliged to make their opinions and attitudes toward their characters as apparent as possible. "What do we really want from a poem?" Tony Hoagland once asked; and answered, "We want to encounter a version of the world and of human nature that is not overly simplified." Oversimplification is a disservice to the serious reader, the one who reads not for comfort but to be led to places of discomfort, the one who reads not to have her beliefs reaffirmed but to be led to reconsider them.

Putting the Reader to Work, Part 2: A Quieter Way (Omission, Implication, Arrangement)

It isn't surprising that younger or naive narrators and madmen are treated with ironic distance. But it isn't necessary to resort to such extremes to lead readers into an active relationship with a first-person narrator, to encourage readers both to listen to her and to question her. I'll look briefly at a few more, ranging from eccentric narrators to those who might more easily blend in among us.

TO SOME READERS, JANINA Duszejko, the narrator of Olga Tokarczuk's *Drive Your Plow over the Bones of the Dead*, might seem nearly as mad as the narrator of "The Tell-Tale Heart." She introduces herself by telling us she makes sure to wash her feet every night, in the event that she might need to be removed from her home by ambulance; that she uses, as a sleep aid, "an infusion of hops"; and that first names and surnames demonstrate "a lack of imagination," so she refers to people by "epithets that come to mind of their own accord the first time I see a Person."

Thus she refers to some of the people she knows as Big Foot, Oddball, Good News, and Dark Coat. Her capitalization is unconventional, and she interprets the world largely through cosmology, or horoscopes, as when she says her neighbor Oddball "generally doesn't say much. He must have Mercury in a reticent sign, I reckon it's in Capricorn or on the cusp, in square or maybe in opposition to Saturn." As the novel unfolds, the logical and philosophical grounding of Janina's beliefs becomes clear. Unlike her neighbors, she is not a Catholic, and she opposes much of what is done in the name of religion (though she appreciates the silent contemplation available during church services). Unlike her neighbors, she is opposed to hunting, and sees the prevailing attitude that human lives are more important than animal lives as a kind of madness. A retired engineer—a bridge builder—she now teaches English, and translates the work of William Blake with a friend. She has no children, and grieves deeply the recent loss of her two dogs.

Framed as a whodunit, the novel falls into that subgenre of murder mysteries narrated by the murderer. In that way, it's related to "The Tell-Tale Heart," *Lolita*, Graham Greene's *The Quiet American*, and even Agatha Christie's *The Murder of Roger Ackroyd*. As in those works, the narrator of *Drive Your Bones* devotes a good deal of time explaining her view of the world, justifying her actions. But while we will never share Humbert Humbert's attitude toward nymphets or Poe's narrator's belief in an old man's evil eye, any number of readers, while stopping short of justifying murder, will agree with Janina's anger over the apparent hypocrisy of those who claim to value life but celebrate killing, the arrogance of those who believe humans should impose their will on all animals, and the twisted logic of a religion that turns a man who was converted by the voice of God as he was about to kill a deer into Saint Hubert, patron saint of hunters. Of course, other readers will disagree with her. But the novel aims first to lure us into an easy dismissal of Janina, emphasizing her eccentricity; then to complicate our response by giving her a seriousness, a moral perspective, and an intellectual rigor that demands our consideration; then to further complicate it by having her take even more drastic action than most readers would condone. Like Humbert Humbert, she surprises us with her self-awareness (as when she says, "I'm not a good Astrologer, unfortunately. There's a flaw in my character"), her insight ("It is at dusk that the most interesting things occur, for that is when simple differences fade away"), and her humor ("The best conversations are with yourself. At least there's no risk of a misunderstanding"; and "Many men come down with testosterone autism, the symptoms of which are a gradual decline in social intelligence and capacity for interpersonal communication…The Person beset by this Ailment becomes taciturn…He develops an interest in various Tools and machinery, and he's drawn to the Second World War and the biographies of famous people."). Even if we don't ultimately agree with Janina about the relative value of animal lives, and we see hypocrisy in Janina's willingness to take human lives, Tokarczuk has created a narrator who challenges us, forces us to reexamine our own beliefs.

THE UNNAMED NARRATOR OF Yoko Ogawa's *The Memory Police* is less assertive and less violent than Janina, but she is, in her way, every bit as disturbing. This narrator is no murderer; rather, she's one of many victims of an authoritarian state on an unnamed and inescapable island. At the outset she tells us that for as long as

she can remember things have disappeared, vanished. We're encouraged to interpret this broadly: she recalls her (disappeared)
mother telling her, "It won't be long now ... Something will disappear from your life." We can't help but agree. But on the narrator's
island, the things that disappear—that are essentially destroyed,
erased, or eliminated—include ribbons, bells, perfume, birds
and, eventually, roses, photographs, fruits, books, and body parts.
By novel's end, the narrator is reduced to a voice, and even that
is fading.

While the narrator is certainly disturbed by these losses, and
while she takes great risks to protect one friend and investigate the
disappearance of another, ultimately she seems passive, helpless.
She's a writer, and over the course of the novel we read excerpts
from her work in progress, the story of a typist who is seduced by
her teacher, held captive in a tower, and rendered voiceless. That
character, whom we associate with the narrator, says that while her
captor has done "truly horrible things ... I can't help feeling a kind
of gratitude." One day, when she's alone in the tower, another typing
student, a young woman, knocks at the door, providing a chance to
escape. But instead the character stays silent. "How can you explain
this?" she thinks. "And even if she did help you, do you really believe
you'd get back all the things you've lost?" That night, her captor says,
"I knew that you were no longer capable of going back out into the
world." She realizes that she is being replaced by the other young
woman, and that they are two in a long line; but instead of expressing anger, she says she's disappointed: "Why doesn't he realize that
my voice, my body, my sensations, my emotions—everything exists
only for him." Soon after that final installment of the novel within
a novel, our narrator tells us that she and "the citizens of the island

had lost everything that had a form, and our voices alone drifted aimlessly."

In contrast to *Lolita* and *Drive Your Plow over the Bones of the Dead*, *The Memory Police* provokes us because of what the character suffers, and because of what she doesn't do. Unlike Humbert Humbert and Janina, she doesn't seem compelled to justify herself; she's simply recounting what happened. We can read the book as a more abstracted and fantastic version of the effects of a totalitarian state than, say, Orwell's 1984; we can read it as a story of psychological and sexual abuse leading to something like Stockholm syndrome; we can read it as an illustration of the dangers of forgetting the past and failing to act to prevent its repeating; and/or we can read Ogawa's novel as an expression of mortality, of the losses we all face, eventually. What we can't do is simply take Ogawa's narrator at her word. While she is absolutely authoritative in her recounting of what's happening around her and what she does, she never explains the relationship of the novel she's writing about the typist in the tower to her own circumstances; in fact, she barely seems to recognize how the two stories intersect. Through this and similar absences, and by the contrast of the narrator's calmness with the horror of what's happening on the island, Ogawa leads us to actively question the narrator and our understanding of her.

A DIFFERENT SORT OF erasure distinguishes Rachel Cusk's *Outline*. While Cusk is often discussed alongside Karl Ove Knausgård as one of the leading practitioners of autofiction, she describes *Outline* as a novel, so we're invited to regard the book's narrator as a created character, no matter the similarities to the author. But that's already misleading: in *Outline*, we aren't really invited to regard the narrator much at all. Even in the large subgenre of observer narrators, Faye—who withholds even her name until very late in the book—is unusual. We know that she's a writer visiting Greece to teach in a summer program, that she's divorced, that she has two sons, and that she's waiting to hear the result of a loan application. That's about it. And unlike most observer narrators, Faye isn't focused on another character (as Nick Carraway is on Gatsby) or a dramatic event. Instead, she recounts a number of conversations she has with strangers, old friends, new acquaintances, and students, with the emphasis on what those people say. We learn about Faye largely through what she chooses to include, and occasionally by how she responds.

While the novel's detractors claim it has no plot—no dramatic chain of events linked by cause and effect—it does have a story, a chronological sequence of events, and it has thematic coherence. Put broadly, the novel focuses on marriage, romantic and familial relationships, questions of identity, reality and illusion, and writing. Most important for our purposes here, it also raises questions about the presentation of the self, the narrator's role in a first-person novel.

At the opening, Faye tells us she was invited to lunch in London with a billionaire. From there she goes to the airport, where she's seated next to, and talks at length with, a Greek man; they discuss two of his marriages and his children. In the second chapter, she is in Athens, in conversation with Ryan, a fellow teacher with a roving eye. Ryan ogles their waitress and talks about his wife and a former girlfriend. Faye reports his attention to the waitress without comment.

In the third chapter we get our first look at the apartment where Faye is staying, as she makes deductions about the owner, Clelia, based on the art and music and kitchen appliances she's left behind. Faye draws some curious conclusions. She tells us, for instance, that the kitchen "was sufficiently functional to give the clear message that Clelia didn't spend much time there," that the presence of model boats is "a metaphor I felt sure Clelia had intended to illustrate the relationship between illusion and reality," that her collection of the complete symphonies of major composers represents "in Clelia's mind…a sort of objectivity that arose when the focus became the sum of human parts and the individual was blotted out," and that the presence of bunk beds in the apartment "made it evident [the owner] had no children." Her logic? The beds' "presence…seemed to suggest something that otherwise might have been forgotten. The bunk beds, in other words, stood for the concept of children generally." Faye has never met Clelia, and doesn't, in the novel, so we have no way of knowing if any of these inferences are accurate; what we do know is that they reveal at least as much about Faye as they do about the absent owner.

While Faye is observant, analytical, and intelligent, her perspective is also idiosyncratic. She inhabits a world constructed by her own beliefs, experience, assertions, and defenses. The same might be said of all of these narrators, and of all of us; the point here is that, while Faye tells us very little about herself in the conventional way—where she grew up, how she met her husband, why their marriage failed, how she became a writer, what she writes about—we learn about her through her observations, and by what she chooses to record. It isn't necessary for us to agree with her about everything, any more than we endorse everything asserted by Ralph Ellison's Invisible Man, or Dostoyevsky's Man from Underground; we only need to be persuaded to engage with the ideas and attitudes she's curated.

Most of the novel consists of extended conversations, making it a bit reminiscent of *My Dinner with Andre*, or a Richard Linklater film, *The Canterbury Tales*, or even Plato's *Symposium*, though Faye is the only character who gets to hear all of the stories she elicits. Faye accepts the invitation of the Greek man from the plane to go out on his boat. They talk more about his marriages and children; they swim; she watches another family, which reminds her of her own; they eat. Faye lunches with an old friend and a woman novelist who has become an international success; we finally see her in the classroom, where she has her students tell stories; she goes out on the boat again, and rebuffs her airplane seatmate's advance; she has yet another meal with the Irishman, a woman of great beauty, and a lesbian poet; we listen to the students in a second meeting of the class. In the novel's tenth and final chapter, Faye finds another woman in her apartment—the next writer who will be staying there for a week. They discuss, among other things, that woman's marriage. A few hours before Faye's flight home, the Greek boat owner calls her, and—nothing happens.

Without relying on dramatic action, how does Cusk lure us into complex engagement with her narrator?

First, perhaps most notably, she denies us nearly all of the introductory and contextual information that makes readers comfortable.

Faye describes other people in great detail—but she has very little to say about herself. We never know what she looks like, despite her attention to the physical appearances of others, and only in response to others, over time, do we learn anything about her feelings regarding being married, then divorced, and living with her sons. As a result, in the same way that she studies the objects in her host's apartment to imagine who she is, we read Faye's narrative alert for clues that will reveal something more about this woman who's writing to us.

While the people she meets talk at great length, Faye reveals relatively little of her own speech; at times, it feels she is more tape recorder than conversationalist. But while we hear the content of what the other characters say, their speech is nearly always told in, or translated into, Faye's language. What elevates the conversations, then, is the lens Faye provides: her language, her vision, her attention.

One of the novel's primary sources of tension is omission. At one point she says she's come "to believe more and more in the virtues of passivity, and of living a life as unmarked by self-will as possible." When we finally see her teach, it seems she'll have to take action, and so be exposed to us: but for the entire meeting, she has students describe things they saw on the way to class. That chapter ends with a punchline: "I don't know who you are," one of the students tells her, "but I'll tell you one thing, you're a lousy teacher."

Characteristically, Faye doesn't respond—to the student, or to us. Only later, in conversation, do we learn that she was hurt. Other moments complicate our relationship to Faye, as when she is on the boat with the man she calls her "neighbor." She's surprised when he moves to embrace her; *our* only surprise is that she didn't see this coming.

Because she omits so much, everything Faye tells us is revealing. When Faye boards the plane in the first chapter, she describes the flight attendants going through the usual demonstrations and required instruction, in the usual manner. This would seem to be entirely uninteresting and unnecessary information. She tells us, "When the recorded voice came to the part about the oxygen masks, the hush remained unbroken: no one protested, or spoke up to disagree with this commandment that one should take care of others only after taking care of oneself. Yet I wasn't sure it was altogether true." Those lines take on significance when we know that Faye is raising her young sons alone, and that until recently she had stayed in the house she had shared with her husband "to watch it become the grave of something I could no longer definitively call either a reality or an illusion." It seems she's still debating who she should take care of first.

In that first chapter, in one of her rare speeches, Faye responds to a question from her seatmate:

> It was impossible, I said…to give the reasons why the marriage had ended: among other things a marriage is a system of belief, a story, and though it manifests itself in things that are real enough, the impulse that drives it is ultimately mysterious. What was real, in the end, was the loss of the house, which had become the geographical location for things that had gone absent, and which represented, I supposed, the hope that they might one day return. To move from the house was to declare, in a way, that we had stopped waiting.

This is as personal, as emotional, and as revealing as Faye will get. We come to understand that what we're reading is, to some extent, a trauma narrative, the story of a life disrupted, of a woman contemplating how to move forward. She tells us, "I was no longer interested in literature as a form of snobbery or even of self-definition… What I knew personally to be true had come to seem unrelated to the process of persuading others. I did not, any longer, want to persuade anyone of anything."

Hence her refusal to discuss her own marriage; hence her teaching by asking her students to talk. What she *can* do is to ask other people about their experiences, and record what resonates—what implicitly speaks to her own experience and interests.

Immediately after that bit about the house, Faye seems to change the topic:

> My younger son...has the very annoying habit of immediately leaving the place where you have agreed to meet him, if you aren't there when he arrives. Instead he goes in search of you, and becomes frustrated and lost. I couldn't find you! He cries afterwards, invariably aggrieved. But the only hope of finding anything is to stay exactly where you are, at the agreed place. It's just a question of how long you can hold out.

We understand that she's still talking about her marriage. She waited in that house for three years; now she's moved on. After that, it's easy enough to consider virtually everything she tells us in light of what she avoids talking about. She reveals herself not by depicting her own image but by carefully depicting the people around her—creating a self-portrait by silhouette, as it were. While on his boat, she tells her neighbor from the plane,

> I thought often of the chapter in *Wuthering Heights* where Heathcliff and Cathy stare from the dark garden through the windows of the Lintons' drawing room and watch the brightly lit family scene inside. What is fatal in that vision is its subjectivity: looking through the window the two of them see different things, Heathcliff what he fears and hates and Cathy what she desires and feels deprived of. But neither of them can see things as they really are. And likewise I was beginning to see my own fears and desires manifested outside myself,

was beginning to see in other people's lives a commentary on my own.

Late in the novel, the playwright moving into the apartment Faye has been living in completes the circle of the narrative by telling her own story about a conversation she had with a man sitting beside her on the plane. Faye tells us,

> It was really their conversation that had set her mind to work around these themes... The longer she listened to his answers, the more she felt something fundamental was being delineated, something not about him but about her... In everything he said about himself, she found in her own nature a corresponding negative. This anti-description, for want of a better way of putting it, had made something clear to her by a reverse kind of exposition: while he talked she began to see herself as a shape, an outline, with all the detail filled in around it while the shape itself remained blank. Yet this shape, even while its content remained unknown, gave her... a sense of who she now was.

Here, it seems, Faye offers us instruction in how to read her narrative. Her friend Paniotis adds, "We expect of our lives what we've come to expect of our books; but this sense of life as progression is something I want no more of." And so Cusk presents us with a different sort of narrative, one that resists the familiar conventions of Aristotle's *Poetics*, Freytag's Pyramid, and epiphany.

IT MAY NOT BE coincidental that these last three novels—*The Memory Police, Drive Your Plow over the Bones of the Dead*, and *Outline*—all written by women, feature women narrators (two of them writers, the other a translator), largely independent, largely concerned with presentation of the self, or the difference between how one is perceived (often, but not only, by men) and how she wants to be seen. Ogawa's narrator is forced into secrecy, and her life is gradually whittled away. Janina knows she's perceived as "a crank," and she struggles with her desire to explain her anger and her competing desire to be accepted, even peripherally, as part of a community. Faye tells us she has "come to believe more and more in the virtues of passivity, and of living a life as unmarked by self-will as possible." But rather than simply depict these struggles and invite us to observe them, each author, using very different methods, creates a narrator that requires us to participate in a consideration of the challenges she faces.

ONE OF THE TRADITIONS of the MFA Program for Writers at Warren Wilson College is for students (and sometimes faculty) to provide musical entertainment at the graduation dinner. Years ago, there was one student who didn't sing, or play an instrument, yet very much wanted to participate. After dinner, then, she went to the front of the room, stood at the podium...and proceeded to do imitations of the program's faculty.

This student imitated faculty members' accents; she imitated their speech patterns, and habits of delivery. She imitated the way one person puffed on a cigarette, squinted, and exhaled; she imitated the way another ground her toe into the carpet as she read. We all immediately recognized the subjects of her performance. To put it another way: the student had noticed and then re-created various tics and habits the rest of us had seen and remembered, when we were supposed to have been focused solely on the content of a lecture or reading. Aspects of the delivery of that material that the individual faculty member had thought (or hoped) had been essentially invisible were now made the focus: the prominent poet reduced to a chin waggle and a stern gaze upward; the famous fiction writer reduced to a nervous foot.

As you might imagine, the atmosphere in the room was electric. Some people even stopped drinking. Others began drinking faster. I wasn't the only faculty member who found the performance excruciating. We each anticipated—well, *dreaded* is the word I'm looking for—our turn as the focus of, let's say, *homage*.

But thinking about that night now, from the safe distance of more than a decade, I realize that student was acting the way my relatives and I had at Vera's funeral, and we—the faculty—were Paul. The mimic offered a reminder that those of us who take the stage are not invisible; that there are limits to our control over the listener's attention; and that there's nearly always another story to tell, if only we take a wider view.

Don't Stand So Close to Her, or Him, or Them, Either

Narrative Distance in
Third-Person Fiction

About two-thirds of the way through *Butch Cassidy and the Sundance Kid*, the two outlaws, having fled the American West to Bolivia, decide to clean up their act, to go straight. They attempt to get work as payroll guards. As part of their job interview, their would-be employer asks if they can shoot. He tosses a tobacco plug, as a target, to test them; Sundance, the celebrated gunslinger, misses badly. Butch looks stunned. Sullen, Sundance asks, "Can I move?" Even as the mine owner asks, "What do you mean, move?" Sundance drops to one side, drawing and firing, and blows the tobacco plug to bits.

As the dust settles, Sundance says, "I'm better when I move."

I DO NOT MEAN to suggest that the narrator of a story or novel is equivalent to a mythic gunfighter seeking work as a payroll guard in Bolivia. But I sometimes think of that scene when I read a story, or a draft of a story, and the narrator seems locked in place—particularly a third-person story when the narrator seems to have yielded all independence and authority, and essentially records the point-of-view character's thoughts and actions.

I had not thought much about the need to make use of shifting narrative distance until a particular discussion in a graduate workshop forced the issue. As we discussed a student's draft, one of the participants noted that we had no idea what the main character did for a living; someone else added, "Or what he looks like." That started the sort of avalanche we sometimes see in workshops: someone else noted that we didn't know who the character's close friends were; someone pointed out that we knew virtually nothing about his past; yet another participant added that the other characters were never physically described. Finally, the author, exasperated, said, "I know, I know—but how am I supposed to get him to think about all of that?"

It turned out that the writer had somehow picked up a strange notion about writing in the limited third person: he believed that once a story indicated that its perspective would be close to a particular character's, it was somehow required to *stay* close to that character, within the confines of that character's thoughts. Even more surprising—to me—was that other students agreed; some went so far as to say it was a "violation" of the limited third-person point of view to include information that might come from a narrator, even when that information was as objective as the color of a character's hair, or the fact that she drove a Camry in disrepair—never mind the fact that her coworkers thought she was irresponsible, or that her mother thought she had a worrisome number of cats.

I was tempted to quote another line from *Butch Cassidy*: "Rules? What rules?"

Even those students who didn't think there was some sort of rule governing the intimacy to the main character one has to maintain in such stories tended not to make much use of their narrators. It seemed there were essentially two reasons for this. The first reason they offered is that any evidence of a narrator at work interrupts the "realism" of a story; furthermore, to create a narrator with an apparent attitude and purpose is risky. The creation of such a narrator often reveals the writer's interests and sympathies, and that exposes the writer to criticism; even worse, it seems suspiciously related to omniscient narration, which, they were sorry to have to tell me, is out of fashion. I asked if they'd read Toni Morrison or Colum McCann, Colson Whitehead or David Malouf, Jenny Erpenbeck or Mohsin Hamid. They *had* read those writers; the real problem, it turns out, is that assuming the omniscient point of view is difficult.

The second reason some writers avoid dynamic third-person narrators is because they find it easier to align themselves with a single character's perspective than to hover above that character, constantly making choices about what to tell the reader when, and why. But ultimately, there is no escaping that responsibility.

A reluctance to accept that narrative responsibility explains why, in a great many drafts of limited third-person stories, it isn't clear who's in charge, by which I mean whose attitude or perspective is being expressed—or if anyone's is. In these drafts, readers wonder whether the tale is aware of the impression it has created of the main character, and whether things that seem implicit are intentional. Too often, the narrator seems to have his or her or their hands off the steering wheel.

The problem might stem in part from the terms we use: "close third," or "third person limited." "Close third" implies, well, closeness; and "third person limited" omits the crucial word, the thing that's being limited: the narrator's omniscience. Every "third person limited" story has an omniscient narrator; and that narrator is—or should be—making choices about what to include, what to exclude, and from what distance the reader is observing the main character.

I've heard some students say that narrative commentary is "unnatural." But what's unnatural is to tell a story about someone else without comment. Just listen, the next time someone tells you a story about a friend of theirs, or a relative. A story like this:

> Patsy had become severely nearsighted in second grade. She avoided sports, sat in the front row when she could, and read with her nose nearly pressed against the pages of books. Glasses were ugly, and everyone knew boys didn't like girls who wore them. When her teachers insisted her parents buy her a pair, she finally understood the reason for telephone poles: there were wires! Still, she never wore her glasses on dates, and certainly not at her wedding: it would have been nice to see everyone, but who wanted to see glasses in wedding photos? When they got to the restaurant where they would have their first dinner together as a married couple, the room was dim, the menu in elaborate script; rather than hold it close to her face, she said, "Oh, you order for me."

This is a mostly true story, about my mother. But I would never tell it that way. Instead, I might write:

Patsy had become severely nearsighted in second grade. She avoided sports, sat in the front row when she could, and read with her nose nearly pressed against the pages of books. *While she would never blame her parents, her father, who had near perfect vision most of his life, made her feel needing to wear glasses was a kind of deficiency; her mother told her boys would find them unattractive.* When her teachers insisted her parents buy her a pair, she finally understood the reason for telephone poles: there were wires! Still, she never wore her glasses on dates, and certainly not at her wedding: it would have been nice to see everyone, but who wanted to see glasses in wedding photos? When they got to the restaurant where they would have their first dinner together as a married couple, the room was dim, the menu in elaborate script; rather than hold it close to her face, she said, *not with embarrassment, but with characteristic submissiveness,* "Oh, you order for me."

In a single paragraph, those additions might not seem terribly significant; but even in a few phrases, we can begin to see the narrator negotiating the distance between reader and character.

When we tell stories about other people, even if we try to represent their thoughts and feelings—and, most crucially, their perspective, their justifications for what they say and do—we tend to add information and, very often, our opinions, our own perspective. So it's helpful to remember that a third-person narrative is being conveyed by a narrator, and that narrator is the one ultimately shaping the story. The narrator is the person who has determined the story has meaning, or consequence, a reason for being told.

Right up to the end of her life, my mother would tell that story about her wedding and honeymoon: to her it was evidence that, like most of us, she had been young and foolish once. When *I* tell that story, I tell it because it's funny and it's sad, and I think it captures something about who my mother was. Even in her eighties, long after she had accepted wearing glasses, long after my father was gone, when we went out to eat, she was happy for me to order for her.

There is nearly always a difference between the story the narrator understands and wants to tell and the story the character would tell. That's why the story is in the third person.

IN HIS ESSAY "FROM Long Shots to X-Rays: Distance and Point of View in Fiction," David Jauss points out that when we talk about point of view, we tend to focus on person, as if the most important distinctions were among first-, second-, and third-person stories. Jauss argues that, instead, "the most important purpose of point of view is to manipulate the degree of distance between the characters and the reader in order to achieve the emotional, intellectual, and moral responses the author desires."

Jauss goes on to make another important point: "Because it is generally a bad idea to shift person in a work of fiction... we leap to the conclusion that point of view should be singular and consistent. In fact, however singular and consistent the *person* of a story may be, the techniques that truly constitute point of view are invariably multiple and shifting." It's nearly as unusual for a story to be told from a single, fixed narrative distance as it is for a film to be shot entirely in close-up, or entirely in a two-shot. Even during a simple television interview, the camera is constantly moving, or an editor is shifting from one camera to another.

With that in mind, we can look at a variety of work in the third person—in this case, stories by Anton Chekhov, Katherine Anne

Porter, Adam Johnson, and Jay Chakrabarti, and a novel by Jenny Erpenbeck—and consider briefly where the narrators stand, how they move, and why, or toward what end.

Framing the Point-of-View Character

Shifts in narrative distance do not need to be frequent or extended to be effective. Chekhov often uses narrative distance in order to lay the foundation for a false epiphany, one of his specialties. Usually we use "narrative frame" to refer to a story that frames another story. Here I'm referring to stories in which the narrator establishes a perception of the main character before moving close to his or her thoughts—and that initial perception instructs us in understanding the story.

In "A Doctor's Visit," we're introduced to the point-of-view character, a professor's assistant, like this:

> [Korolyov] had been born and had grown up in Moscow, he did not
> know the country, and he had never taken any interest in factories,
> or been inside one, but he had happened to read about factories, and
> had been in the houses of manufacturers and had talked to them; and
> whenever he saw a factory far or near, he always thought how quiet
> and peaceable it was outside, but within there was always sure to be
> impenetrable ignorance and dull egoism on the side of the owners,
> wearisome, unhealthy toil on the side of the workpeople, squabbling,
> vermin, vodka.

And that is quite enough to tell us what we need to know: Korolyov is content to make sweeping assumptions based on secondhand information. He is one of Chekhov's ineffective intellectuals.

From that point on, Chekhov's narrator does not intervene; and in fact we have no reason to question Korolyov's observations and conclusions: the factory feels oppressive, the woman of the house is caught up in social pretension, and so on. Korolyov understands that his patient, the young heiress of the factory, is lonely and weary and unhappy because she is well aware of her privileged status and deeply uncomfortable with it. But this is what he tells her:

> Your sleeplessness does you credit; in any case, it is a good sign. In reality, such a conversation as this between us now would have been unthinkable for our parents. At night they did not talk, but slept sound; we, our generation, sleep badly, are restless, but talk a great deal, and are always trying to settle whether we are right or not. For our children or grandchildren that question—whether we are right or not—will have been settled. Things will be clearer for them than for us. Life will be good in fifty years time…You are a good, interesting woman. Goodnight!"

One imagines that if he were alive today, Korolyov would be very active on Facebook. It might help to enter the moment by imagining that the story is instead set in the current day, and the young woman is despairing about climate change, or the humanitarian crisis at the border with Mexico, or domestic violence; she confides in her yoga instructor, and the instructor says, "Well, at least you're losing sleep over it—that's something! See you next week."

As Korolyov drives off, in the story's final line, the young woman is pale and exhausted, but he has put her situation out of mind, and thinks "of the time, perhaps close at hand, when life would be as bright and joyous as that still Sunday morning, and he thought how pleasant it was on such a morning in the spring to drive with three horses in good carriage, and to bask in the sunshine."

In other words, Chekhov has given his story a beautiful happy ending—but his introduction has told us not to believe it. The professor's assistant has missed the point; he's like someone who thinks renewing his subscription to *The Nation* is striking a blow for progressivism. Korolyov has done nothing, and when he leaves, his patient is no better off than when he arrived. Our understanding of the story depends on that small but significant wedge Chekhov's narrator inserts between us and Korolyov at the very start.

The (Nearly) Claustrophobic Third Person

It might seem contradictory to advocate standing even closer to your point-of-view character, but in the same way that standing too close to a stranger in conversation—violating that person's "personal space"—creates tension, deliberately limiting the reader's perspective can be useful. "Deliberately" is the key word—for any of these techniques to succeed, our proximity to the point-of-view character has to be intentional, strategic, in service to the story's ultimate purpose. These narratives stand so close to their point-of-view characters that we don't know what the characters don't know, we can't see what they can't see—until the narrator chooses for us to see, or understand, something more. The key to this strategy is to make the reader aware that we're so close to the main character that we're missing something—and then finding a way to supply it.

A classic example, an extreme case, is Katherine Anne Porter's "The Jilting of Granny Weatherall." Porter's narrator tells, with remarkable economy, the story of a tough eighty-year-old Texas woman as she lies on her deathbed. Due to some combination of age, illness, and her mind's deterioration, Granny is disoriented, confusing past and present, uncertain of her surroundings. And Porter narrates the short story so close to Granny's perspective that, unless we read carefully, we too might be disoriented and confused.

To encourage us to read carefully, Porter draws our attention to something curious in the story's opening lines: "She flicked her wrist neatly out of Doctor Harry's pudgy careful fingers and pulled the sheet up to her chin. The brat ought to be in knee britches. Doctoring around the country with spectacles on his nose! 'Get along now! Take your schoolbooks and go! There's nothing wrong with me.'" Immediately, we know something is wrong. Either "Doctor Harry" is a child's odd nickname, or our to-this-point unnamed character has a strong bias against young doctors, or there's some other explanation. We've been confronted with a minor mystery.

Granny's protest earns this response: "Doctor Harry spread a warm paw like a cushion on her forehead where the forked green vein danced and made her eyelids twitch. 'Now, now, be a good girl and we'll have you up in no time.'" Doctor Harry's calm, perhaps even condescending reply suggests that he's used to this woman's outbursts, or at the very least, he doesn't take offense. But Porter has immediately drawn our attention to telling details, things that are wrong with this picture: Doctor Harry is *not* a schoolboy, the patient he's treating is *not* a girl, and despite what she claims, we feel fairly certain that there *is* something wrong with her, thanks to that forked green vein that makes her eyelids twitch. Porter hasn't just limited our access to information; she's drawn our attention to those limitations, to the distortions in the information we're given. Our challenge, we understand, is to figure out what's really happening—whom to believe about what.

In the lines that follow, Porter gives us broader indicators—we're told "Doctor Harry floated like a balloon around the foot of the bed"—even as fighting through the thicket of Granny's thoughts and perceptions gets trickier: characters are named but not identified, they may or may not actually be in the room. But when Granny recounts the past, she's lucid:

> They had been so sweet when they were little. Granny wished the old days were back again with the children young and everything to be done over. It had been a hard pull, but not too much for her. When she thought of all the food she had cooked, and all the clothes she had cut and sewed, and all the gardens she had made—well, the children showed it. There they were, made out of her, and they couldn't get away from that. Sometimes she wanted to see John again and point to them and say, Well, I didn't do so badly, did I? But that would have to wait. That was for tomorrow.

While we don't have the context necessary to immediately understand everything Granny is thinking, her memories are offered as valid evidence: in them, doctors are not schoolboys, and no one floats around rooms. While this occasional lucidity might seem like an inconsistency, (a) it's true to the way that older people often recall the distant past more readily than they do the recent past, and (b) a narrative's primary responsibility is not to be consistent—it's to do whatever needs to be done to convey the story.

When we return to the present, clarity is often provided by secondary characters. When Granny's daughter, Cornelia, says that Doctor Harry has come to see her, Granny says, "He just left five minutes ago." Cornelia corrects her and, in doing so, orients us: "That was this morning, Mother. It's night now." Later, we hear what Granny says to Doctor Harry, but we also hear someone reply, "She's saying something," which tells us Granny is mumbling, or slurring her words, or barely speaking at all. But even in the present she has moments of lucidity: "So, my dear Lord, this is my death and I wasn't even thinking about it. My children have come to see me die." So we have no reason to doubt the story's final line, or its implication: "She stretched herself with a deep breath and blew out the light."

This use of the third person allows Porter to situate us very close to Granny's perspective, even as she uses secondary characters and our knowledge of cultural conventions—we understand that the priest is not tickling her foot but administering last rites—to convey to the reader information Granny either doesn't have access to or can't fully comprehend. Far from merely documenting Granny's thoughts as she declines, Porter's nimble narrator gives us access to an understanding of events greater than any one of the characters can possess.

Claustrophobia with a Twist

Granted, it's not so often that we write about characters who are hallucinating, or deeply delusional. But there's a fairly common variation on the claustrophobic stance used in less dramatic situations. In these stories, the narrator positions us so close to the main character that we have trouble seeing anything the character can't see—but the narrator also obscures things that the character *can* see. The result is that sometimes we feel stranded, abandoned, unsure of what to make of what we're reading; but the best of these stories pay off brilliantly.

In "A Funny Thing Happened on the Way to the Information Dump" I discussed Adam Johnson's "Hurricanes Anonymous," which also happens to be an excellent example of this approach toward narrative distance. To a large degree, the story reads like a straightforward close third-person narrative. But Johnson puts that "closeness" of the close third person to use in at least two surprising and significant ways. Johnson's narrator is something of a trickster, carefully manipulating what we know and what we think we know about Randall, the point-of-view character.

At the start of the story, Randall has a problem to solve: he's trying to find the mother of his son, and to learn how long he's supposed to take care of the boy. For the most part we have access to the information he has access to, and our knowledge and understanding is limited the way Randall's understanding is limited; when he's surprised, we're surprised. This is important to the story because Randall is a thoughtful observer and a sympathetic character—and yet he has serious blind spots that lead him to make a terrible error in judgment. Johnson's job—one we often run up against—is to make that error surprising but believable, consistent with everything we've been told earlier. The reader needs to feel surprised but not cheated.

Johnson doesn't necessarily explain to the reader things that Randall knows but has no reason to think about. A simple example comes in the first two sentences: "[Randall] pulls up outside Chuck E. Cheese's and hits the hazards on his UPS van. The last working cell tower in Lake Charles, Louisiana, is not far away, so he stops here a couple of times a day to check his messages." We don't know why Lake Charles has been reduced to one working cell tower; Randall does, and he's been living with the fact for a while, so there's no explanation.

This sort of withholding is not uncommon in the opening of a story. More surprising is what happens in the scene we looked at earlier: Randall and his girlfriend, Relle, are in a bar when she slips a cotton swab into his mouth. He's surprised, then realizes she's taking a sample for a DNA test, hoping to prove that the boy he's taking care of is not his own. This should tell us quite a lot about Relle's interests, but Johnson distracts us from the significance of the act: neither Randall nor Relle discusses it at any length, and Randall's UPS van is swarming with live crawfish. "We'll talk about it tonight," Randall says. Relle says, "At A.A.?" "Where the hell else," Randall answers.

When we get to the AA meeting, it comes as a surprise that neither Randall nor Relle is a recovering alcoholic; they attend the meetings because AA offers childcare, and that allows them the opportunity to make love in Randall's van. The surprise to us is the result of a clever move on Johnson's part: Randall knows perfectly well why they go to the meetings; but he had no reason to "think it" while he was corralling crawfish. Johnson's narrator didn't let us draw a false conclusion by mistake—he set us up for a surprise. Throughout the story, this sort of intentional withholding of information keeps the reader slightly off-balance, building tension and suspense.

As we saw in Porter's story, one of the challenges of the claustrophobic third person is conveying what the point-of-view character doesn't know, or fails to recognize, in a way the reader can trust. In "Hurricanes Anonymous," Johnson uses repetition—specifically, the repeated, consistent perceptions of secondary characters.

Three times in the story—at the beginning, in the middle, and in the last third—a minor character indicates to Randall, and so to us, that he or she is concerned about his son's condition. Early on, Randall makes a delivery to a friendly electrical engineer who makes conversation with the boy and reveals he has a son the same age. We see the scene from Randall's perspective, as he observes the work site, so we're caught off guard when the engineer says, "Obviously, you two are in some kind of situation, but seriously, the boy can't be running around in his jammies. Look at the glass and nails. He needs some boots and jeans, something." Until that moment, we didn't know the boy was barefoot, and Randall had taken no notice of the glass and nails.

At the AA meeting, after Randall and Relle make love, they go to collect the boy and find that the older women have done much more than babysit—they've given him a bath and a haircut and a hand-me-down set of overalls, and "they've applied thick cream to his sunburned face." Until that moment, we had no idea that he was so obviously in need of a bath and a haircut, or that he was sunburned. Now we understand that the earlier scene with the friendly engineer wasn't an exception: despite all the attention Randall gives his son, he is not up to speed on some of the basic elements of parenting.

At the end of the story, Randall asks Dr. Gaby, a woman who works at the halfway house where his girlfriend lives, to take care of his son while they go to visit Randall's father. Randall insists that he's coming back, and he's sincere; but Dr. Gaby clearly believes otherwise: "You understand that if you leave this boy with me, I'll have to do what's best for him. That's what will make the decisions." She has him write out a note giving her temporary guardianship; but first she says, "Randall. Do you know what you're doing?"

Randall believes he does. But thanks to his interactions with the engineer, the women at the AA meeting, and Dr. Gaby, we've slowly come to understand that he does not; and through scenes with his girlfriend, Relle, we understand something else he does not: she has been lying to him about her plans for their future.

And so, at the end of the story, Randall—a character we've come to like—abandons his son. To help us understand why and how this good-hearted young man makes such a terrible mistake, Adam Johnson needs to carefully guide us throughout the story, allowing us to see the world as Randall sees it but not limiting our perspective to what Randall notices, comprehends, or focuses on.

That's what stories with shifting narrative distance have in common: they allow us to see what the point-of-view character sees, but also something more. While we might call the point of view "limited" third person, because it gives us access to only one character's thoughts, the story itself is not limited to the point-of-view character's understanding.

As in Porter's story, in Johnson's we see the adept use of secondary characters to direct the reader's attention. Often, problems with third-person limited stories stem from our aligning ourselves with the perspectives of our main characters to the point that we don't fully consider how the world they're in might challenge them, or conflict with their attitudes and actions. (If you think you've gotten too close to one character's perspective, you might ask yourself, What does each character in this story think of every other character? Why? What does he or she disapprove of? How does that character express her reservation?)

The Compassionate Stance: Free to Move

Chekhov often offers us compassionate insight into a character who is alone—emotionally and psychologically, if not physically. This stance is important to study because most often we have a sympathetic understanding of our main characters, even a rooting interest in them; and while we need to reveal their flaws, we want our readers to understand the characters the way we do. In other stories, we may write about characters whose actions are questionable, even despicable; even in those cases, we want our readers to understand the characters the way we do.

One of the key advantages to writing about these people in the third person is that we have the freedom to do things the character simply can't. For instance, we can use diction and syntax and figures of speech that the character wouldn't; and we can guide our readers' attention in ways the character cannot, or would not. Fully assuming the narrator's role allows us to construct the story in ways that have little to do with the character's perspective, and everything to do with what we want to tell, or show, the reader.

Earlier I discussed Jai Chakrabarti's use of images and motifs in "A Small Sacrifice for an Enormous Happiness." The story is also a useful model for the subtle control of narrative distance. It takes as its subject a man consumed by desire and, perhaps, ego, and invites us to understand him, even extend our compassion, if not our approval. Chakrabarti's technique is Chekhovian: he draws us close to his main character, withholding any overt judgment, instead guiding us so that we see the character's flaws, and allowing his narrator to give the story not only shape but depth through the careful selection of detail. While we have intimate access to the main character's thoughts, we are also allowed to see around him, as it were; our reading is being guided by someone who sees and understands more than the character.

The writing is also beautiful. And there's a wonderful sex scene, but we will aim to stick to our topic.

To reiterate: "A Small Sacrifice for an Enormous Happiness" is set in Kolkata in or soon after 1979. Nikhil, the main character, is a wealthy landlord, probably in his forties. He has an elderly, hard-of-hearing servant, and for the past three years he has had a younger lover, Sharma, a blacksmith. To disguise their relationship, Nikhil and his servant arranged for Sharma to marry an uneducated woman named Tripti. Sharma visits Nikhil every Thursday—ostensibly to play backgammon, though in the story no backgammon is played. To clarify the cultural moment, we're told that when two young men in another town were discovered to be lovers, locals threw acid on their faces. And so Nikhil and Sharma must keep their relationship a secret.

The story begins as Nikhil watches the streets from his balcony awaiting Sharma's weekly visit. He goes inside to check on the pyramid of sweets he has made and arranged—when Sharma arrives, he recognizes this must be a special occasion.

While we're in the dark about the nature of this special occasion, Chakrabarti has grounded us in Nikhil's anxiety: "Nikhil breathed deeply to calm his heart. He feared the words would be eaten in his chest, but he'd been planning to tell Sharma for days, and there was no going back now. As evening settled, the air between them became heavy with the sweetness of secrecy, but secrecy had a short wick." Then he delivers the news: "My dearest, fairest boy," he said. "I want our love to increase…I desire to have a child with you."

On the one hand, we've been at a significant distance from Nikhil, because we didn't know why he had prepared the elaborate sweets, or why he was watching for Sharma from the balcony so eagerly. This creates the sort of suspense useful to a compelling scene. On the other, we've been told exactly how Nikhil feels. And then, on the third hand, the narrator tells us something that conveys meaning to us but not to Nikhil:

Nikhil had trouble reading Sharma's expression in the waning light, so he repeated himself. His fingers were shaking, but he took Sharma's hand anyway, gave it a squeeze.

"I heard you the first time," Sharma said.

Nikhil doesn't get it. Chakrabarti has established ironic distance, and his narrator has served notice: we need to be attentive to the signals Nikhil misses.

In order to convey his seriousness about this new step in their lives, Nikhil gives Sharma a gift: "his dead mother's necklace. It had been dipped in twenty-four carats of gold by master artisans...A piece for the museums, a jeweler had once explained, but Nikhil wanted Sharma to have it." And Sharma seems touched by this gift, of all the gifts Nikhil has given him. In exchange, Nikhil asks him to "dream about a child" with him, and "toss the idea to [his] wife. Get Tripti used to the matter."

Sharma does that thing again, the repeating thing we understand but Nikhil does not: he says, "Toss the idea to my wife. Get Tripti used to the matter."

In Nikhil's mind, we're told, Tripti should be grateful: she comes from a poor family, and the marriage to Sharma has given her a life she never could have achieved otherwise. Sharma's a looker, too—we're told he resembles a Bollywood movie star.

While he waits for Sharma to agree, Nikhil worries over questions about where the child will be raised and how she'll receive a proper education. His imaginings distract him from all his routines. The next Wednesday, Nikhil goes so far as to buy a white dress with a lacy pink bow for the girl he dreams of having, whom he's already named. Then, in defiance of their agreement, and at real risk, he goes to the foundry to show Sharma the dress. Could there be a more Chekhovian moment of bathos? A man brings a little white dress to a foundry to show it to his lover—a man wearing welding gloves. Sharma acts as if Nikhil is merely a customer, then whispers, "Have you lost your soup?"

Sharma does not visit Nikhil the next day.

Sharma does return the following week, though. He says, "Tripti and I have been discussing the issue of the baby."

> *Tripti and I.* He so rarely heard the name Tripti from Sharma's lips, but that she could be in league with him, discussing an *issue?* Unjust, was what it was.

You see how important it was for Chakrabarti to establish that ironic distance early—when we get to this moment, we understand that despite our intimacy with Nikhil, his view and the narrator's view—so his view and ours—are distinct. Nikhil finds his lover's relationship with his wife "unjust"; but we, with the narrator, are more attentive to what this attitude reveals about Nikhil.

As the scene goes on, then, we continue to study Nikhil's reactions. Sharma explains that he and Tripti "do not do" the physical act.

> "Don't worry," Nikhil said. "I shall do the deed." ... While it was unpleasant to imagine the act of copulation itself, he'd studied the intricacies of the reproductive process and believed his chances were excellent for a single, well-timed session to yield its fruit.

> "But you can barely stand the smell of a woman." What passed over Sharma's face may have been described as amusement, but Nikhil refused to believe his lover wasn't taking him seriously—not now that he'd opened his heart like a salvaged piano.

"Sharma," Nikhil said. "It shall be a small sacrifice for an enormous happiness."

The narrator provides explicit guidance in order to make the moment clear: "What passed over Sharma's face may have been described as amusement, but Nikhil refused to believe his lover wasn't taking him seriously." This is one of the very few moments in the story that the narrator actually tells us how to understand something, but it's critical, because in addition to everything else, we need to know, we need to believe, that these men love each other. They meet every week despite the real risk of exposure and, as we know from the anecdote early in the story, physical violence. There's nothing idle or thoughtless about their continued meetings. And they do love each other; but they each see their relationship differently.

Eventually, Nikhil decides to take a train to the small town where Sharma lives, to try to sell Tripti on his plan. Nikhil is used to having things his way; this resistance, this questioning, is an unpleasant novelty. What's worse, when he gets to the house, Tripti is not humbled—she rejects the idea out of hand. She tells Nikhil she's planning to go to university to become a teacher. Nikhil has already thought that she looks vaguely like a Neanderthal; now he finds it "improbable that she would be able to absorb the principles of higher learning." We're seeing him at his worst. But what he says is that if she has the child, he'll help her, he'll pay for tutors.

"Whose happiness are you after?" she asks. "Yours, and yours only?"

Nikhil is so shocked at what he perceives as her disrespect that he says, "Perhaps you should enroll in a school for proper manners."

We are not surprised when she tells him to leave.

The final sequence is the most Chekhovian of all. Nikhil reaches the village station just as a train is arriving, and he conceals himself, watching for his lover. Squatting behind the begonias, sweating, Nikhil does in fact see Sharma get off the train. The younger man is talking to someone, and he's laughing hard, in a way Nikhil has never seen him laugh in all their nights together. Another writer might have given Sharma another lover, so might have made the betrayal more explicit and dramatic; but Chakrabarti knows that this evidence of the fact that Sharma is simply more relaxed, more freely himself, with another person, is more subtly and delicately painful.

It turns out there are no more trains to Kolkata that night, and this rural town has no hotels, so Nikhil returns to Sharma's house. Standing outside, trying to decide what to do, he sees Sharma and Tripti making dinner together. When they take their food to the table, he steps close to the window—and there, on the kitchen counter, is Nikhil's mother's necklace. The jewelry so beautiful and valuable that it belongs in a museum has been left beside the dirty dishes. Outraged, hurt, Nikhil reaches through the window, grabs the necklace, and runs off. Sharma, who has seen only the hand coming through the open window, yells, again and again, "Thief, stop." The story ends, "Nikhil almost called back, but too much distance lay between them. Whatever he said now couldn't be heard."

Those final lines are one more reminder of what the author has done: those are Nikhil's thoughts, but he means them literally; we understand them figuratively. We also understand that Nikhil has been rudely, painfully enlightened; the future he imagines will not come to pass.

When we talk about creating distance from a main character, there is sometimes an assumption that we would only want to do that if the character were unlikeable. But by carefully negotiating narrative distance, Chakrabarti's narrator moves us to a compassionate understanding of a flawed man.

THAT SEX SCENE, COME to think of it, is not unrelated to this topic. Nikhil has just stuffed Sharma with sweets. Then: "Nikhil was pulled back to the divan. Sharma, lifting Nikhil's shirt, placed a molasses square on his belly, teasing a trail of sweetness with his tongue. Nikhil closed his eyes and allowed himself to be enjoyed. Down below, the rum sellers negotiated, the prices of bottles fluctuating wildly."

Flaubert would be proud. At that moment, Nikhil is not paying attention to the fluctuating prices of rum. That little bit of sonic wit, and the unpredictable euphemism, are gifts from the narrator to us.

Exceeding the Limits: or, Moving toward *Un*limited Omniscience

Chakrabarti's story, like the others I've discussed so far, employs a narrator who does his work, for the most part, without drawing attention to himself. The narrator in the next example makes bolder choices, is more assertive, but still stops short of expressing opinions or telling the reader what to think.

Jenny Erpenbeck's *Go, Went, Gone* tells the story of Richard, a widowed and recently retired classics professor in Berlin who becomes aware of African refugees staging a hunger strike. He chooses to learn more about them. Over time, he interviews many of the men, helps them find ways to make money, and to get health care, and to get necessary legal representation; eventually he invites several of them to live with him. But that summary sounds overly romantic: what Richard and the reader come to understand is that the struggle of most of these men is, if not futile, nearly Kafka-esque in its frustrations, as European laws make it very difficult for African refugees to become citizens, or even to be legally employed.

To some extent, Richard is a stand-in for the reader: we learn what he learns, and the book largely follows his curiosity, his discoveries, and his decisions. For the great majority of the novel, we are, if not in Richard's head, his close companion. The book begins with his thoughts and ends with an admission he makes only as a result of a conversation with his closest friends and several of the African refugees he's taken in.

Along the way, though, Erpenbeck shifts narrative distance, sometimes almost imperceptibly, sometimes dramatically. These shifts ultimately govern the novel's thematic development, its meaning-making. Erpenbeck prepares us for them, subtly, from the very beginning:

Perhaps many more years still lie before him, or perhaps only a few. In any case, from now on Richard will no longer have to get up early to appear at the Institute. As of today, he has time—plain and simple. Time to travel, people say. To read books. Proust. Dostoyevsky. Time to listen to music. He doesn't know how long it'll take him to get used to having time. In any case, his head still works just the same as before. What's he going to do with the thoughts still thinking away inside his head?

The opening paragraph continues along these lines, situating us very close to Richard, creating intimacy through colloquial syntax, approximating his thoughts, but without adopting his voice.

The opening section closes, "From his desk, he sees the lake." At first, this seems like an innocuous detail—he has a nice view. But Erpenbeck ends the section with that fact to give it emphasis. Over the course of the novel, the lake will become a powerful metaphor. But it isn't a metaphor for Richard (at least, not yet); for him, it's simply a lake. Two pages later, he contemplates what he should wear and how he should take care of himself now that he "no longer goes out in human society on a daily basis." He thinks he can stop shaving: "Let grow what will. Just stop putting up resistance—or is that how dying begins?" He rejects that notion, but his thoughts immediately turn to the lake. Or rather—that's what the narrator suggests. Here's the passage:

> Just stop putting up resistance—or is that how dying begins? Could dying begin with this kind of growth? No, that can't be right, he thinks.
>
> They still haven't found the man at the bottom of the lake . . .

The narrator goes on to tell us that the man, a swimmer, drowned in June; since then, the lake has been "perfectly calm," in part because of the weather, in part because locals have avoided going into the water since the accident. Only outsiders, people who don't know about the drowning, swim in it.

> Richard has never mentioned the accident to an unsuspecting visitor: what would be the point? Why ruin things for someone who's just

trying to enjoy the day? Strangers who walk past his garden gate on their outings return just as happy as they came.

But he can't avoid seeing the lake when he sits at his desk.

It's up to the reader to draw the conclusion that the lake represents not only the death of a stranger, but Richard's inevitable demise. That suggestion is made entirely by the narrator, in the rewording of a statement of fact.

The lake will take on greater meaning as the novel progresses.

IN THE NEXT SECTION—STILL in the first chapter—we learn that local gossip has it that some people were out in rowboats when the man drowned, but didn't try to rescue him—either they didn't understand the seriousness of his trouble, "or maybe they were afraid the man would pull them down with him, who knows." That casual "who knows" might throw us off the scent, and this early mystery—the identity of the drowned man and the circumstances of his death—is never resolved. Instead, Erpenbeck lets these early references to the drowning establish a darkness in the background, one that she'll develop in ways that Richard never fully recognizes, or at least never acknowledges.

As you might already have intuited, the anecdote about the drowned swimmer in the lake is analogous to the story of the African refugees in the middle of Berlin. Some people ignore them; some may not understand their plight; and eventually they're moved out of sight. But this analogy can't be evident to the novel's reader—not yet—because the African refugees haven't even been mentioned.

The ambiguous distance between narrator and point-of-view character is more fully defined in the second chapter, when the narrator tells us that ten men, who speak English, French, and Italian, as well as other languages "no one here understands," and whose skin is black, have gone on a hunger strike. Some of the men have also decided not to speak, not to answer questions put to them by the police and others. She tells us, "The silence of these men who would rather die than reveal their identity unites with the waiting of all these others who want their questions answered to produce a great silence in the middle of the square."

In the next paragraph, the narrator asks, "Why is it that Richard, walking past all these black and white people sitting and standing that afternoon, doesn't hear this silence?" That quickly, the narrative has established a much longer view, distant from the main character. Only in the third chapter, when Richard sits down to watch the news at home, does he learn part of what the narrator has been telling us about the African refugees.

From that moment we might expect the novel to operate differently; we might think the narrator has more she wants to tell us, that she might start interjecting like Tolstoy, or Dickens. But for the most part the novel stays close to Richard's thoughts, questions, concerns, and actions. Erpenbeck has established her options, though, and her narrator occasionally draws back to tell us more that Richard doesn't know, as in this passage:

> The professor emeritus, who's hearing so many things for the
> first time that it's as if he's become a child again, now suddenly
> understands that Oranienplatz is not only the square designed in the
> nineteenth century by the famous landscape architect Lenné, not only

the square where an elderly woman walks her dog every day, or where a girl on a park bench kissed her boyfriend for the first time. For a boy who has grown up among the nomads, Oranienplatz—where he made his home for a year and a half—is one station on a long journey, a temporary place, leading to the next temporary place.

"The professor emeritus" is Richard; Erpenbeck uses that label to signal a shift to the stance she introduced much earlier—here, to underscore the fact that Richard's is the story of an education, even if the man being educated is a retired professor.

Late in the novel, Erpenbeck puts this greater distance to dramatic use in two ways.

In the final scene, during a party at Richard's house, he learns that the wife of one of his best friends, who has been ill, is now close to death. The friend, the woman's husband, is at the party; and when the news spreads, all of the guests, German and African, fall silent. (A reminder: all of the African refugees are men.)

One man now thinks about how his wife always kissed him on his eyes.

One thinks how well the woman he loves always fits in his embrace.

One man thinks about her running her hand through his hair, and another how good her breath smelled when her face was beside his.

One thinks how his wife stuck her tongue in his ear...

All of them think for a moment about women they have loved, who once loved them.

This leap to the other men's thoughts is surprising; at the same time, we realize the narrator has prepared us for it, has given herself the option of telling us things Richard doesn't know, since that moment in the second chapter, when she asked why Richard hadn't seen the men in the plaza, and each time she's moved briefly into the perspective of another character.

On the final page, Erpenbeck does something even more surprising. If you haven't read the book, it would significantly impact your experience of it. So I'll say only that Erpenbeck first tells us something that Richard may or may not know; then she tells us something that he certainly knows, something he has known all along, information about his past that dramatically changes what we thought we knew about him. It's as if something long suppressed has forced itself into view. The novel ends with these lines:

> I think that's when I realized, says Richard, that the things I can endure are only just the surface of what I can't possibly endure.
>
> Like the surface of the sea? asks Khalil.
>
> Actually, yes, exactly like the surface of the sea.

All of the refugees have had to cross the sea; many of them saw friends and family members drown. And of course Richard can't avoid looking out at the lake, which the narrator tells us "will forever remain the lake in which someone has died, but it will nonetheless remain forever very beautiful."

And so at the end of the novel Erpenbeck draws together multiple narrative threads, but also the pain of knowing, the impossibility of forgetting, temporary forgetting, and the unbearable knowledge that lies beneath ordinary, and even beautiful, surfaces. She's done that by leading us deep into the thoughts and experiences of a compassionate, curious, educated, and clearly flawed man; and she's done it by allowing us to see most but not all of what he sees; more than he sees; and differently than he sees. The result is a novel that demands, and rewards, the reader's active participation.

Erpenbeck's narrator doesn't tell us what to think, doesn't explicitly pass judgment; she guides us almost entirely through the selection and arrangement of information.

YOU'RE PROBABLY FAMILIAR WITH the old science experiments involving rats in mazes. The maze was a big box made of wood with a transparent lid on top, so the researchers could watch the rats. One of the earliest experiments involved putting a piece of cheese somewhere in the maze, and having the rat find it through exploration—then, sometime later, putting the same rat in the same maze with the cheese in the same place, and seeing if the rat found the cheese any more efficiently. The idea was to see if the rat could "learn," or remember, how to reach the goal.

At some point in the drafting and revision process, we have a main character, and we know that character is going to make certain right and wrong moves, certain decisions, and encounter certain obstacles, and we know where that character is going to end up. And that's when the trouble starts—because we might, in fact, write a story that is the equivalent of putting a GoPro on a rat, documenting his or her journey.

But here's something to keep in mind: any number of rats outwitted that first experiment. In one case, a particularly ingenuous or impatient rat, placed for the second or third or fourth time at the start of the maze, simply stood up, raising the lid, and walked directly to the cheese.

After observing this sort of behavior, in the 1930s, Edward Tolman proposed that rats were capable of "building [mental] representations of their environment." The cognitive map a rat made "wasn't just a strip map of the particular paths that led to the food but a comprehensive map that included the location of food and the surrounding space, enabling [it] to find novel routes." Novel, indeed.

In other words, Tolman thought rats were a lot like us. The first "aerial view" maps of cities were made long before the airplane was invented, long before hot air balloons; in *Arctic Dreams*, Barry Lopez includes a detailed map of part of the Alaskan coastline as seen from above, drawn by a Native fisherman who had never left the ground. This is what all of us, and particularly artists, do—construct an understanding of the world larger than a mere documentation of our own experience. We intuit, we infer, we gather information. Among other things, this allows us to imagine effects of actions we might take, and it allows us sympathetic understanding. It allows us to create fiction and poetry that, even if it is based in some way on our experience, extends beyond that, and speaks to readers we've never met—many of them quite different from us.

After studying rats, Edward Tolman shifted his focus to people. He promoted the notion of "broad cognitive maps," maps that he hoped would lead us to recognize, for instance, that the well-being of all people is mutually interdependent.

This is something to bear in mind when we think of the narrators of our stories and novels. While our characters might very well be narrowly focused, we, as writers, and our narrators, need to continue to build broader maps of the world of our stories—so that, when it's necessary, we can create a few roadblocks for the reader; and when it's helpful, we can raise the lid and point straight to the cheese.

(Don't) Stop Me If You've Heard This Before

Storytelling Characters

Like a lot of writers, I discovered a love of reading early in life. That was thanks to my mother, primarily, as she read to my sister and me every night when we were young. Once I started reading on my own, she fed my habit with books she bought at the grocery store—the Hardy Boys, mainly—and took us to the Baltimore County Public Library, where I would check out stacks of books I could barely see over as I carried them to the car.

My mother's only regular opportunity to read came once a week, while she sat under the dryer at the beauty shop. For a while, when I attended college and then graduate school—opportunities she never had—she read books I recommended. As our tastes grew further apart, she would buy me books she knew I wanted but that she would never read. I wish I had been as generous, and spent more time talking with her about books she enjoyed—books by Baltimore writers or about growing up Catholic—that for one reason or another weren't high on my list. She continued buying me books long after I could afford all the ones I wanted, dating and inscribing them. To this day I'm surprised when I go to my shelves and see her handwriting in, say, Larry McMurtry's *Some Can Whistle,* or Gabriel García Márquez's *The General in His Labyrinth.* Surprised and grateful, reminded of how she supported me on a journey she knew she wouldn't be going on.

Depending on his mood, our father was either mystified or exasperated by all my reading. TV shows he understood; ditto movies on TV (especially war stories and westerns). (Movies in theaters? Unnecessary extravagance.) Cops and robbers, heroes and villains. Perry Mason and John Wayne. *McHale's Navy* and Gomer Pyle. Books? Suspicious. Our father was a storyteller, though. Like a lot of storytellers, he tended to dramatize, to mythologize, whether he was recounting a golf game, reminding us how, even though he had no relevant experience, he got a job as a barber when he joined the Marines, telling about the day, with our mother navigating, they nearly drove onto an active runway at Friendship Airport, or polishing tales of his youth, like the one about the time he and his friends broke into a railroad freight car, ate the watermelons they found inside, got caught, and were taken to their parents, who made them eat watermelon until they were sick.

Despite some questionable claims in those stories, we never questioned them. Our father could be hot-tempered, but when he told stories he was in good humor; we laughed and laughed. Like pool players at a jukebox, we would call up old favorites. My sister especially liked that watermelon story, to the point that she could tell it herself.

In our family (like most families?) there were talkers and there were listeners. My father and sister were talkers, gregarious, never hesitant to strike up conversation with strangers, always ready with a story. My mother and me, not so much. But a few weeks before she died, I persuaded our mother to tell us some of the stories we thought we knew. After decades of listening to our father, I wanted to hear her version.

DEMURE OR OUTSPOKEN, THE truth is, all of us tell stories: about our day at work, about what happened while we waited at the DMV, about visiting family over the holidays, name it. We tell stories in celebration and in grief; we tell them to entertain, to vent, and to be understood.

It makes sense, then, that characters in fiction would be storytellers. But often, possibly due to the influence of movies and television, writers seem worried about having characters speak for long, as if all dialogue should be short and pithy or glib. Of course, every first-person narrator is a storyteller, but my particular interest here is the storytelling that happens in dialogue, and in scenes. (Something I won't get to: stories told by one character on behalf of another. This happens when Nick Carraway tells us the story of Gatsby's past, as Gatsby told it to him the night before he was murdered; when the narrator of "Breakfast at Tiffany's" tells the story of Holly Golightly's youth; and throughout Rachel Cusk's *Outline*. Here stories are being translated, even co-opted, reframed by the teller for his or her own purposes.) Sometimes the stories characters tell are clearly purposeful, but not always. Sometimes they're meant to be taken at face value; in other cases we have reason to interpret them differently than the teller does. Some stories are incomplete; others are contradictory. Some characters, like Coleridge's Ancient Mariner, are obsessed by a story, in need of someone to tell it to; others require prodding, reveal their tales reluctantly.

It can be useful to think about what sorts of stories a person tells, to whom, and how; and about what stories that person is reluctant or unable to tell. (It can be just as useful to consider what stories someone wants to hear, from whom, and why.) Among the options, characters can

1.   refuse to tell their story;

2.   tell part(s) of their story;

3.   tell a complete and unquestioned story;

4.   tell a deliberately distorted version of their story;

5.   tell an unintentionally inaccurate or distorted version of their story; or

6.   tell substantially different, even contradictory versions of their story.

When characters tell stories, several things happen at once. The teller is characterized by the telling: her voice, her allusions and figures of speech, what she includes, what she omits, what she emphasizes. Occasionally we forget this and allow a character to tell *her* story merely for the sake of *our* story; that is, we fail to process the narrative through the character's perspective. Occasionally, we forget to allow the story to have a demonstrable effect on the characters who hear it. A story can reveal as much about its audience as about its teller. Does the listener react inappropriately? Does he ask questions? Does he ask questions that would be unnecessary if he had listened carefully? Does he try to interrupt? If so, what do those interruptions reveal about what's on his mind? How do they influence the rest of the telling?

STORYTELLING WITHIN NARRATIVES GOES back at least as far as *One Thousand and One Nights*, *The Odyssey*, and *The Canterbury Tales*. Scheherazade, possibly the most famous tale-teller in literature, told stories to save her life. Odysseus needs to be encouraged, but it doesn't take much: "Who are you? Where did you come from across the watery depths?" asks the Cyclops; "Please explain why you were crying," says Alcinous; "Who are you? Where is your city? And who are your parents?" asks Circe, and off Odysseus goes again. Depending on the circumstance, he answers discreetly or sincerely, nearly always strategically. For both Homer and Odysseus, storytelling is purposeful. Chaucer's pilgrims tell stories to pass the time, but their tales reveal personality, attitude, and motivation. Their storytelling also forms a sort of dramatic action of its own, as the pilgrims interrupt each other, bicker, and use their stories to respond to one another, as when the Summoner attacks the Friar. As Chaucer's readers, we are meant to recognize the interplay, to form opinions about the tellers, to hover above it all, beside the author.

1. A Taxonomy

In storytelling mode, our father bore some resemblance to Jackie Gleason: a solid working-class man, hair cut tight to his head, fully assuming his role as head of household, talking loudly, gesturing broadly, giving expression to a wide range of emotions. Our mother played the role of sidekick, mostly called on to confirm certain claims, very rarely contradicting or correcting, even more rarely initiating a story herself. Stories had to be drawn from her. I didn't expect her to reveal some shocking new insight about that episode at Friendship Airport, which always had the earmarks of a simple anecdote—they made a wrong turn, panicked—writ large. That day in the nursing home, my sister and I asked her to tell stories mostly to keep her mind off her pain. But I had a secondary motive. My son, who was there with me, was engaged to be married, and while we couldn't say it, none of us expected my mother to live until the wedding. So I asked a question I thought she could answer without being overcome by sadness, one I genuinely wanted to hear her answer to: Exactly how and when had our father proposed?

"It was 1953," my mother told us. "We were in the car, in the driveway. He said 'You should marry me.'"

"Always the romantic," I said.

"And I said, 'I don't think so.'"

News to me. "You told him no?"

"Three other boys had already asked me that year," she said. "And I had told them yes."

AS WRITERS, WE GRAVITATE to what we feel are untold stories, unheard voices. Often we do this to get a truth or perspective we feel hasn't been recognized. This sort of storytelling appears as a conceit in the earliest detective stories. The people who seek out Sherlock Holmes feel, for one reason or another, they can't tell their stories to the proper authorities. They need someone who will listen, someone who will take action. The typical Sherlock Holmes story begins when one of those people comes to 221B Baker Street with a story to tell, one that ends with a request. For Holmes, accepting the case typically requires journeying to the scene of prior events, and interrogating people: getting them to tell their stories. While all of those stories within the story supply useful information, many are incomplete, or misleading. At the end of each tale, Holmes solves the case by discovering the true and complete story.

Arthur Conan Doyle's narrator, Dr. Watson, consistently directs our attention to Holmes, the embodiment of knowledge, logic, and methodical problem-solving, rather than to the original storyteller, the person with a problem. That changes, to varying degrees, in the hard-boiled noir novels of James M. Cain, Raymond Chandler, and Ross McDonald, where character psychology and motivation—who tells what story, and why—become more central.

Toni Morrison's *Song of Solomon* begins as dramatically as any murder mystery: insurance agent Robert Smith is about to "fly" from the roof of Mercy Hospital. Smith's suicide and the song sung by a woman in the crowd are two early pieces of a puzzle that will be fully assembled only in the book's final pages. In Morrison's novel, client, detective, and even potential murder victim are one and the same: Macon "Milkman" Dead, born after Robert Smith's appearance on the roof sent his mother into labor. Milkman has multiple mysteries to solve: mysteries about his parents and his aunt, about his ancestors and his best friend. Who killed Macon Dead, Milkman's grandfather? Why does Milkman's father hold his wife and his sister, Pilate, in such low regard? What's in the bag Pilate calls her inheritance? Where is the gold they thought she carried? What do the insurance agent, Milkman's sister's lover, and Milkman's best friend, Guitar, have in common? By drawing out the people around him, encouraging them to tell their stories, Milkman eventually forms a coherent narrative—one that includes a secret society, a cache of gold, a sack of bones, ghosts and golden-eyed dogs, encoded names and Flying Africans. Milkman discovers information sometimes by chance, sometimes through persistence. While he thinks he's pursuing mysteries about the people around him, ultimately he is on a journey of self-discovery. In other words, he is less like Sherlock Holmes than he is like us.

Examined closely, *Song of Solomon* offers a taxonomy of many of the ways and reasons characters can tell stories within a larger narrative.

(Tantalizingly) Fragmented Stories

This option, most famously attributed to Scheherazade, is a staple of mysteries, and can help fuel plot boldly or more subtly. Morrison begins *Song of Solomon* with a story told in the form of a note tacked to his front door by the insurance agent:

> At 3:00 p.m. on Wednesday the 18th of February, 1931, I will take off from Mercy and fly away on my own wings. Please forgive me. I loved you all.
>
> (signed) Robert Smith,
>
> Ins. Agent

This brief note echoes a very short story attributed to Hemingway ("For sale: baby shoes, never worn") but raises even more questions. Fly how? What does he mean, "my own wings"? Forgive him for what? Who "all" did he love?

The note sends us forward in search of answers.

Incrementally Assembled Stories

A fragmented story doesn't necessarily need to be completed. *Song of Solomon* doesn't investigate Robert Smith's life at length, as he is, ultimately, a peripheral character. When fragmented stories are continued or completed, they form incrementally assembled stories. In that first scene, a woman sings,

> O Sugarman done fly away
>
> Sugarman done gone
>
> Sugarman cut across the sky
>
> Sugarman come home

That song will return in various places and forms (Pilate and Reba will sing some of it, children jumping rope will sing a different version) until it reveals itself, very late in the novel, to be an encoded version of the story of Milkman's grandparents and great-grandparents.

A related story, also gradually assembled, is about how and why Milkman's grandfather was killed. Milkman works to learn all he can about that event from the past. Various people, including his Aunt Pilate, his father, Reverend Cooper, and Susan Byrd, know pieces of it. Pilate tells part of what she knows as a digression during a larger story and acknowledges, "I don't know who and I don't know why" he was killed. (The narrator tells us, "Guitar felt like a frustrated detective.")

Midway through the novel, Macon tells Milkman, "A long time ago, I told you about when I was a boy on the farm. About Pilate and me...I never finished the story; I never told you all of it." He goes on to tell what he believes is "all of it"; Milkman will learn more from other sources. The desire to complete that narrative is central to both the novel's story (what happened?) and its plot (why?).

Story as Warning

Freddie, a janitor and one of Macon's tenants, tells part of a story with ominous implications: Guitar and Empire State, unlikely companions, have recently been spending time together; and Freddie thinks Empire State has committed murder. "Keep your eyes open...Some strange things going on round here." Freddie connects this to the insurance man who jumped off the hospital roof years earlier: "It was some strange stuff then, too." He then tells Milkman to ask his sister Corinthians what she knows—to add to the story.

Eventually we'll learn that Guitar and Empire State, as well as the insurance agent Robert Smith and Porter, another of Macon's tenants, are (or were) members of the Seven Days, a secretive group avenging the murders of Black people by murdering White people.

A story as warning creates dramatic tension in part through foreshadowing, in part through mysteries or ambiguities in the telling ("Some strange things going on...").

Stories Told through Conversation/Interrogation

Even in detective novels, an interrogation doesn't necessarily occur in a police station or courtroom; often the detective confronts a witness or suspect and asks questions, eliciting a story that might or might not be accurate, honest, and/or complete. The person doing the questioning has something they want to know, which reveals what they feel is important; the person answering can have any number of reasons for responding in a particular way (withholding information out of self-interest, offering information out of self-interest, telling the story the speaker believes the listener wants to hear, etc.). This kind of storytelling is most effective when the two people in conversation have different understanding or motivation—when there's some impediment to the free flow of information.

Early in *Song of Solomon*, Freddie tells Macon Dead, Milkman's father, that Porter is drunk and threatening to kill himself. This particular story is energized by the need for someone to take immediate action. As Macon closes up his office and takes out a gun, he asks Freddie a series of questions—a kind of interrogation—that serve to fill us in on what's happened so far. This is a way of dramatizing what might otherwise be an extended passage of exposition.

A potential pitfall of an interrogation is what Paul West used to call "Q&A dialogue." At its worst, Q&A dialogue feels less like conversation than like someone filling out a form:

"Do you want to go out tonight?"

"Sure."

"Dinner?"

"How about a movie?"

"What do you want to see?"

And so on.

Morrison avoids this in several ways. Most notably, Macon and Freddie have different ideas about what needs to be done: Freddie wants violence to be avoided, but Macon—who is taking a gun to confront a man who claims to be on the verge of committing suicide—wants the money he's owed. Meanwhile, though Macon asks, "Who's crazy enough to sell [Porter] any liquor?" the narrator tells us he knows the wine came from Pilate, his sister. This adds to the tension of the scene, as one story is unfolding in dialogue while a significantly different version is unfolding in narration. Freddie eagerly supplies information in short, excited bursts, while Macon asks questions to learn about the situation, tells Freddie what he intends to do ("If he don't toss me my rent, I'm going to blow him out of that window"), and withholds information.

An interrogator doesn't need to be explicit or even honest about his motives. In this scene, we learn that Macon cares more about collecting his rent than about the well-being of his tenant, and that he actively disassociates himself from his sister.

Communal Storytelling

Communal or Cooperative Storytelling is a common feature of Richard Russo's novels, where people gather in diners and bars and bond over card games, and of August Wilson's plays. (George C. Wolfe, director of the film adaptation of *Ma Rainey's Black Bottom*, calls Wilson's storytelling speeches "blues arias." "It's the storytelling equation of human beings…'I may not be in charge of my life, but I'm in charge of my narrative.' That's what all of these characters are talking about…It's a human impulse we all have.")

Morrison uses this technique throughout *Song of Solomon*, usually to convey the bonds among various groups of characters. The first time Milkman and Guitar go to Pilate's house, Hagar, her daughter, asks, "Why they call you Guitar?" The question elicits an answer in the form of a story from his childhood and leads to the claim that Reba is lucky (she wins contests), which leads to the story of her being "the half a millionth person to walk into Sears and Roebuck," which is ultimately a story of racial discrimination. Communal stories often shift focus as well as teller. "Hagar and Pilate pulled the conversation apart," Morrison writes, "each yanking out some thread of comment more to herself than to Milkman or Guitar."

Another example occurs in Tommy's Barbershop, as Milkman, Guitar, and others learn about the death of Emmett Till on the radio. While this might seem more a kind of communal listening than communal storytelling, the two are related. The men debate the story and how it will be covered in the newspapers, and they support their arguments with stories of their own: "The men began to trade tales of atrocities...A litany of personal humiliation, outrage, and anger."

A communal storytelling scene later in the novel has a different tone. When men gather at Reverend Cooper's house to tell Milkman what they remember of his father and Pilate, "they talked on and on, using Milkman as the ignition that gunned their memories." While their stories provide information to Milkman, their memories of his father, whom they see as a successful Black businessman, serve a different purpose, giving them hope: "See? See what you can do?"

Communal storytelling can define a group through shared interests; it can also illustrate each individual's allegiance to or wariness of that group.

Story as an Act of Sympathetic Understanding

While the men in Tommy's Barbershop superficially disagree about the news coverage of Emmett Till's murder, their storytelling is also an act of mutual support during a time of rage and grief: "They laughed then, uproariously, about the speed with which they had run, the pose they had assumed, the ruse they had invented to escape or decrease some threat to their manliness, their humanness." During that first visit to Pilate's, Milkman thinks, "It was the first time in his life that he remembered being completely happy. He was with his friend, an older boy...He was sitting comfortably in the notorious wine house; he was surrounded by women who seemed to enjoy him and who laughed out loud." At Reverend Cooper's, the mutual storytelling is a sign of pride but also consolation: "Even as boys these men began to die and were dying still. Looking at Milkman in those nighttime talks, they yearned for something."

Similarly, an individual can share a story as a gesture of understanding. After Milkman, defending his mother, strikes his father, and his father tells him a story about Ruth lying in bed, naked, with her father's corpse, Milkman seeks out Guitar, both to unburden himself and to try to make sense of all that's just happened. "I can understand how you feel," Guitar says, and goes on to tell a story about shooting a doe. The story is an admission of shame. "So I know how you felt when you saw your father hit your mother," Guitar concludes. "It's like that doe." Milkman nods, "but it was clear to Guitar that nothing he had said made any difference." Feeling his gesture failed, Guitar asks Milkman to tell him in more detail about the altercation with his father. Asking for a story can also be an act of sympathy and generosity.

When Ruth goes to visit Pilate, Pilate tells the story of her childhood in a manner very much influenced by her audience: she speaks mother to mother, woman to woman. She also has an unspoken motive: she tells "her life story...making [it] deliberately long to keep Ruth's mind off Hagar."

Stories Forced into the Light

Characters can withhold stories for all sorts of reasons. They might not understand the value or meaning of a story to someone else, they might repress a story out of fear or shame, they might doubt their memory, they might fear repercussions (for themselves or others), and so on. Forcing these stories to light can involve a sort of emotional violence, but the telling can also be therapeutic, healing.

One of the great mysteries for Milkman is why his father treats his sister, Pilate, and his wife, Ruth, with such disrespect. When Milkman finally works up the nerve to question him about Pilate directly, his father thinks, "Maybe it was time to tell him things." He begins by telling his son what he has intentionally withheld, but that leads to what we might call recovered memories—details only the telling brings to mind. And while he means to defend his past actions, the act of telling changes him: "His voice sounded different to Milkman. Less hard, and his speech was different." The story brings them closer.

This kind of storytelling can fall flat dramatically, especially if it seems the writer has simply waited to allow a character to explain himself, and the reader feels the withholding of information is artificial. Morrison avoids this in several ways. For one, Macon's story raises new questions. When Milkman asks "What was [your father's] real name?" Macon doesn't answer; he doesn't know. For another, the story creates new tension. When Macon tries to explain his feelings toward Pilate by telling an allegory about a baby snake, Milkman thinks, "His father had explained nothing to him." In *Song of Solomon*, stories are often misunderstood or unappreciated by the listener. The distinction between the listener's perspective and the reader's helps to keep each story from being simply expository.

This revealing of suppressed stories is common in theater; it's a type of drama that directly reveals character. What stories does a character suppress? Why? What suddenly allows him to release them? How do various characters interpret events differently? Why?

The day comes when Milkman can no longer tolerate his father's abuse of his mother. When Macon punches his wife, Milkman yanks him by his collar, knocking him into the radiator. "You touch her again, one more time," he tells his father, "and I'll kill you."

Later that night, his father comes to his room and says, "If you want to be a whole man, you have to deal with the whole truth." His need to justify his violence in the kitchen finally forces him to tell a dark story from the past, one Macon believes to be a damning revelation about Macon's mother's relationship with her father. ("Goddam," Milkman said aloud. "What the fuck did he tell me all that shit for?")

Story as Corrective

Later, Ruth will say, "I don't know what all your father has told you about me…But I know…he told you only what was flattering to him." She then tells her version of the same story. The disparities between the two accounts is never resolved, but this is a novel, not a criminal case—determining exactly what happened isn't the point. Here, the competing stories help us understand how Macon and Ruth justify their actions, and why they each feel misunderstood.

Similarly, Milkman's sister Lena will bring him into her bedroom to tell him her version of an event we saw played out early in the novel, a story that erupts from her. During a family drive, she was asked to lead her little brother away from the road so he could urinate; he turned and peed on her dress. To Milkman, the act was accidental; he's forgotten about it. But Lena has harbored that memory like an oyster with a pearl: to her it's the defining illustration of how Milkman treats her, her sister, and their mother.

Story Charged by Dramatic Context

The early scene involving Freddie and Macon, where Freddie's story about Porter is drawn out of him via interrogation, has dramatic urgency because Porter is still sitting in the window, holding a shotgun, threatening to kill himself. In a lesser novel, that scene would be all about the action: Is Porter going to commit suicide, or possibly hurt someone else? Instead, Morrison uses the high stakes of the situation to reveal the character of the listener. With another man's life at stake, Macon is most interested in (1) his money and (2) his reputation.

At another point, Pilate tells a story about things she's done to protect Reba in the past. The story is charged by the fact that she tells it to a man who has just hit Reba, and Pilate is standing immediately behind him, pressing the tip of a kitchen knife through his skin, just above his heart.

Most stories and novels will have relatively few moments of such high drama, but a story told when a character's life is threatened, or when she's taking bold action, is clearly charged with significance: when the stakes are high, this is what the character wants to say. Even when the stakes are less than life or death—on a first date, say, or when a man is trying to persuade his wife not to leave him—the story someone chooses to tell at that moment, and how they choose to tell it, can be deeply revealing.

Story Influenced by Context

Communal storytelling relies on some degree of shared experience. A lack of shared experience or beliefs—or a lack of trust—can also influence a storyteller.

Milkman and Guitar are arrested after they steal from Pilate's house what they think is a sack of gold but is in fact a sack of bones. At the police station, Pilate shuffles, stoops, changes her voice, quotes from the Bible (which they never knew she had read), and tells the police the bones are those of her late husband—which is to say, she creates a story and a way of telling it to a particular audience to serve an immediate end. Once the boys are released, on the ride home, "Pilate was tall again…And her own voice was back…In a conversational tone, like somebody picking up a story that had been interrupted in the telling, she told her brother something quite different from what she told the policemen." To Macon she tells the story of returning to the cave where he killed a man when they were young and gathering the bones she has carried with her in the sack ever since. "The dead you kill is yours," she tells him. "They stay with you anyway, in your mind. So it's a better thing…to have the bones right there with you wherever you go."

Much later, Milkman will learn that while Pilate believes that story to be true, the bones are likely her father's.

When Milkman first visits Susan Byrd and Grace, Susan withholds and distorts much of what she knows; when he returns, Susan says, "I just said that in front of *her*…She talks so much, you know." She goes on to tell him a great deal more.

Disguised or Encrypted Story

For a variety of reasons, as when Pilate goes to the police station, a character might feel compelled to fictionalize a story, or obscure its origins or details. Morrison's narrator tells us, Milkman "began to describe to Guitar a dream he had had about his mother. He called it a dream because he didn't want to tell him it had really happened."

One more example of an encrypted story: at one point Pilate's father "comes to her" (as a ghost) and says "Sing, Sing," and "You can't just fly on off and leave a body." Pilate interprets his words to mean she should sing, and she should collect the bones of the man Macon killed. Eventually we learn Sing was Pilate's mother's name, and her father was referring to his own bones. Whether stories are presented complete or in fragments, they can be encoded, encrypted, or ambiguous; and the act of interpretation can reveal some aspect of the listener's character or interest.

In Helon Habila's *Travelers*, a man named Matteo who fell in love with an African refugee, then deceived her, sees the opportunity to unburden himself to a stranger. "I'll tell you a story," he says. "It is about a woman…Think of it as a fairy tale." His listener never doubts that the man in the story is Matteo, and when he's finished, Matteo doesn't deny it. But telling the story in the third person, as if it were about a stranger, is the only way he can admit to what he knows was a terrible wrong.

Stories as Currency

Earlier in Habila's book, another character, Manu, thinks, "Details have a way of piling up, layer upon seductive layer, making you think you know the person, until one day you realize you don't. Stories are made up and traded as currency among homeless, rootless people… something to disarm you with." Stories can serve as currency even when they're true. In *Song of Solomon*, when Milkman anticipates stealing what he thinks is the sack of gold from Pilate, he imagines how the story of his deed would elevate his status: it would reveal "a self that could join the chorus at Railroad Tommy's…He could tell this."

2. Too Good to Be True vs. Complex Truth

Song of Solomon won the National Book Critics Circle Award and was cited by the Swedish Academy when Toni Morrison received the Nobel Prize. Even so, some feel it isn't her best book. One reservation some readers have is the neatness with which all of the stories within the novel add up. Ultimately, the mysteries are explained, the fragments assembled.

In John Irving's *The World According to Garp*, the title character, a fiction writer, expresses frustration at psychiatrists: "There was no one Garp tended to sneer at as much as he sneered at psychiatrists—those dangerous simplifiers, those thieves of a person's complexity...The psychiatrist approached the mess without proper respect for the mess. The psychiatrist's objective was to clear the head...Garp knew the trick is to *use* the mess." While assembly narratives, or stories that result in understanding or explanation, can be rewarding and enjoyable, at some point readers may begin to distrust them. Our desire to see the parts made into a satisfying whole is in competition with our desire for fiction to mirror the messy complexity of our lives.

We know from experience that we can talk to everyone we want and still not come to complete understanding of an event, or a person's motivation. A subcategory of assembly narratives rejects the notion that there is a single truth to be discovered. Perhaps the most famous example is Ryunosuke Akutagawa's short story "In a Grove," the inspiration for Akira Kurosawa's film *Rashōmon*. "In a Grove" is presented as an unmediated series of seven transcriptions: of testimony given by four secondary witnesses to a high police commissioner, and testimony of the three eyewitnesses, the people involved. Seven first-person narratives, all focused on the death of a samurai, the involvement of his young wife, and a brigand. Established as fact is that the samurai was killed, that the brigand was apprehended—the first five transcriptions appear to be part of his trial—and that the young wife, defiled before the murder, ran off.

The story begins with a woodcutter telling the police commissioner, "Yes, sir. Certainly, it was I who found the body." "In a Grove" was published while Arthur Conan Doyle was still writing about Sherlock Holmes; and if it ended after the brigand's confession, it would read like a fairly primitive mystery story. But Akutagawa offers the reader several surprises in quick succession. The first surprise appears in the sixth transcript: it's the story of the samurai's wife, whom we know to be missing, so not involved in the trial; the next is that she claims *she* killed her husband. Even more unexpectedly, the seventh transcript is "The Story of the Murdered Man, as Told through a Medium." From the grave, the samurai confesses to the murder—or, rather, suicide. There the story ends.

Given that "In a Grove" has no mediating narrator, and no character who responds to the seven speeches we read—no equivalent to Sherlock Holmes or Milkman Dead—it leaves us with a puzzle and three conflicting solutions. Which is to say, no solution, if what we want to know is whoreallydunnit, or what happened that day in the grove. While the testimonies contradict one another, we have no evidence that would prove any of the three confessions to be false. Rather than focusing on solving the crime, Akutagawa's story raises questions about our expectations of fiction and about the subjectivity of experience. Akutagawa suggests that it is naive to think that there is one true story; there are as many true stories as there are tellers.

To be fair, Toni Morrison suggests the same when Milkman hears contradictory stories from his parents, and from his father and Pilate; but the overall experience of reading *Song of Solomon* is one that emphasizes the pieces fitting together, the truth being discovered. In other novels, including *A Mercy* and *Beloved*, Morrison balances the pleasures of assembly with uncertainty, irreconciliation, and ongoing mystery.

An extraordinary demonstration of the power of this sort of contradictory, unreconciled storytelling is *A Separation*, by Iranian director Asghar Farhadi, which won the Academy Award for Best Foreign Language Film in 2012. The film's strategy is demonstrated in the opening sequence. A woman, Simin, is pleading her case to a judge: she wants to leave Iran with her husband and daughter, but he refuses, so she wants a divorce. As she makes her case, we begin to feel that her husband is unreasonable and oppressive. We take her side.

But then Nader, her husband, speaks, and we learn that he's the only caretaker of his father, who has Alzheimer's. How can he leave his father behind? Immediately, we understand there's more to the story: another perspective, other factors to consider, greater complication. A lesser narrative would become a simple he said, she said, but *A Separation* keeps opening outward, introducing new characters, revealing new complications and additional perspectives. Just when we think we know who's right, who's wrong, we're given not just new information but a new way of considering what we've already been told. People do bad things, make regrettable choices; but they're allowed to tell their stories, explain their justifications. As viewers, we're denied facile conclusions. What we're given instead is compassionate understanding of a group of people trying to do what they believe is right, but suffering nonetheless.

3. Possessed by the Unspeakable: When Stories Matter Most

What had begun as conversation turned to interrogation, that day in the nursing home. Later I discovered that as soon as our mother said, "Three other boys had already asked me, and I said yes," my son had activated the voice recorder on his phone. So while I could recount the conversation verbatim, I'll just say this: I started by asking the obvious. What happened with those three other boys? The answers were incomplete and out of sequence. According to our mother, the father of one boy disapproved, because she was Catholic. Our grandparents put a halt to the interest of another young man: "Mother and Daddy wouldn't hear of that, because he wanted me to ride on the back of his scooter." More likely their concern had to do with the fact that she was eighteen. He was twenty-six.

The third name she mentioned was familiar. A neighbor, he had been just a few years older and joined the Navy after graduating from high school. The two of them kept in touch. When I was young, we had all visited him and his wife in Florida. Much later, when I learned the word "subtext," I immediately thought of that trip.

While my sister and I pressed for answers, recollecting led our mother in other directions. She tried to remember names, told us about other boys who had joined the military, jumped ahead to her first meeting with our father's parents, who met her at their door and asked, "What are you?" Not Italian, they meant. So how had our father prevailed?

"He was always there!" When our mother went out on dates with other young men, he would go to her house and ingratiate himself with her parents; when she got home, he'd be waiting for her.

That didn't answer our questions, but it was all the answer we got.

YEARS AGO, A WOMAN told me she wanted to write about the unspeakable in fiction. I wish I could tell you what was wrong with me; maybe I was too young, maybe I just wasn't thinking well. But I responded by saying something like, "What's unspeakable? If you can think it, you can put it into words." I wasn't being mean, just thoughtless. She was and is a serious person, with serious concerns, and she wanted to write about the stories that are so important, so potentially dangerous or revealing, so foundation threatening, that we don't know how or to whom to tell them. Since then, I've come to believe that most of us have such stories.

Unspeakable stories are related to a category I referred to earlier: Stories Forced into the Light. The difference is that these stories never come to the surface, or not entirely; or that the emergence of the story creates a new kind of damage. Having characters confront the need to tell them can make for powerful fiction.

IN ANTON CHEKHOV'S "MISERY," a sleigh driver, or cab driver, Iona Potapov, sits in the falling snow "white as a ghost." He and his "little mare" have been still so long that they are nearly covered in snow—as if, Chekhov tells us, they are both lost in thought. Iona is startled by an officer who needs a ride. Other drivers shout at him as they move along, and when the officer makes a sympathetic comment—"What rascals they are! They are simply doing their best to run up against you or fall under the horse's feet"—Iona blurts out the thought that had kept him motionless: his son has died. The officer asks what he died of, and when Iona turns to explain that his son had a fever and was hospitalized, he nearly runs into another sleigh; the driver yells at him, and this time the officer says "Drive on!...Hurry up!"

Two hours pass. Three young men hire Iona to take them to the Police Bridge. The men insult Iona, criticizing his driving, in the spirit of young men out on the town. The effect of this banter is surprising. We're told Iona "hears abuse directed to him, he sees people, and the feeling of loneliness begins little by little to be less heavy on his heart." To be involved, even to be insulted, is better than being buried alone under the snow. Iona now feels he can share his story. He tells the three men that his son has died. One of them asks if he's married, to which Iona replies, "The only wife for me now is the damp earth...The grave, that is!...Here my son's dead and I am alive...It's a strange thing, death has come in at the wrong door...Instead of coming for me it went for my son." He turns to tell them more, but they've reached their destination. When the men are gone, "The misery which has been for a brief space eased comes back again and tears his heart more cruelly than ever." Looking out at the crowds in the street, he thinks, "Can he not find among those thousands someone who will listen to him? But the crowds flit by heedless of him and his misery."

Despairing, Iona decides to go back to the yard, where some of the drivers sleep around a dirty stove. When one of them awakens to get a drink, Iona tells him his son has died, but the man falls back asleep. "Just as the young man had been thirsty for water," Chekhov tells us, he thirsts for speech. His son will have been dead a week, and he has not really talked to anybody yet...He wants to talk of it properly, with deliberation. He wants to tell how his son was taken ill, how he suffered, what he said before he died, how he died...He wants to describe the funeral, and how he went to the hospital to get his son's clothes. He still has his daughter Anisya in the country...And he wants to talk about her too...Yes, he has plenty to talk about now. His listener ought to sigh and exclaim and lament.

IONA ATTEMPTS TO TELL his story three times—to the officer, to the three raucous young men, and to his fellow driver. We're told he "cannot think about his son when he is alone...To talk about him with someone is possible, but to think of him and picture him is insufferable anguish." How threatening is it for Iona to think of his son? How desperate is he to talk with someone? The story ends with the sleigh driver feeding his little mare a bucket of oats:

> "That's how it is, old girl...Kuzma Ionisch is no more...He's gone and died...Now, let's say you had a little foal, and you were its mother...And what if your little foal went and died...You'd be sorry, wouldn't you?"
>
> The little mare munches, listens, and breathes on her master's hands. Iona is carried away and tells her all about it.

You might argue that while Iona is clearly obsessed by the story he wants to tell, this is not quite a case of the unspeakable; it's more a matter of not having the right listener. To that I'd reply: (1) You're right, and (2) The two are related. We find certain stories unspeakable not because we can't imagine putting them into words but because we fear how a listener might react: that they'd criticize us, dismiss us, think less of us, turn us in to the authorities, name it. More than one writer has had family members refuse to speak to them after publication—not because what the writer wrote was inaccurate, or even explicitly revealing, but because the writer made public something the family believed to be private (which is to say, unspeakable, outside of a close circle).

In other cases, like Iona's, we can find no listener. Iona needs to give voice to his grief, and for his grief to be recognized. His loss is amplified by his isolation, his inability to share the story that is breaking his heart. Chekhov reminds us that characters not only *want* to tell their stories but *need* to tell their stories. He shows us this again and again, in "About Love," "The Man in the Case," "Gooseberries," and "A Doctor's Visit." In "Lady with the Pet Dog," Gurov feels "an overwhelming desire to share his memories with someone." Why? Because he has a secret, and he believes this secret is the most important thing in his life. In every one of those examples, when the character tries to tell his or her story, they are misunderstood. The attempt only underscores their isolation.

REPRESSED STORIES DISTORT A character's surface. What secret is forcing its way out? What shameful desire? The effort to get a story told, or to resist telling it, is a particular kind of action; the more important the story is to the teller, the greater the tension created by each frustrated attempt to tell it, or each near exposure.

The stakes are raised in Katherine Anne Porter's "Noon Wine," where the inability to tell a story kills a man.

It isn't enough for Mr. Thompson to be heard; he needs to be believed. And while no one tells him, to his face, that they don't believe him, he knows they don't. Worse yet, he doesn't believe himself.

The story begins in 1896, on a small South Texas farm owned by the Thompsons. One day a stranger, Olaf Helton, walks up and says he needs work. Mr. Thompson comes to terms with him.

The farm is in debt. Mr. Thompson is the sort who spends long hours rocking on the side porch, wondering how he could ever get more work done. Appearances mean a great deal to him and his wife. He declines to do many jobs because he feels they are not men's jobs; it wouldn't look right for him to do them. Mr. Helton, by contrast, is a perpetual motion machine: he milks the cows, churns the butter, slaughters hogs, makes sausages, and over the course of a few years turns the farm into a money-making enterprise.

Years pass. One day, Mr. Thompson is on the porch when another stranger comes to the farm. This man, Mr. Hatch, asks if there is an Olaf Helton nearby. It turns out Mr. Helton recently sent his mother in North Dakota several hundred dollars, thus revealing his whereabouts. Mr. Hatch claims that, years ago, Mr. Helton killed his brother. Mr. Hatch is a bounty hunter: he wants to take Helton back to North Dakota, where Hatch will receive a cash reward.

Over the course of the conversation, Mr. Thompson grows irritated, to the point that "he wanted to turn around and shove the fellow off the stump, but it wouldn't look reasonable." What does happen happens with the agonizing irrevocability of any life-changing accident. Angered, Mr. Thompson orders Mr. Hatch to leave. At the sound of raised voices, Mr. Helton comes around the corner, "arms swinging." Mr. Hatch "drove at him, knife in one hand, handcuffs in the other." Mr. Thompson "saw it coming, he saw the blade going into Mr. Helton's stomach"; he grabs the ax he had been using to cut wood and brings it down on Mr. Hatch's head, killing him. When the sheriff and his men come to the farm, Helton flees; in the process of subduing him, they wound him so badly that he dies in jail.

Mr. Thompson is cleared of the crime of murder. He knows, though, that this looks bad—and as we've seen, appearances mean a lot to the Thompsons. In the days that follow, he drives his wagon to his neighbors' homes and farms and, with his wife, tells his story. Or at least, he tells a version of it. Even standing on his porch, immediately after striking Mr. Hatch, he told himself a lie: "He killed Mr. Helton!" But Mr. Helton ran away.

Mr. Thompson tells his story so many times that people know what to expect when they see him coming. He tells it to everyone he knows well, then starts telling it to people he has never called on in his life. But the telling brings no satisfaction; his obsession with explaining himself makes things look even worse. Even his lawyer doesn't "seem pleased to see him."

One night when his now sickly wife wakes up screaming, his teenage sons run in and ask, "What did you do to her? You touch her again and I'll blow your heart out!" Mr. Thompson tells them he never did his wife any harm "on purpose." He knows she's suffering from the gossip, from what their neighbors think of them. The boys listen but do not speak, the depth of their accusations clear. When his wife is resting again, he goes downstairs, gets a lantern, a pencil, a piece of paper, and his shotgun, rides to "the farthest end of his fields," and kills himself.

"NOON WINE" ECHOES "MISERY"—A man is in search of someone to tell his story—and it echoes "In a Grove." Someone was killed.

Three people were at the scene. In this case, Mr. Hatch can't speak, and Mr. Helton won't speak (then dies). That leaves Mr. Thompson to grapple with contradictory information: what he knows he did (strike Mr. Hatch), what he's certain he saw (Mr. Hatch stab Mr. Helton), and what he has been told (that Mr. Helton wasn't injured). In addition, he knows his response to Mr. Hatch was influenced by the fact that the bounty hunter was abrasive and irritating, and quite possibly dishonest (he's deceptive about where he's from, and he claims to have "mislaid" a new shirt and a cake Helton's mother sent for her son). The truth of what he saw, and of his motivations for what he did, is difficult even for Mr. Thompson to determine. And while "Noon Wine" is told by an omniscient narrator, that narrator is careful not to explain too much, or to suggest whether Mr. Thompson's act was justified. Like Akutagawa, Katherine Anne Porter puts the reader in the position of juror, and she's complicated the situation so as to make our job difficult—to force us to confront "the mess," as John Irving puts it.

Porter imagines her characters as people with stories to tell. Early on, Mrs. Thompson "wanted to believe in her husband, and there were too many times that she couldn't." There is a divisive silence between them. The first night Mr. Helton eats with them, Mr. Thompson, in an attempt to break the awkward silence, tells a joke. "Mr. Helton did not seem to hear. Mrs. Thompson laughed dutifully, but she didn't think it was very funny. She had heard it often before...and it had never been a story that Mrs. Thompson thought suitable for mixed company." Later, they argue about his telling that joke. We will remember this dinner when the Thompsons go around to their neighbors, Mr. Thompson tells his not-entirely-true story of the killing, and Mrs. Thompson unhappily plays her part.

Mr. Helton rarely speaks. The Thompsons find themselves living with someone, dependent on someone, they can't talk to, except
for the most fundamental exchanges. We are not allowed access to
Mr. Helton's thoughts, which is to say the reader is also kept at a
distance by his silence. These poor people have the semblance of
family but none of its comfort; they are as isolated as Chekhov's
Iona.

Mrs. Thompson sees Mr. Helton shake her sons after they have
touched his prized harmonicas, but "she was afraid to ask them for
reasons. They might tell her a lie, and she would have to overtake
them in it, and whip them. Or she would have to pretend to believe
them, and they would get in the habit of lying. Or they might tell
her the truth, and it would be something she would have to whip
them for. The very thought of it gave her a headache." She imagines
the stories they might tell, imagines her responses, but she remains
silent. More repression, more tension.

Mr. Thompson lies to himself. Some of his lies seem deeply
ironic, but they are not unlike lies we may have told ourselves. Early
in the story he complains about his sons: "Mr. Thompson sometimes grew quite enraged with them, when imagining their future,
big lubbers sitting around whittling or thinking about fishing trips.
Well, he'd put a stop to that, mighty damn quick." Later we're told,
"They were such good boys Mr. Thompson began to believe they
were born that way, and that he had never spoken a harsh word to
them in their lives, much less thrashed them. Herbert and Arthur
never disputed his word."

Mr. Thompson tells himself two stories about his sons. We
know the second one is a comforting "belief," rather than the truth,
and if it were presented differently, we might see it as an example

of forgiveness, even love. But Mr. Thompson isn't forgiving, he's forgetting; and one thing Porter's story cautions us about is the danger of self-deception.

When Mr. Hatch, the bounty hunter, arrives, Mr. Thompson tells him, "I never take any man for a suspicious character 'til he shows hisself to be one. Says or does something." But he's already suspicious. It would be excusable, even admirable, if he were covering his suspicion with a bit of social grace, but by now we understand that Mr. Thompson believes many of the lies he tells about himself. Porter has arranged the events of the story to force him to confront that.

Mr. Thompson gets so irritated with Mr. Hatch that he considers assaulting him even before their argument escalates and Helton arrives. What most irritates Thompson is the way Mr. Hatch "had a way of taking the words out of Mr. Thompson's mouth, turning them around and mixing them up until Mr. Thompson didn't know himself what he had said." This irritation, combined with the threat of depriving the family of Mr. Helton's industriousness, leads Mr. Thompson to take violent action when Hatch pulls out his knife. The narrator clearly tells us that Mr. Thompson truly believes he "saw the blade going into Mr. Helton's stomach"; that is not a lie, although it is not true. The narrator also makes it clear that Mrs. Thompson only goes out to the porch *after* Mr. Thompson kills Mr. Hatch: "She saw first Mr. Helton, running all stooped over through the orchard...[then] a man Mrs. Thompson had never seen, who lay doubled up with the top of his head smashed."

Near the end of the story, Mrs. Thompson tells her sons, "I don't know what good it does, but your papa can't seem to rest unless he's telling how it happened." Mr. Thompson has become obsessed with his tale, obsessed with the need to get it right: "His eyes [are] hollowed out and dead-looking" from days of "see[ing] the neighbors to tell them his side of the story." That night, Mr. Thompson is unable to rest:

> [He] kept saying to himself that he'd got off, all right, just as Mr. Burleigh had predicted, but, but—and it was right there that Mr. Thompson's mind stuck, squirming like an angleworm on a fishhook: he had killed Mr. Hatch, and he was a murderer. That was the truth about himself that Mr. Thompson couldn't grasp...If he was given a chance he could explain the whole matter. At the trial they hadn't let him talk...they never did get to the core of the matter...[Since the trial he] had taken Ellie with him to tell every neighbor he had that he never killed Mr. Hatch on purpose, and what good did it do? Nobody believed him.

In each of these tellings, Thompson has turned to his wife and said, "You was there, you saw it, didn't you?" and she has said, "Yes, that's the truth. Mr. Thompson was trying to save Mr. Helton's life." In every telling of "what really happened," Mr. Thompson has lied, and forced his wife to lie. Each time she stiffens "as if somebody had threatened to hit her." "I remember now, Mr. Thompson," she tells their neighbors. "I really did come around the corner in time to see everything. It's not a lie, Mr. Thompson. Don't you worry." And the neighbors reply, "Why, certainly, we believe you, Mr. Thompson, why shouldn't we believe you?" and "Well, now, natchally, Mr. Thompson, we think you done right." Nonetheless, "Mr. Thompson was satisfied they didn't think so."

In "Misery," while people hear the few words Iona is able to share, they don't acknowledge the import of his son's death, or of his grief.

Mr. Thompson has listeners, but they reflect back to him his own doubt and uncertainty, compounded by the lies he's constructed. His story can provide no consolation because he lacks the ability to recognize, much less speak, the complicated truth.

Porter tells us, "It still seemed to him that he had done, maybe not the right thing, but the only thing he could do, that day, but had he? *Did he have to kill Mr. Hatch?*" Thompson tries to imagine other versions of the story. He imagines getting rid of Hatch "peaceably," or overpowering him and turning him over to the sheriff, or saying something that would convince him to leave. He finds himself imagining "how it might all have been, this very night even, if Mr. Helton were still safe and sound." This self-torment leads him back to his anger at Mr. Hatch. Lying in bed, Mr. Thompson clutches his fists "as if they seized an ax handle," and startles his wife awake.

Porter has Mr. Thompson try to tell his story one last time. After he leaves the house, he sits with his back against a fence post and writes:

> "Before Almighty God, the great judge of all before who I am about
> to appear, I do hereby solemnly swear that I did not take the life
> of Mr. Homer T. Hatch on purpose. It was done in defense of Mr.
> Helton. I did not aim to hit him with the ax but only to keep him off
> Mr. Helton. He aimed a blow at Mr. Helton who was not looking
> for it. It was my belief at the time that Mr. Hatch would of taken
> the life of Mr. Helton if I did not interfere. I have told all of this to
> the judge and the jury and they let me off but nobody believes it.
> This is the only way I can prove I am not a cold-blooded murderer
> like everybody seems to think. If I had been in Mr. Helton's place

he would of done the same for me. I still think I done the only thing there was to do. My wife—"

Mr. Thompson stopped here to think a while. He wet the pencil point with the tip of his tongue and marked out the last two words. He sat a while blacking out the words until he made a neat oblong patch where they had been, and started again:

"It was Mr. Homer T. Hatch who came to do wrong to a harmless man. He caused all this trouble and he deserved to die but I am sorry it was me who had to kill him."

In this final version of his story, the only one we see in its entirety, Mr. Thompson aims for a new standard of honesty. The sentence beginning "My wife" may have started as a repetition of the now familiar lie ("My wife saw it all, and she won't lie") or it may have been the beginning of a more painful admission ("My wife says she believes me, but she doesn't"). Mr. Thompson refuses to allow himself the lie, and he isn't prepared to admit to another painful truth. Instead, he signs his name to the truest version of the story he can tell, and then "trembling…his head…drumming until he was deaf and blind," he fumbles "for the trigger with his big toe."

Thompson's suicide, rather than proving his innocence, will only confirm the suspicions of his neighbors. Porter's story is not only about vanity, or an overdependence on appearances, and it isn't only about the failure to recognize the truth, which she reminds us can be deeply complicated. "Noon Wine" is about what happens when the stories we tell ourselves about ourselves conflict and we are unable to imagine new ones. "Noon Wine" illustrates our need to tell stories that allow us to go on with our lives not by simplifying or forgetting but by accepting complication and uncertainty. Whether they succeed or fail, a character confronted with the need to create the story that allows them to survive is deeply compelling.

THE EXPRESSION OF A suppressed story—one believed to have been unspeakable—might lead to some degree of healing; it might, as in the case of Mr. Thompson, have devastating results; or it might have multiple, powerful effects on a number of people, as in Javier Marías's *A Heart So White*, which focuses on the listener to such a story, rather than the teller. The novel could be described as a trauma narrative, or as an aftermath narrative; it focuses not on the explosive events that occurred before Juan, the narrator, was born, however, but on the story he hears his father tell about those events. He finds the story so overwhelming that it takes him nearly 250 pages to share it with us. While the novel includes many storytelling characters, the focal story is a warning, incrementally assembled, told through conversation and interrogation, forced into the light.

The book begins, "I did not want to know, but I have since come to know..." and goes on, in a tour de force opening chapter, to tell us part of the story: Juan's father's second wife killed herself immediately after their honeymoon. Throughout the book, Juan (whose mother is his father's third wife) reminds us that he did not want to know about the past; and on the few occasions when he asks about his father's earlier life, Ranz, his father, says either that he has no interest in talking about it or that he can't remember. But despite his professed lack of interest, Juan's curiosity, his anxiety related to his own recent marriage, and his father's advice on the day of the wedding ("If you ever do have any secrets or if you already have, don't tell her") haunt him, to the extent that they color virtually everything he describes. Among other things, the novel is about the relationship of support and coercion; of the one who acts and the one who, deliberately or not, encourages the action; and of the storyteller and the listener ("at our backs," Juan writes, "is the person urging us on, the person who whispers in our ear...his tongue at once his weapon and his instrument").

> An instigation is nothing but words...The same actions that no one is even sure they want to see carried out...are always involuntary... while words can be reiterated and retracted, repeated and rectified... One is guilty only of having heard them, which is unavoidable, and although the law doesn't exonerate the person who spoke, the person who speaks, that person knows that, in fact, he's done nothing, even if he did oblige the other person with his tongue at their ear, his chest pressed against their back, his troubled breathing, his hand on their shoulder, with his incomprehensible but persuasive whisper.

That passage occurs after Juan has heard a politician allude to *Macbeth*. In time we'll learn why he feels urgently connected to it.

The novel is something of a detective story, except that the dramatic events happened decades ago, and there is someone who can explain them: Ranz. One question is whether he will; another is whether Juan wants to hear what he has to say. Juan's wife, Luisa, has grown close to his father.

> What she was clear about was that it had to be her, not me, who asked Ranz, not so much because she was so sure that he'd confide in her, but because she was sure he wouldn't confide in me..."Who knows[, Luisa says], maybe he's been waiting all these years for someone like me to appear in your life, someone who could act as an

intermediary…Everything can be told. It's just a matter of starting, one word follows another."

Finally, Luisa elicits the story, which rests heavily on something Ranz shared with his second wife, Teresa, on their honeymoon. He says,

> I could have kept silent forever, but we believe that the more we love someone, the more secrets we should tell them, telling often seems like a gift, the greatest gift one can give, the greatest loyalty, the greatest proof of love and commitment…The person speaking is as insatiable as the person who listens, the person speaking wants to hold the attention of the other for ever.

To tell a story is to act on the listener; in this case, after hearing what he had to say, Teresa "couldn't stand [him], couldn't bear to be with [him] for a day or a minute longer." This of course leads Luisa to ask, "What did you tell her?" She waves off Ranz's concern that by telling her what he told Teresa, he might alienate her too.

> "The other day," said Ranz, "the other day was the day on which I killed my first wife in order to be with Teresa."
>
> "Don't tell me if you don't want to. Don't tell me if you don't want to."

Of course, it's too late—for her, and for Juan, who is in the next room, listening. Changing course, she continues to tell her father-in-law that he doesn't need to go on; but he does go on, recounting in incriminating detail the story he's suppressed for most of his life. Although Luisa had said that nothing he could say would change her feelings for him, when the conversation is finished Ranz has lost his appetite and Luisa is weary. In the final chapter, Juan tells us that his father now seems "almost an old man, which he never was before." The two of them haven't acknowledged what Juan now knows—in that way, the story remains unspeakable. But listening has drawn Juan and Luisa closer. Even if, one day, Luisa were to have an affair and the other man said, "It's him or me," Juan tells us, "I'd be happy simply for her to come out of the bathroom and not lie there on the cold floor with her breast and her heart so white... I would support her."

A Heart So White illustrates the power of stories to cause great harm, to heal, even to change the course of our lives; and it contemplates the complex roles of teller and listener. When should we tell what we know? When should we remain silent? And what does it do to us to hear someone else's story?

MY PARENTS MARRIED YOUNG, and they were from different worlds. Each of their families disapproved of the other. And maybe their parents were right to be wary. While our mother and father told themselves they were in love, there would be hard years ahead; they were very different people. It's not for me to say whether their marriage was unhappy. It may just be that the darkest days made the deepest impression.

But I can tell you this: After our mother died, my sister and I learned that what she had always called the cedar chest—a piece of furniture once known as a hope chest, used by young, single women to store things for their future marriage—had been a Christmas gift from that third suitor, the neighbor boy who joined the Navy. For the rest of her life, it stood, silently, at the foot of her bed.

Archimedes's Lever

Setting a Narrative World in Motion

The great mathematician and engineer Archimedes, born in Sicily, is remembered for many things, among them lowering himself into a hot bath, realizing that the displacement of water could be used to calculate volume, and jumping out of the tub, shouting "Eureka!" meaning "I have found it." Archimedes also wrote a Law of the Lever, describing the relationship of the weight of an object and its distance from a fulcrum, or pivot point; and he is reported to have said, "Give me a lever and a place to stand, and I shall move the Earth"—his point being that, at least in theory, if one had a lever long enough, and exerted force on it, a single person could physically move something as large and heavy as a planet.

This should be heartening to anyone writing a novel, as nearly every novelist has days—even years—when it seems impossible to set such a large thing in motion. Archimedes suggests that the essential challenge is the preparation: finding the lever and calculating where one needs to stand, or how much force one needs to exert, to get things rolling. The novelist's challenge is even more complicated. It isn't enough to set something in motion; the goal is to send the narrative and the reader moving on exactly the right course.

In *The Art of Perspective*, Christopher Castellani discusses what he calls "narrative strategy": "By narrative strategy, I mean the set of organizing principles that (in)form how the author is telling the story. If perspective is a way of seeing, and narration is perspective in action, then a narrative strategy is the how and why of that seeing." Narrative strategy, he goes on to explain, isn't the choice of point of view, or verb tense, or whether dialogue is put in quotation marks, and it's more than the division of a novel into books or chapters, the use of white space, the movement of narrative through time, or even the narrator's attitude toward the characters and their actions; it's all of those things and more. "It's the unique philosophy behind the construction of a work of fiction that applies to that work alone… The narrative strategy doesn't determine every choice an author makes…but every choice an author makes must answer to the narrative strategy. Its greatest virtues are consistency and internal resonance; its archenemy is the arbitrary."

The fact that every novel or story has (or should have) its own narrative strategy can make it hard to decide how to make use of models. While there are certain default choices related to point of view, movement through time, the use of chapters, and much more, simply to rely on those conventions, or to make use of certain approaches without fully considering their effects, is a disservice to the work. And of course it's pointless to set out to write a book just like *Don Quixote*, or *Beloved*, or *Lolita*, or *Visitation*, or *Outline*, or *A Visit from the Goon Squad*, or *Drive Your Plow over the Bones of the Dead*; those books are already written, and distinguished by their unique qualities. But it can benefit us to study any books we admire, to see what they do—what makes up their narrative strategy, and how and why that strategy is deployed—then turn back to our own work with ideas not just about specific choices we might make, but about how the sum of our choices can guide our readers.

EARLIER IN THIS BOOK I've discussed the openings of several novels. I'll look back at two of them, briefly, to illustrate how those openings prepare us for the whole—how they not only set a world in motion but also send the reader in a particular direction—then look at a few additional examples.

The first section of Colson Whitehead's *Underground Railroad* mimics the opening of a traditional biography, the kind that tells us about the main character's ancestors (at length) before eventually getting to the great man or (less often) woman who is the book's subject. But in addition to covering the history of his main character's grandmother concisely, Whitehead charges the information by presenting it as the explanation for dramatic action: "The first time Caesar approached Cora about running north, she said no. This was her grandmother talking." Everything that follows serves to explain why Cora rejects Caesar's proposal—why an enslaved woman refuses to attempt to escape to freedom. In other words, the omniscient narrator's thumbnail biography of Ajarry, Cora's grandmother, does much more than explain how Cora got to where she is: it explains one specific (and crucial) decision. And as we saw earlier, Whitehead makes that biographical information dynamic in a number of ways, among them alternating brief scenes with vivid exposition and making general assertions (as when he tells us she was married three times) then providing brief, essential explanation.

That opening section does several other important things. It defines Cora's story around her ultimate decision to "run north"; it establishes the narrator's authority; more specifically, it prepares us to trust the narrator even when information seems to be withheld or delivered in surprising sequence; it prepares us for a novel in which characters (like Ajarry) will be introduced, serve their purpose, and then essentially disappear; and, through Ajarry's story, it establishes the individual stakes for Cora's attempt at escape, not just freedom from slavery but an attempt to be recognized as an individual (unlike Ajarry, whose life after her kidnapping was, we're told, a series of appraisals), an attempt to redefine "the fundamental principles of [her] existence." Cora's grandmother ultimately believed such a thing was impossible. Her mother hoped it might be. Cora sets off to discover the answer for herself.

In the opening of the novel, then, Whitehead introduces several components of his narrative strategy, his narrator's stance toward his material and characters, and the primary focus that will drive the novel from first page to last.

WHILE A MERCY ALSO has an omniscient narrator and a relatively large cast of significant characters, Toni Morrison's approach is quite different. Her novel begins with a section narrated by Florens, in the first person; and as we saw earlier, far from clearly articulating the novel's primary concerns, Florens seems to present the reader with a series of puzzles. It's in the second section, which is focused on Jacob, and which begins before he meets

Florens, where the narrator asserts her presence and addresses us clearly, meaningfully. So why start with Florens?

For one thing, she's at the center of the story's dramatic action: she's the one sent by her sick mistress on a perilous journey to fetch the blacksmith, whom her mistress believes can cure her. For another, while Florens, as an enslaved Black woman, would be historically silenced, here she's able to tell her story, writing it on the walls of Jacob's decaying mansion, the monument to himself built with profits made possible by slavery. Starting with Florens also gives the opening the immediacy of her impassioned direct address (though she's addressing the blacksmith, it feels as if she's addressing us), which is useful given that the novel is set in the distant past—we become attached to a person, a woman speaking with urgency, before we learn she lived hundreds of years ago. And while the novel's opening is full of mystery, the narrative eventually answers all of the questions it raises. Another way of putting that: the opening pages pose questions, and we read to discover the answers. The final answer—the explanation of why Florens's mother effectively gave her to Jacob—is provided in the novel's final lines.

A Mercy is a highly expository novel. We spend most of our time learning the background, circumstances, and concerns of each of the point-of-view characters. Morrison uses Florens's story as the dramatic focus, the spine to which she attaches all of the expository ribs; and the mystery that haunts and embitters Florens, the question of why her mother entrusted her to a stranger, leads us directly to what Morrison called "the human gesture" that gives the book its title.

AS I SAID IN "A Funny Thing Happened on the Way to the Infor-mation Dump," writers often worry about losing readers' atten-tion with extended expository passages. It's worth noting, then, that there is no immediate, present action in the opening pages of *Underground Railroad* and *A Mercy*. Whitehead alludes to a con-versation—Caesar asking Cora to run north—and that conver-sation has dramatic implications, but it's still only a two-sentence summary of a conversation in the recent past, and what follows is a summary of events from the more distant past. All of the momentum comes from the narrator's syntax and his attention to the dramatic highlights of Ajarry's life. In those opening pages of *A Mercy*, Florens is describing past events in a way we can't fully appreciate, but the urgency of her concerns is immediately apparent.

Before moving on to two openings in scene, let's look, briefly, at one of the most renowned expository openings, one that not only makes no effort to convey a sense of urgency but also suggests that the novel's world is essentially mired, stagnant:

London. Michaelmas Term lately over, and the Lord Chancellor sitting in Lincoln's Hall. Implacable November weather. As much mud in the streets as if the waters had but newly retired from the face of the earth, and it would not be wonderful to meet a Megalosaurus, forty feet long or so, waddling like an elephantine lizard up Holborn Hill. Smoke lowering down from chimney-pots, making a soft black drizzle, with flakes of soot in it as big as full-grown snow-flakes— gone into mourning, one might imagine, for the death of the sun. Dogs, indistinguishable in mire. Horses, scarcely better; splashed to their very blinkers. Foot passengers, jostling one another's umbrellas, in a general infection of ill-temper, and losing their foot-hold at street-corners, where tens of thousands of other foot passengers have been slipping and sliding since the day broke (if the day ever broke), adding new deposits to the crust upon crust of mud, sticking at those points tenaciously to the pavement, and accumulating at compound interest.

Fog everywhere. Fog up the river, where it flows among green aits and meadows; fog down the river, where it rolls defiled among the tiers of shipping and the waterside pollutions of a great (and dirty) city. Fog on the Essex marshes, fog on the Kentish heights. Fog creeping into the cabooses of collier-brigs, fog lying out on the yards, and hovering in the rigging of great ships; fog drooping on the gunwales of barges and small boats. Fog in the eyes and throats of ancient Greenwich pensioners, wheezing by the firesides of their wards; fog in the stem and bowl of the afternoon pipe of the wrathful skipper, down in his close cabin; fog cruelly pinching the toes and fingers of his shivering little 'prentice boy on deck. Chance people on the bridges peeping over the parapets into a nether sky of fog, with fog all around them, as if they were up in a balloon, and hanging in the misty clouds.

Charles Dickens begins *Bleak House* with the essentials of time and place, then seems to be offering a more detailed look at the setting, focused on the "implacable November weather." Then the narrator turns fanciful, suggesting the circumstances are fitting for a dinosaur. The figurative language intensifies as "flakes of soot [are] as big as full-grown snow-flakes—gone into mourning, one might imagine, for the death of the sun." Dogs and horses are made indistinguishable, people are irritable. The narrator allows himself more hyperbole: "Foot passengers losing their foot-hold at street-corners, where tens of thousands of other foot passengers have been slipping and sliding since the day broke (if the day ever broke)." Then we get a paragraph devoted to the movement of the fog and all it obscures, which leads to this:

> The raw afternoon is rawest, and the dense fog is densest, and the muddy streets are muddiest, near that leaden-headed old obstruction, appropriate ornament for the threshold of a leaden-headed old corporation: Temple Bar. And hard by Temple Bar, in Lincoln's Inn Hall, at the very heart of the fog, sits the Lord High Chancellor in his High Court of Chancery.
>
> Never can there come fog too thick, never can there come mud and mire too deep, to assort with the groping and floundering condition which this High Court of Chancery, most pestilent of hoary sinners, holds, this day, in the sight of heaven and earth.

The narrator has guided us—led us by hand—not only to a particular place at a particular time but to a vision of that place, one defined by the figurative fog of the High Court of Chancery. What more does it tell us? That this narrator has a lot to say; that he's going to take his time saying it; that much of the pleasure of the journey is going to come from the narrator's editorializing; that he has a sense of humor; and that the story he's about to tell us is focused, in some way, on the court, which reflects what surrounds it. Like many expository openings, this one means to establish the novel's world, the context for the characters and events to come; and by doing so it tells us that the novel is as interested in the broader implications of what follows as in the specific people and scenes.

THE OPENING OF BLEAK HOUSE has a cinematic quality, even though it predates cinema: Dickens opens with a wide establishing shot, leads us through the streets of London, then settles into "the Lord Chancellor's court this musky afternoon," a seemingly endless trial well underway. E. L. Doctorow offers a different sort of cinematic moment to begin *The March*: the sort of scene so highly populated and buzzing with such action that it hardly has time for explanation.

> At five in the morning someone banging on the door and shouting, her husband, John, leaping out of bed, grabbing his rifle, and Roscoe at the same time roused from the backhouse, his bare feet pounding: Mattie hurriedly pulled on her robe, her mind prepared for the alarm of war, but the heart stricken that it would finally have come, and down the stairs she flew to see through the open door in the lamplight, at the steps of their portico, the two horses, steam rising from their flanks, their heads lifting, their eyes wild, the driver a young darkie with rounded shoulders, showing stolid patience even in this, and the woman standing in her carriage no one but her aunt Letitia Pettibone of McDonough, her elderly face drawn in anguish, her hair a straggled mess, this woman of such fine grooming, this dowager who practically ruled the season in Atlanta standing up in the equipage like some hag of doom, which indeed she would prove to be. The carriage was piled with luggage and tied bundles, and as she stood some silver fell to the ground, knives and forks and a silver candelabra, catching in the clatter the few gleams of light from the torch that Roscoe held. Mattie, still tying her robe, ran down the steps thinking stupidly, as she later reflected, only of the embarrassment to this woman, whom to tell the truth she had respected more than loved, and picking up and

pressing back upon her the heavy silver, as if this was not something Roscoe should be doing, nor her husband, John Jameson, neither.

Doctorow begins *The March* midscene, replicating the chaos and confusion felt by his characters. Like the opening of *A Mercy*, this one draws us forward in part by raising questions (Who's banging on the door at this hour? Where are we?), in part through the urgency of the prose. Here the first sentence is 168 words long. It introduces five characters, two horses, and the narrator. Chaos is evoked by the active verbs (banging, shouting, leaping, grabbing, pounding, pulled, flew, rising, lifting, showing, standing), yet the sentence is orderly. While at first the syntax might throw us off-balance, the sentence is carefully focused on one of those five characters. Mattie is introduced by the pronoun "her" in "her husband, John"; then she appears by name immediately after the colon, as if all the banging, shouting, leaping, grabbing, and pounding is about her—and it is about her, in the sense that it's around her, and she is at the center, taking it in. The organization of the sentence locates us beside her. To reinforce her importance, she pulls on *her* robe, *her* mind prepared, then takes action, flying to see.

What does she see? That information is delayed just a bit, as Doctorow both sustains the suspense (What's out there?) and defines the action through Mattie's perspective: she sees through the open door, at the steps of the portico, the two horses "their eyes wild," the driver (the pejorative "young darkie" reflecting Mattie's language), and then *her* aunt. Mattie is at the center, all of the action coming to her, all that's seen viewed from her perspective, virtually everything in the sentence belonging, in some way, to her. Mattie is the eye of the storm.

Mattie's eyes—and ours—are ultimately drawn to her aunt, who is introduced like royalty (Letitia Pettibone of McDonough) in a Shakespearean tragedy ("her elderly face drawn in anguish, her hair a straggled mess, this woman of such fine grooming...standing up in the equipage like some hag of doom"). Even in an opening sentence intent on communicating action, and a sense of imminence, Doctorow provides necessary contextualizing information without slowing things down. We learn that Letitia is "of fine grooming" and "practically ruled the season in Atlanta," but now "her face is drawn in anguish, her hair a straggled mess," and when she stands, hastily packed silver tumbles to the ground. Something seriously disturbing is happening. Earlier in the first sentence Doctorow told us Mattie's mind was prepared for war, but now she feels it in her heart. That abstraction is made concrete in her sympathetic response to her aunt "whom...she had respected more than loved." And so Doctorow's opening paragraph, while thrusting us into the action, also grounds us in an individual.

Mattie is not the novel's main character; she is one of many. To prepare us for a book with a very large cast, the opening sentence introduces those five characters (and two horses), but it also introduces the narrator, our guide. The narrator is introduced at the very end of the sentence, when we draw back from Mattie's point of view for just a moment: Letitia Pettibone is standing "like some hag of doom, *which indeed she would prove to be.*" That brief flash forward is provided by someone not a part of this frantic moment; it is provided by the omniscient narrator. The next sentence continues the action before the narrator steps in again, to tell us more: "Mattie, still tying her robe, ran down the steps thinking stupidly, as she later reflected, only of the embarrassment to this woman, whom to tell the truth she had respected more than loved." The narrator is elbowing in, beginning to provide background information.

Doctorow does a few other interesting things in his opening chapter, which is just twelve pages long.

The second paragraph shifts the focus to Letitia, who makes the novel's opening speech:

> Get out, get out, take what you can and leave...And I know him! She
> cried. He has dined in my home. He has lived among us. He burns
> where he has ridden to lunch, he fires the city in whose clubs he once
> gave toasts, oh yes, someone of the educated class, or so we thought,
> though I never was impressed! No, I was never impressed, he was
> too spidery, too weak in his conversation, and badly composed in
> his dress, careless of his appearance, but for all that I thought quite
> civilized...[but] he is no more than a savage with not a drop of mercy
> in his cold heart.

This is a model introduction for a particular sort of character, a larger-than-life villain. First, we see people in terror. We're made to understand one of them is a matriarch of society, one of the last people who would allow herself to be seen with her hair undone, or who would leave home with her valuable possessions poorly packed, but even Letitia Pettibone has been driven to distraction. Who or what could be responsible? Someone she knows—someone she's socialized with, someone she believed, with reservations, to be part of "her people." Letitia is not just afraid—she feels betrayed. The fact that this man is referred to only by the indefinite pronoun might suggest God, or Satan, and that suggestion is intentional. General Sherman himself will not appear in the novel for quite a while, but the threat and effects of his action are evident from the first page. His importance has been underscored by the fact that he literally needs no introduction. When Sherman finally appears, his actual presence is much less powerful than his implicit and symbolic presence. He is, for all he's done, just a man; the army he's created and the campaign it's waging seems inhuman, an incomprehensible force. As these opening two paragraphs suggest, the novel isn't about a famous military figure; it's about the devastating action he set into motion.

The novel's opening chapter consists of six sections separated by ellipses, providing the novel with not one but six openings. The first focuses on Mattie; the second, while staying close to Mattie's perspective, focuses on her husband, John; the third focuses on an enslaved girl, Pearl; the fourth focuses on a group of ten enslaved people; the fifth focuses on Clarke, an officer from Boston; and the sixth brings the enslaved people, Clarke, and Pearl together.

Doctorow distinguishes among his point-of-view characters not only by name, circumstance, and attitude, but by the language associated with them. We've already seen how Mattie is introduced as the still center of a cascading sentence, language rushing toward her and then away from her. A few pages later we meet Clarke, the well-trained officer. Clarke is purportedly in control of the men who caused the furor of the first sentence. The language around him is calm, orderly. "Clarke had in his foraging party a two-wagon train, a string of three extra mules, and twenty men mounted. General orders specified no fewer than fifty men. He was several miles off the column, and so, coming upon the plantation, he resolved to make quick work of it…He shook his head…He posted his pickets." When Clarke is being described by the narrator, this shift in diction and syntax is taken to an extreme: "For Clarke, all of this was unsettling. He liked order. Discipline. He kept his own person neat and clean-shaven. His uniform brushed. His knapsack packed correctly." There is no arguing with those sentences, or with those sounds: "His knapsack packed correctly." The sentences are clear and direct, firm and crisp.

Pearl, the enslaved girl, is one of the novel's most important characters, and the language associated with her is particularly interesting—and, to my mind, problematic. Her voice is conveyed through dialect in ways that are stereotypical and distracting. On top of that, Doctorow's intentional misspellings don't always create clear sonic effects, as when he spells Pearl "Porhl" and your "yore." Over the course of the novel, as Pearl becomes an adult and spends time with other people, her voice will change, which might explain why Doctorow exaggerates her voice early on. It's his execution rather than his strategy that's regrettable.

The second chapter introduces an entirely new set of characters. Will and Arly are the novel's Shakespearean clowns, and Arly, in particular, has a voice all his own, one created not by misspelling but by diction and syntax:

> Supposing it happens we are reprieved? Won't do you no good if
> you're too weak to march out the door. Me, I will eat their maggoty
> salt pork and beans and politely thank Prison Sergeant Baumgartner
> down the corridor there for the fine vittles, though in fact he is as deaf
> as a doorpost. What was your affront, young Will?

No one else in the book talks this way.

Sherman's army on the move—what history knows as Sherman's march—is something like a character in the novel: it acts with purpose (if also unpredictably), it influences other characters, and it is acted upon. Doctorow focuses our attention not on specific military maneuvers or the names of wings and corps, divisions and brigades, regiments and companies, but on individual characters and the march itself, which is introduced in the final line of the first chapter, indirectly (similar to how Sherman was introduced), as a "column of sunlit dust pushing southeast in the Georgia sky." Doctorow's challenge is to present the reader with the overwhelming force of the army, the enormity of the historical event, and these individuals. He has to continually remind us of both the forest and the trees. Toward this end, he characterizes the army through variations of that early image:

> What they saw in the distance was smoke spouting from different points in the landscape, first here, then there. But in the middle of all this was a change in the sky color itself that gradually clarified as an upward-streaming brown cloud risen from the earth, as if the world was turned upside down. And, as they watched, the brown cloud took on a reddish cast. It moved forward, thin as a hatchet blade in front and then widening like the furrow from the plow. When the sound of this cloud reached them, it was like nothing they had ever heard in their lives.

This enormous, anonymous force, described as a perverse force of nature, is at the heart of the book—it represents both the army and its effects. Smoke spouts from the landscape—a bad sign. Dirt rises into and discolors the sky. The world is turned upside down. The brown of the earth turns to red, or blood. The cloud is thin as a hatchet and wide like the furrow of the plow—comparisons drawn from the plantations it will destroy. It is like nothing these people had ever heard or seen or been a part of.

In addition to opening with propulsive action, then, the first pages of Doctorow's novel establish important characters and motifs, serve notice that this will be a highly populated novel with multiple narrative lines, and essentially promise us that the narrator will be standing by, to serve as our guide. Those small bits of exposition (the flashes forward from Mattie's perspective, Letitia's memories of Sherman) also prepare us for longer passages of explanation and backstory, which is essential: Doctorow doesn't want to move us at high speed for three hundred pages.

All of those specific decisions and effects are in service to the larger whole. Among other things, Doctorow needs to persuade us to read another Civil War novel. Even for people eager to read *any* Civil War novel, Sherman's march is well-covered material. What will this book add to what we've read before? Doctorow answers that in the first pages: his focus will be on a wide range of individuals—men and women, soldiers and civilians, White and Black, rich and poor, northern and southern—and how they were impacted by the force of the march.

MOHSIN HAMID'S *EXIT WEST* is, on the surface, a very different sort of war novel. There are no scenes of battle, barely any mention of combatants. But it's similar to *The March* in that its focus is on individuals, in this case civilians, whose lives are changed by forces beyond their control. It is also one of countless twenty-first-century novels that contradict the misguided notion that omniscient narration is a dusty relic, one better suited to the nineteenth century; and it makes use of devices often associated with genre fiction to tell a story about love, exile, contemporary world politics, and the things we have in common, despite all our differences. Most relevant to the current discussion, it establishes its narrative strategy in the opening pages. It starts like this:

> In a city swollen by refugees but still mostly at peace, or at least not yet openly at war, a young man met a young woman in a classroom and did not speak to her. For many days. His name was Saeed and her name was Nadia and he had a beard, not a full beard, more a studiously maintained stubble, and she was always clad from the tips of her toes to the bottom of her jugular notch in a flowing black robe. Back then people continued to enjoy the luxury of wearing more or less what they wanted to wear, clothing and hair wise, within certain bounds of course, and so these choices meant something.

This opening couldn't be much more different from the super-charged, action-packed, propulsive opening of *The March*. Hamid's narrator is calm. He's providing information, and appears to be in no particular hurry. He draws our attention to two characters, but there's no scene yet; they aren't doing anything. And yet the paragraph is rich with foreshadowing, full of tension, complex and playful. Let's take a closer look: "In a city swollen by refugees but still mostly at peace, or at least not yet openly at war, a young man met a young woman in a classroom and did not speak to her."

"In a city swollen by refugees" is a meaningful opening for this book, as all of its settings will be cities swollen by refugees. Also meaningful—and a critical choice by Hamid—is to leave this city and country unnamed (while Nadia and Saeed will eventually go to

Crete and London and Marin, California, their country of origin will never be named). This might seem coy—and we might make assumptions about where people named Nadia and Saeed might live, or where a Pakistani author might set his novel—but we come to understand the larger purpose: the book isn't about a particular conflict, or a particular nation's people; it's about all of us.

"—but still mostly at peace" is the novel's first hint of foreshadowing, and "at least not yet openly at war" more or less confirms our suspicion that war is coming. The narrator could tell us, "In the days just before the war," but that would be a static piece of information. Worded as it is, the sentence captures a sense of uncertainty, of imminence, of a city trembling on the verge. The sentence also introduces an engagement with time that will continue throughout the book, and ultimately lead to one of its largest claims. There's a present, when the city is swollen with refugees; there's an implied future, when the city will be—or could be—openly at war; and there's an implied past, because the narrator seems to be looking back; he already knows what happens next. (Almost certainly, Hamid has read *One Hundred Years of Solitude*, the famous opening line of which does something similar: "Many years later, as he faced the firing squad, Colonel Aureliano Buendía was to remember that distant afternoon when his father took him to discover ice.")

"—a young man met a young woman and did not speak to her." Suddenly the sentence has taken on the air of a fairy tale or folk tale; at the same time, there's a playfulness to "and did not speak to her." Of course he's going to speak to her—why would the narrator draw our attention to them, otherwise? This feels like the beginning of a romantic comedy, though one set in a potentially war-torn city. Hamid is going to attempt something difficult in this book:

he's going to ask us to engage with these two characters, and to care about them, but not to focus on them exclusively. He's interested in something larger than their story. But now he moves closer: "His name was Saeed and her name was Nadia and he had a beard, not a full beard, more a studiously maintained stubble, and she was always clad from the tips of her toes to the bottom of her jugular notch in a flowing black robe."

We get to know more about these characters, moving cinematically from a distant two shot ("a young man met a young woman") to a startling close-up—he draws our attention to the stubble of his beard and her "jugular notch." "Jugular notch" is much more arresting, and sonically interesting, than "neck"; that choice in diction, along with "clad" and "studiously maintained," begins to give us some idea of how this narrator looks at the world. He sounds a bit old-fashioned, even though he's writing from the future: "Back then people continued to enjoy the luxury of wearing more or less what they wanted to wear, clothing and hair wise, within certain bounds of course, and so these choices meant something." Again he serves notice that things are going to change; and if people lose the freedom of choosing what to wear, it certainly feels like a change for the worse. The narrator, at least, has gotten to some future time safely; will Nadia and Saeed survive the war? And in the meantime, how will their implied romance play out? In just a few sentences, Hamid has set a great deal in motion.

In the second paragraph, the narrator stands even farther back from the characters and philosophizes: "One moment we are pottering about our errands as usual and the next we are dying, and our eternally impending ending does not put a stop to our transient beginnings and middles until the instant when it does." Here he makes a claim not just about his characters' lives but also about ours. Hamid's novel is ultimately not just a call for compassion for others, for people we might think of as refugees; rather, it asks us to recognize that, as his narrator later says, "We are all migrants through time." The suggestion here is that given how relatively short life is, how difficult it can be, we might work a little harder to be our best selves, especially when it comes to appreciating the difficulties others face. That might seem like a truly modest proposal, but in order to put us in the place of refugees, not only to see but to feel their losses, he needs for us to identify with Nadia and Saeed, needs to build a bridge from us to them. That work starts on the novel's first page.

After having teased us, the narrator finally gives us the scene we've anticipated: Saeed approaches Nadia and asks her to join him for coffee. We are not at all surprised that she declines; the narrative flirtation will continue. But Hamid isn't using the familiar template of romantic comedy simply for fun. Nadia asks Saeed if he says his evening prayers; hedging, he says, "Not always." She says, "I don't pray," and then, "Maybe another time," suggesting that her refusal is linked to their different attitudes toward religion; and religious differences will be one of the factors that ultimately drives them apart. Hamid plants the seeds of the trouble in their first meeting.

It certainly isn't necessary—or possible—for a novel to lay the groundwork for everything to come in the first few sentences, even in the first pages; but as Christopher Castellani writes, it's important for those opening sentences to be consistent with what's to come, and vice versa. The opening of *Exit West* suggests a fairy tale, and a romance, which prepares us for another trope of genre fiction that will be introduced gradually, over the first several chapters: we'll learn that characters can move from one city to another, from one country to another, via black doors. Exactly how the doors work is never explained; and as the novel goes on, people are able to use them in different ways. While it might seem the introduction of magical black doors is a departure from the world set into place in the novel's opening lines, Hamid prepares us for the surprise.

The first chapter establishes the novel's form: its fifteen pages contain nine short sections separated by white space. In the fourth of those sections, the novel makes an abrupt departure: "As Saeed's email was being downloaded from a server and read by his client, far away in Australia a pale-skinned woman was sleeping alone in the Sydney neighborhood of Surry Hills." We're told the woman's husband is away on business, that she's wearing only a T-shirt, that the home alarm isn't turned on, that the bedroom window "was open, just a slit," and that a man is emerging from the bedroom closet. In short, Hamid is borrowing heavily from another genre, murder mystery. He focuses our attention on a vulnerable woman (asleep, barely clothed) and a potentially dangerous figure. But then he defies our expectations: the man simply slips out the window. We'll never see that woman (or the mysterious man) again; what's actually being introduced are the portals, the doors that allow transit from one place to another. There will be a similar scene set far from Nadia and Saeed's city in the second chapter, and another in the third; it won't be until the fourth chapter that we get some explanation. The withholding builds tension, and it invites our participation. We can't help but wonder what these apparently unrelated scenes are doing in the book, how they relate to the rest of what we're reading. At the same time, they work with that first paragraph to remind us that this novel is about more than Saeed and Nadia.

Hamid relies on the universal appeal of romantic pursuit as the primary engine pulling us forward, coupled with the explicit foreshadowing—the promise—of danger and destruction. By the end of the first chapter we know the city will be damaged and that Saeed's parents' "life together" will end, though we don't know exactly what that means, just as we don't know what will happen to the city, or how Nadia and Saeed will be impacted. Characters, plot, theme, form, voice, and the omniscient narrator's stance have all been established; the unique world of *Exit West* has been set in motion.

ONE MIGHT REASONABLY ASK why this discussion of beginnings would come at the end of a book on writing. Like many things in these pages, that decision was made with a former student in mind—in this case, one who said, "How could anyone possibly think about all that when they're starting a novel?" While there may be exceptions, effective openings are nearly always the result of rewriting that can only take place when the author fully understands the story that's going to be told, and so how the reader needs to be guided. In many cases, the opening pages are the last to be revised before a book is done. Decisions about the best place to start—what information, what scene, what detail, what sentence—will be informed by all the discoveries along the way. That isn't to say that the first scene in the first draft can't possibly be the scene that starts the final one; only that, in its ultimate iteration, that first scene, or that first passage of exposition, will be informed by everything that follows it. The reader might not know that, might not see exactly how that's true, especially on first reading; but a well-considered opening will convey the authority that results from knowing exactly where the story is headed.

APPENDIX A

Out of the Workshop, into the Laboratory

No matter whether you enroll in a degree program, join a class at a writing center, or assemble a group of friends, if you're a writer, odds are good that at some point you'll be part of a writing workshop. Joining one certainly isn't necessary, but workshops are available, and they can be helpful.

They can also be harmful. Some days it seems everyone has workshop horror stories: stories about rude behavior, savage "advice," someone trying to dictate how someone else should write, writers in tears, writers enraged, friends who feel obliged to "defend" each other's work...the kinds of experiences that led Flannery O'Connor—who attended the Iowa Writers' Workshop—to write:

> I don't believe in classes where students criticize each other's
> manuscripts. Such criticism is generally composed in equal parts of
> ignorance, flattery, and spite. It's the blind leading the blind, and it
> can be dangerous. A teacher who tries to impose a way of writing on
> you can be dangerous too. Fortunately, most teachers I've known have
> been too lazy to do this. In any case, you should beware of those who
> appear overenergetic.

Then there's the creaky complaint, repeated by people who haven't spent any time in a decent writing program, that such programs lead writers to produce one particular kind of fiction—and not very good fiction, either. O'Connor, again:

> In the last twenty years the colleges have been emphasizing Creative writing to such an extent that you almost feel any idiot with a nickel's worth of talent can emerge from a writing class able to write a competent story. In fact, so many people can now write competent stories that the short story as a medium is in danger of dying of competence. We want competence, but competence by itself is deadly. What is needed is the vision to go with it, and you do not get this from a writing class.

Dare I point out a contradiction? "We want competence," she admits. Most introductory writing classes focus on competence—and should, just as an introductory dancing class should help you avoid stepping on your partner's feet. "But competence by itself is deadly": overstatement, but true. No one rushes to a gallery to see competent paintings, or to a concert hall to hear a competent band. "What is needed is the vision to go with it, and you do not get this from a writing class." Absolutely true. A good class might recognize, even encourage a writer's vision, but vision can't be taught; and all of us who have taken or taught writing classes know that a truly distinctive voice—Gertrude Stein's, say, or Virginia Woolf's, or Kafka's, Nabokov's, or García Márquez's, or O'Connor's—might *not* be recognized, or welcomed. If we aren't careful, a writing class can reduce distinctive work to familiar-looking work.

Roughly fifty years after Flannery O'Connor weighed in, Madison Smartt Bell wrote, in *Narrative Design:*

Fiction workshops are inherently almost incapable of recognizing success. The fiction workshop is designed to be a fault-finding mechanism; its purpose is to diagnose and prescribe. The inert force of this proposition works on all the members... Whenever I pick up a few pages without defect, I start to get very nervous. Because my job is to find those flaws. If I don't find flaws, I will have failed.

As for the other students, they are just as influenced by the factors above as the teacher, and on top of that, there's the probability that in confronting a successfully realized piece of fiction, the classmate has to cope with a certain amount of conscious or unconscious envy...

Take that to its logical extreme and you see that the student as writer has been assigned the task of Sisyphus. There is no way to ever finish anything.

Since then, there has been no shortage of books and essays proposing alternatives to workshops, or at least to the long-standing format that involves a teacher and a group of students discussing another student's work while that student endures the conversation in silence. Some writing teachers have adopted Liz Lerman's Critical Response Process, which originated in dance and theater, or even more author-centered approaches. David Mura and Matthew Salesses, among others, have written about the unspoken assumptions and inequities baked into the original workshop model, the definition of "craft," and even the use of the term "the reader" (as if it were possible to generalize about all readers). In *Craft in the Real World*, Salesses writes: "As craft is a set of expectations, the workshop needs to know which expectations, whose expectations, the author wishes to engage with, if the workshop is to imagine useful possibilities for the story... To silence the author is to willingly misinterpret the author. It is to insist that she must write *to the workshop.*" He goes on to describe several alternate approaches, and to encourage experimentation. He summarizes his argument simply: "It is time for workshop to change."

I agree. My own practice has changed significantly over the past forty years, and continues to change. For example:

- ✦ Long ago, I made the mistake of discussing students' manuscripts as early as the second day of class, giving them what they (thought they) wanted. People are nearly always eager to get to the discussion of their work; but with every new group it's important to establish the tone as well as the terms of the conversation. Now, we'll often devote several meetings to terminology, guidelines, and work by other writers. During those meetings, I aim to model the approach we'll take to student drafts, and to have students practice that approach with no writer's ego at stake.

- ✦ For decades "the workshop method" required the writer to sit in silence while everyone else discussed the manuscript. One justification was that when the work is published the writer won't be able to sit next to every reader and explain it, so this was an opportunity for the writer to hear how people understand the work on its own. I still suggest that the writer have the rest of us *begin* by describing the work, but the writer is free to ask questions, answer questions, offer clarification, and redirect the discussion. Often the writer chooses to listen to what everyone has to say. If that's the case, at some point I make sure to ask, "How can we be useful to you?"

✦ About fifteen years ago I wrote out what I recognized
as some of the common pitfalls of workshops, as well as
good practices. (I had been thinking and talking about
workshops before that; the change was formally articulating
those thoughts for students.) I revisit that document every
year. What follows is the latest version. I encourage my
graduate students who are teaching, or who plan to teach,
to do the same thing, beginning with their own experience.
When have you found workshops most useful? Most
frustrating? What would you want to be able to tell, or
ask, all of the participants? What's your notion of an ideal
writing class?

I offer this version of my workshop guidelines not because I
think everyone should embrace them but because I encourage anyone leading or participating in a workshop to engage in a similar
exercise. Whether you're in a degree program, a standalone class,
or an informal writing group, what do you want from it? What do
you want from your fellow participants? What kind of participant
do you hope to be?

No matter what model you employ, the spirit of the engagement
is what matters most—a combination of seriousness, respect, hu-
mility, and generosity.

Workshop Guidelines

A workshop should be as useful as possible to as many of its participants as possible as often as possible. Ideally, everyone will leave
the room each day excited about writing, with new ideas to apply
to their work. Those might be ideas for a particular story, but they

might also be broader ways to think about fiction and its components.

The label "writing workshop" is curious. We typically think of a workshop as a place where things are made. But if Santa ran his workshop like a writing workshop, nobody would get any toys, ever. None that worked, anyway. And the elves would not be singing. Stories do not get written in workshop.

The writing workshop is sometimes presented as a place where you can bring a draft of a story or novel to a group of fellow writers who will read it carefully and help you see where it's working effectively, where it isn't, and how you might fix it. That assumes a story is a like a car and the workshop is your friendly neighborhood service station. But this analogy is deeply flawed. When you take your car to a service station, the assumption is that the car was running as it should, then it wasn't, and that it can be repaired, or returned to the state it was in. But the story you submit to workshop wasn't working just fine; if it had been, you wouldn't have submitted it. (A workshop is not the place to bring work you feel is finished and have no interest in revisiting. It's a place to bring work to which you truly want to hear people's responses.) Also: when you take your car to a service station, while different mechanics may offer different diagnoses, they aren't likely to tell you that your Honda Civic should be a tractor, or that it would be more interesting with fewer windows. ("Spare me," no mechanic says. "Four doors, steering wheel on the left, rubber tires—have we not all seen this a million times before?") You and your mechanic share an understanding of what a Honda Civic is, what it can be, and what it isn't.

The writing workshop is less like a service station than it is a place to bring cars that fell off the assembly line, or, more accurately, cars that are still being designed. For all we know, the twelve-page story you bring to workshop might turn into a novella, or a chapter for a novel, or you might end up using a few of the characters in something altogether different. And even if it remains a twelve-page story, it will change in ways that are by no objective standard "right," the way a Honda Civic can be made right. Your story means to be unique. The writing workshop is not a place for repair, or correction, because fiction doesn't get repaired or corrected.

If a writing class or group isn't a workshop, what is it? Perhaps something more like a laboratory, a place where hypotheses are tested, experiments are carried out, beakers sometimes explode, fruit fly colonies hatch unexpectedly, and people stand around, examining projects in various stages, rubbing their chins, saying "Hmmm" and "What if we try this?" Occasionally, as Madison Smartt Bell warns, people enter a workshop thinking the goal is to either "approve" a draft as complete and wholly satisfactory (almost never happens) or to point out all of its shortcomings. But passing judgment isn't the point. Of course, most of us are excited to read work we find interesting, surprising, moving, provocative, etc., and disappointed when the work seems hastily constructed or overly familiar. But the primary purpose, for the writer and everyone else, is to consider what a draft is doing and what opportunities it suggests. To learn something.

Preparation

When you look at your own drafts, it's best not to ask, in any narrow, limiting sense, "How can I fix this?" but instead to ask, "Where can I improve this?" or "How can I build on this?" The same attitude is useful in approaching someone else's story. What is this? What's most interesting about it? What are some exciting possibilities it suggests for the next draft?

To answer those questions thoughtfully, careful preparation is key. Reading a manuscript hurriedly just before the group meets is likely to lead to an unsatisfactory experience for everyone, especially the writer.

In what follows, the manuscript will be referred to as a story, but it might also be an excerpt, or a chapter, novella, or novel.

1. Start by reading the story from beginning to end. Resist the urge to make notes.

2. When you've finished, try to articulate what Stephen Dobyns, in "Writing the Reader's Life," an essay in *Best Words, Best Order*, helpfully calls the intention of the work. This is more challenging than it might sound. It's difficult to identify with confidence the intention of a piece of writing that isn't fully realized. Chances are good that the author has some idea of their intention for the work but that it is still being discovered and refined.

3. What we aren't trying to do: guess what the writer was thinking. Rather, we're describing what the draft we've been given appears to be aiming for, based on the words on the pages— because it's true, ultimately the story will need to stand on its own, without the author nearby to explain it.

4. Another reason to start by considering the story's intention: we can only assess the effectiveness of the parts if we have some understanding of the whole. While readers might agree that a particular description is "hysterically funny," a particular scene "shocking," a particular character "familiar," it's impossible to

say whether that's a good thing or a bad thing without having considered the work's intention. For example: "So we beat on, boats against the current, borne back ceaselessly into the past" is a world-class last line—for *The Great Gatsby*. It would be an awkward last line for *Moby-Dick*, and it would be an absurd last line for *The Adventures of Huckleberry Finn*. The margin comment "Great line!" is not useful without consideration of the context. What does the story seem to be about? What effect or effects does it seem to mean to have on the reader? What assumptions does the writer seem to make? Who does the story seem addressed to?

5.   We might be inclined to say a story is written for "the general reader" or even "everyone." But that's never the case. The language the story is written in begins to define its intended audience; then there's its treatment of setting (If the story is set in Houston, does it describe Houston? If not, what does it seem to assume the reader knows about Houston? If it's set in an anonymous suburb, what assumptions does it seem to expect the reader to share about suburbs?), its treatment of character, the conventions and rituals it takes for granted or treats as exotic, and so on.

6.   So keep in mind that you may not be part of the work's intended audience. Workshops are often gatherings of strangers: people with different backgrounds, different concerns, and different goals. Of course, each of us can respond only from our own knowledge and experience. We might say, "I'm not a scientist; I got lost in the lab scenes"; "I don't know anything about jai alai, which may be why the descriptions of the matches felt awfully

long"; "I know there are castes in India, but I was confused by the references to *varna* and *jati*"; "The depiction of the guys working on their low riders felt stereotypical; I couldn't tell if that was the narrator's bias showing or the story's." That isn't to say the author is obliged to revise the work in response to such comments. We have no reason to demand the work speak to us, explain its terms and assumptions to us. Ultimately, that decision is up to the writer.

7. With an idea of what the story seems to be trying to do, for whom, read it again. (Be prepared to revise your understanding of the work's intention.) This time, make notes: on aspects of the draft that seem particularly effective as a part of the whole, as well as on aspects that seem less so. Before preparing comments for the writer, though, keep in mind that it can be tempting to mistake a draft's most effective passages or elements for its most important ones, or the ones the rest of the work should be developed around. We've all written stories that had wonderful moments early on that had to be cut from the final draft, appealing characters who turned out to be distractions, clever sentences that turned out to be too clever. Conversely, a draft's less effective moments, or "problems"—shifts in voice or point of view, an unaccountable leap in time, an overly long scene, extended attention to a minor character—may reveal where the writer has stumbled onto something interesting. You've probably had the experience: the very "problem" you've been trying to "fix" turns out to be the key to a story you didn't realize you needed to write. A draft's apparent "failures" might indicate where the story is breaking free from the author's

(misguided?) plan, from what the author finds it easiest to do, or from what we're used to reading.

8. Finally, write comments for the author in complete sentences and paragraphs. Resist the urge to begin those comments with anything like "I love the way this story—" or, worse, "My problem with this story is—." Instead, begin by describing the work to the writer as objectively as you can—like a scientist peering through a microscope, trying to report accurately what's on the slide. "It's ugly" won't cut it in science class or the workshop. And while "It's beautiful" might be intended sincerely, try to begin objectively. The goal isn't to tell the author what they already know ("This is a story about a man who loses his job") but what you, as a thoughtful reader, believe the story is doing ("This is a story about a man who defines himself through his work, and about how financial uncertainty can tear a family apart").

9. Go on to note what you find most interesting, effective, promising, beautiful, etc., in the draft. It can be tempting to hurry through this, because it doesn't seem necessary to explain why something good is good. It can also be difficult to explain why something is effective. But while every writer would be happy to read the comment "Great dialogue!" that isn't particularly helpful for the author or the reader. What makes the dialogue effective? How could recognizing that help the author revise another scene where the dialogue isn't working as well? How could it help you, in your work?

10. Identify a few possibilities for further exploration, development, or an alternate approach. Remember: if you identify

something you feel is unclear or ineffective, you're obliged to make a suggestion. (You say a scene is sluggish? How would you energize it? You say a character feels stereotypical? How could the writer move past that conception?) If the draft seems to be in the very early stages, don't bombard the author with dozens of concerns. Choose a few. If an apparent problem is recurrent, you can make the point generally without flagging every instance.

11.   You may find yourself with questions you can't answer. That's perfectly fine. Other readers may have answers; or, perhaps even more profitably, the entire group may need to grapple with difficult questions.

The Discussion

At the outset, we need to keep in mind that to share work in progress is to make oneself vulnerable. Everyone in the room is trying to do something difficult. The workshop isn't a competition; we're trying to help each other. To do that, we'll work to create and sustain an atmosphere of respect and support for the writer and seriousness about the writing.

Offering respect and support is different from offering hollow or hyperbolic praise. False praise can actually be condescending, in that it suggests the writer isn't capable of hearing a more honest response. But recognizing the strengths of a piece of writing is as important as recognizing where it has room to grow.

1.   With all of that in mind, the discussion can begin by asking how the author prefers to make use of their time. Does he

want to begin by asking us questions? By hearing our initial impressions of the piece? What follows is what we do if the author says, "I want to hear what all of you thought, before I say anything." That's often a good idea. It can be hard to find readers sympathetic with the difficulty of creating an original piece of fiction who will take the time to carefully articulate their understanding of what you've written. And once you start explaining what you want the piece to do, or thought it was doing, you've lost the chance to hear some of those first impressions.

That said: in most workshops, each participant gets a limited number of opportunities to have work discussed, and some of those discussions can feel brief. So it can be helpful for the writer to tell the group, "I want to hear what you think, but I know the ending is a mess; it's just a placeholder. I can't really write the final scene until I figure out a few more things about these characters"; or "The women from Botswana speak to each other in Tswana, and I decided not to translate their dialogue; in addition to whatever else comes up, I'm interested in how that conveys the experience of the American businessmen." Now we can focus our attention.

2. The group should begin by simply describing the work. If the draft is complex or potentially unclear, a summary might be called for. The group can avoid wasting time by clarifying things at the outset. In any event, the description must move beyond the obvious (so not "This is a story about a man who has lost his job" but "Ultimately, all of these people are angry, or sad, or both; and while they share some of the same fears,

they all have reasons for being unable to confide in one another. While Henry thinks he is isolated in his despair, everyone in the family is hurt by what's happened—even the dog. The loss of his job has exposed deep rifts in this family.").

Be sure to identify the formal means of the work. These might include the story's organization, action (events, story, plot), primary characters, secondary characters, setting, imagery, point of view, and language (diction, syntax, sentence variety) among other things. Too often, fiction workshops focus on character and event to the exclusion of other decisions the writer has made, matters of strategy or presentation.

Not all aspects of craft are equally important in every story. It's our job to identify and focus our attention on the ones that seem most important to the particular piece and its goals. The fact that the town where a story is set isn't named may be a distraction in one story and of no great consequence in another; if we were discussing Shirley Jackson's "The Lottery," we might decide that ambiguity of setting, among many other ambiguities, is a crucial choice, one that helps determine the work's intention.

This opening part of the discussion should lead the group to some shared understanding of what the story wants to reveal, consider, or convey. Ideally, the majority of readers will describe something like what the author had in mind; but it isn't uncommon for different readers to have very different understandings of the work. This is good for the writer to know. While that can be frustrating, there are times when readers will receive the work in a way the writer hadn't anticipated but seems worth pursuing.

If the conversation doesn't begin by trying to recognize the work's intention, there's a great risk that the suggestions that follow will be suggestions for ways to make the story what each reader thinks the story should be.

In the event that readers have significantly misunderstood the work, this may be a time for the writer to intervene, so the group can focus on the cause of confusion.

3. Because Madison Smartt Bell is right—many discussions of drafts turn into fault-finding missions—the next step should be to identify passages, devices, and choices that seem most effective. Many workshops do this in a perfunctory way. There are several reasons for this. When we talk about what's working, we tend to identify details—a sentence, a line of dialogue or description, a character's gesture—rather than an aspect of the work. The tendency is to praise the sentence or line or description and then move on. But it is important to recognize general choices that are serving a story well—say, its modular structure, or its internal clock—even if that aspect of the story isn't working perfectly in every detail. Recognizing effective passages or choices can also be difficult because it's harder to explain why something that works works than it is to discuss why something that fails fails. You know your Honda Civic isn't working because when you turn the key the engine won't start. When your car is working well, you don't think about it. Somewhere, though, designers, engineers, and mechanics gave a lot of thought to making your car run well. As writers, when some part of a work in progress is working well, we should consider why. (And "working well" doesn't mean the same thing

for every story, any more than "running well" means the same for a lawn mower and a Porsche.)

4. Now we come to the point where far too many workshop discussions begin (and, in the worst cases, end): identifying passages, devices, or choices that seem at cross-purposes with the rest of the work, or not as fully realized, clear, detailed, or graceful as they need to be. Identifying those aspects of the work that are not functioning clearly or effectively or persuasively is absolutely useful, but it is only one of many parts of the conversation; and because it is the easiest part to indulge, we must be wary of allowing it to dominate, at the expense of our other responsibilities. When discussing a draft's shortcomings, contradictions, missed opportunities, etc., it's important to keep in mind that we aren't passing judgment on a final draft; our goal, always, is to be constructive.

There's a justified taboo in workshops about being "prescriptive." We have no business being prescriptive; the work belongs to the author. But we certainly can—and should—offer suggestions when we see opportunities for development. If several readers agree that a certain character, or scene, or decision in a story is troublesome, all of us—author included—might devote a few minutes to brainstorming solutions.

With that in mind, we can speculate about changes or additions—again, not to satisfy our own taste or preference, but in light of the work's purposes. If we remember that our job is to generate ideas, possibilities for the next draft, we won't prescribe but suggest. For ourselves, we can generate all sorts of possibilities from the story in front of us; for the writer and the group discussion, we should restrict our suggestions to those which seem most clearly related to the work's apparent goals, or the writer's stated interest.

5. The discussion ends with an opportunity for the writer to ask final questions, or to respond to the group's questions or suggestions. When your work is discussed, you shouldn't hesitate to make use of the chance to hear more from people who have read your work carefully; but you should feel no obligation to explain yourself, and if all has gone well there's no need to "defend" the work, as it hasn't been attacked.

That template is meant as a general guide, not a rigid form. In practice, a workshop conversation is likely to return to a discussion of the story's overall effects, one person's suggestion for an addition might remind someone else of what they think is working effectively, and so on.

Final Notes

Beware of the tendency to think of a workshop in terms of "your time"—when your writing is being discussed—and "their time." It's often easier to identify problems and opportunities in other people's drafts. Ideally, every day of preparation for workshop, and each group discussion, will serve the development of your fiction. The question to keep in mind, always, is "What can I learn from this draft?"

That isn't to imply that every draft is a jewel in the rough. Some drafts, we all know from experience, are a mess. Some trees in the forest need to die, fall, and rot, to nurture the others. But somewhere in the process of recognizing what the work is, considering what it could be, assessing what's effective, determining what isn't yet effective, and posing possibilities for its evolution, we should be able to learn something.

The ideal workshop is one where all of us leave the room eager to write.

APPENDIX B

Annotations, or, Reading like a Writer

One of the best ways to learn the craft of writing is to study the work you admire. The key is to truly study it, rather than simply admire it. (It's also possible to learn from work you don't admire, but when you have the choice, learning from the former is usually preferable.) To put it another way, the key is to read like a writer, not (merely) like a reader. To truly understand how a piece of writing works, or even how one small part of it works, it's important to articulate your observations and understanding precisely.

I had heard this general advice as a student, but it wasn't until I began teaching in the MFA Program for Writers at Warren Wilson College that I was introduced to the annotation as a defined form. There an annotation is a brief analysis of a piece of writing intended to help the writer learn about some aspect of craft. Annotations are meant to be practical, directly serving the development of your own work.

For years I had the job of explaining to students how to make the best use of annotations. Since then, I've introduced annotations to writers at every level. Writing good annotations efficiently takes practice. It's also useful to have the right tools for the job—in this case, a good understanding of the terms used by writers to discuss how fiction works. And it's often helpful to generate possible topics, and consider how they might be developed, before plunging in.

The close readings of stories and novels in the essays in this book illustrate the same sort of analysis. In some cases, a topic came to mind, and I went in search of useful examples; in other cases, some feature of a particular story or novel caught my attention, and I looked to see how other writers had used the same tool or technique differently.

This guide focuses on annotating fiction, but the same general approach can be applied to poetry, nonfiction, plays, screenplays, and songs.

Where to Start

1. Start with a craft topic suggested by the work, such as

    a. An element, technique, device, or choice obviously essential to the story (and throughout this list, "story" means short story, novella, novel, chapter, excerpt, etc.)

    b. An element, technique, device, or choice that is unusual in some way

    c. An element, technique, device, choice, or effect that is either puzzling or for some other reason interesting to you

or

2. Start with a craft topic suggested by your own work, and look to see how that element, technique, device, etc., is used in a story you've read. This can be

a. Something you've been working on in your own fiction or having trouble with

b. Something you've been hesitant to try but feel you should attempt

c. Something you've been using almost out of habit, to the point that you worry you've neglected to examine all its possibilities

d. Something that came up in a discussion of your fiction and seems important to pursue

or

3. Start with a craft topic suggested by a class or lecture or essay about writing (or even about something analogous to writing), and work to understand how the story you've read illustrates or demonstrates what the lecturer/author said.

For example:

1a. You've read John Updike's "A&P." You realize that one of the story's strengths is the way it is grounded in setting—not just in a grocery store but in an A&P near the beach as seen through the eyes of the teenage narrator. So you ask, "How does Updike use concrete detail to convey setting and atmosphere—and, simultaneously, to characterize the narrator?"

1b. You've read Sarah Shun-Lien Bynum's *Ms. Hempel Chronicles*. You notice that the stories move fluidly through past, present, and future, in no predictable pattern. You thought only Alice Munro did that. Focusing on one story, you ask, "What is the effect of Sarah Shun-Lien Bynum's manipulation of time in 'Yurt'? Specifically, why does it end with a memory, and what does that reveal about the present?" Or you ask, "How does Sarah Shun-Lien Bynum move so nimbly and unpredictably through time without confusing the reader? Specifically, how does she guide us with transitions, repetition, and temporal markers?" Or, "How does Sarah Shun-Lien Bynum use present action to lead her character to reconsider her past?"

1c.   You've read Yuri Herrera's *Signs Preceding the End of the World*. The novel contains words you've never seen before, words you can't find in any English or Spanish dictionary. At first this is annoying; but then you realize that you have a pretty good idea of what the words mean because of how they're used. You begin with a question: "What's the point of using words no reader knows?" Then you consider that the novel is about a woman crossing the border from Mexico into the United States, and the fact that, as a telephone operator in a small town, she also serves as a translator. Your question now becomes, "How does Herrera's use of neologisms put the reader in the position of one or more of his characters?" Or even, "How do Herrera's neologisms and use of invented place-names influence how we read his novel?"

2a.   You've written a story about a man who loves his wife and children, who is good at his work, volunteers at a literacy center, and is much admired by everyone, including your readers. In your story, a coworker gradually persuades the man to betray his wife and children, embezzle from his employer, and steal the wheelchair from his elderly neighbor. The problem: your readers don't believe that the good man on the first page has become the deeply flawed man on the final page. Happily, you've read Anton Chekhov's "Lady with a Pet Dog," a story about a married man who enjoys adulterous flings but who discovers true love when he meets Anna, the lady with the pet dog. You realize that one of the great challenges for that story is to persuade readers that Gurov, an apparent cynic, can in fact be moved by relatively naive Anna. So you ask, "How is Gurov's character established, and how does Chekhov persuade the reader that he is vulnerable to change?" Or you ask, "What are the significant steps in Gurov's transformation? Where do they occur?" Or, more specifically, "How is Gurov's transformation played out over each section of the story?" Or you ask, "How are narrative commentary and access to Gurov's thoughts combined to create our understanding of him?" (For an even more direct analogue, you might examine Chekhov's "Misfortune.")

2b. You've become oddly obsessed with the way you account for the passing of time. You feel you're constantly writing sentences that begin, "Later the same day…," "The very next morning…," "Wednesday of that same week…," etc. You ask yourself, "What other ways are there to account for the passage of time?" You search through a story you've read, looking for alternatives. While everyone tells you that "said" is "invisible" in passages of dialogue, you can see it in yours, and it bothers you. You wonder how other writers attribute dialogue—what verbs they use and where they place them. You also wonder what some of the options are for indicating the identity of a speaker without providing an attributive. You go back through a story you've read to see how the speakers of dialogue are identified.

3. You read an essay suggesting that interesting things can happen when characters tell stories. One of the books mentioned

is Helon Habila's *Travelers*, which is new to you. You read the novel and see that a lot of the characters tell stories, some of them quite long. You find two of them particularly engaging, and notice that they're conveyed very differently. You examine what makes each of them compelling, attending not only to content but also to how they are told.

4. You read something in one of the "Resources for Fiction Writers," or another book or essay on craft, that seems enlightening, insightful, provocative, surprising, and—the bottom line— potentially useful, and you look to see how that craft-related insight might be applied to a specific story to further your own understanding.

Once You Have the Topic and the Text

As should be clear by now, you don't necessarily need to focus on an entire story, chapter, or novel. In fact, one of the keys to this sort of examination is narrowing the field, both defining the topic precisely (so not "characterization," but "How Character X Is Made Convincingly Complex," or "How Secondary Characters Are Used to Reveal the Main Character") and focusing on one or a few representative passages. If, for instance, you're writing about depictions of setting, there's no need to look at every setting in a novel; look at one or two you feel are noteworthy, and look as closely as you can at what the writer has done.

Then: Read the story or novel passage at least three times. The first time, you're simply reading for content and first impressions. The second time, focus on those passages—words, phrases, sentences, paragraphs, scenes—that seem most directly relevant to your topic, and most likely to illuminate it. Your topic might require demonstrating progression or variety; if so, carefully select enough illustrative passages to demonstrate the progression or variety, without turning the annotation into an enormous list, or repeating yourself. In most cases, three or four passages will be sufficient; in some cases, one is sufficient (if, for example, you're examining how the terms of a story are established in its opening paragraph, or how plot, meaning, and character are resolved in its final paragraph). You might underline or highlight the most apparently useful passages, but it can be even more useful to write or type them out.

At this point you have a topic and relevant excerpts from the text. The next step is to analyze—to attempt to understand and explain—those passages. Keep in mind that an annotation can record the act of exploration, or the process of moving toward understanding. You don't need to assert knowledge you don't have; you should feel free to pose questions, so long as you try to answer them.

It may be easiest to think of analysis in terms of a few simple steps:

1. Describe what you see.

2. Explain the local effect of what you see.

3. Explain how that local effect serves one or more of the story's larger goals.

If the passage you're analyzing is difficult or complex, or if you're studying a small-scale aspect of craft (say, the long sentences in Mohsin Hamid's *Exit West*), it may be useful to devote much of your time to description (the diction, syntax, tone, placement, etc., of those sentences). If the local effect is fairly apparent, it may be more useful to spend most of your time considering how the author's choices serve the larger story. When in doubt, looking at less material carefully will usually be more beneficial than looking at a lot of material generally. Some excellent annotations have been written about single sentences.

That said, if your topic requires looking at the whole—if, for instance, you want to understand the structure of Jenny Erpenbeck's *Visitation*—the key is to focus on the defining aspects of that structure, and not to get distracted by plot summary, character development, and other issues. For a topic like that one, it might be helpful to begin with a list or outline.

If you're studying several passages, you're likely to note similarities and differences. When you do, consider a logical order for your examples (simplest to most complex? similar components to distinct variations?). A common mistake is to simply track an aspect of craft—say, description of setting—from the beginning of the story to the end, when a more illuminating organization would emphasize the most significant descriptions, or the changes in setting, or the story's repeated use of certain descriptive words or phrases.

Conclude with a paragraph explicitly discussing the immediate or potential relevance of the annotation to your own fiction.

Before you consider the annotation complete, read the story once more, both to see if you've overlooked anything and to make sure the conclusions you've drawn are clearly supported by the text.

Varieties of Annotations

None of this is meant to be restrictive; you might very well discover other effective approaches to generating topics and to composing annotations.

Annotations can range widely in tone and voice. They can be written in the third person, with formal diction, for a larger, unidentified audience of Interested Others, or in the first person, more conversationally, essentially for yourself (though it might be more helpful to imagine that you're trying to explain what you've found to a friend who is also a writer). The important thing is that they serve you, help you understand what you've read in ways that might serve your own writing.

On some occasions, it may be appropriate to write an annotation that is largely descriptive, or one that looks something like a list, or catalogue—say, a discussion of various types of surprise, from syntax to plot, in Flannery O'Connor's "Revelation." On other occasions, it may be appropriate for an annotation to be an argument. An "argument" in this context is (most often) not an attack against a certain choice or strategy in a particular story, but a reasoned defense of a thesis (for instance, "In *One Hundred Years of Solitude*, Gabriel García Márquez writes expository paragraphs that have the vividness and emotional impact of scenes," or "While David Malouf's *Remembering Babylon* inhabits the thoughts of many characters, ultimately it tells the reader a story that no one character fully understands"). If your annotations tend to be general, or superficial, or if you tend to make sweeping judgments, you may need to attempt to suspend judgment entirely and concentrate on looking at the text more closely, describing what you observe more precisely. If your annotations are merely descriptive, or if you simply ask questions, you may need to turn your questions into assertions, then work to support those assertions.

Usually, annotations focus on a single craft topic in a single short story, novella, or novel. Over time, you might find it helpful to write at greater length to compare a particular aspect of two or more stories.

Once you feel comfortable annotating work by other writers, you might try annotating one of your own stories, to help you become a more objective reader of your own drafts.

Common Problems

+ The craft topic isn't clearly stated or defined.
+ The craft focus isn't sufficiently narrow.
+ The craft focus is well chosen, but the annotation wanders from it.
+ The annotation doesn't investigate its stated topic in sufficient detail.
+ The annotation doesn't cite specific passages/examples from the text.
+ The annotation consists largely of plot summary.
+ The annotation is primarily about theme or meaning.
+ The annotation lists examples but doesn't provide analysis or comment.
+ The analysis isn't clearly expressed.
+ The annotation emphasizes opinion, or the passing of judgment, without sufficient supporting analysis.
+ The annotation isn't clearly organized.

It doesn't matter if other people already understand the thing that you're trying to understand. Your job is not to add to the world's collective knowledge, or to think of an annotation topic no one else has ever written about. Your sole responsibility is to add to your understanding of how to write a story, and to articulate your discovery.

A Very Limited Beginning of a List of Possible Annotation Topics

The best topics are the ones that you feel directly address issues for your own work and that are well illustrated by the text you've chosen. If you're not sure where to begin, though, here are some possibilities:

+ The effect of point of view

+ The use of interior monologue

+ Shifts between point-of-view characters

+ Shifts in narrative distance

+ The distinctions between the perspective of the narrative and the first-person narrator (or third-person point-of-view character)

+ Narrative intrusions

+ Dramatic irony

+ The balance of scene and exposition

+ The effects of active verbs

+ Diction

+ The effects of sentence structure / sentence rhythm

+ Effective repetition

+ Parallel structure

+ Tension and surprise in the syntax

+ Compression

+ The effects of sentence variety

- The intentional use of clichés
- Wordplay
- The effects of adjectives and adverbs
- Irregular punctuation
- The use of figurative speech
- The absence of figurative speech
- Modulation of tone
- The gradual revealing of character
- The influences of secondary characters on the main character
- The influence of minor characters on plot
- Counterpointed characters
- Consistent inconsistency and surprise in characters
- Multiple perspectives of the main character provided
- Intentional use of stereotype
- Variation on stereotype
- The effectiveness of character names
- Plot development
- Multiple plotlines, or braided structure
- Unresolved plotlines
- Effective variation on a familiar plot
- Foreshadowing
- Tension and suspense
- The control of mystery
- The controlled release of information

+ Effective use of short scenes
+ The use of space breaks
+ Omitted or reported scenes
+ Effective use of extended dialogue
+ The relationship between setting and character
+ Effective use of epiphany
+ Characterization through dialogue
+ Tension between the said and unsaid
+ Conflict conveyed by characters saying no
+ Jargon, slang, and technical vocabulary
+ The use of foreign words and phrases
+ Conveying foreign-ness in English dialogue
+ Descriptions of faces
+ Physical descriptions of characters
+ The creation of atmosphere
+ Description of setting
+ Description filtered through point-of-view character
+ Conflicting descriptions
+ Generic settings
+ Accumulating descriptions
+ Patterns of imagery

APPENDIX C

Resources for Fiction Writers

The books listed below—a small selection of what's available—range from introductory guides to handbooks to extended discussions of craft in the broadest sense.

Alison, Jane. *Meander, Spiral, Explode: Design and Pattern in Narrative.* New York: Catapult, 2019.

Barthelme, Donald. *Not Knowing: The Essays and Interviews.* Edited by Kim A. Herzinger. Berkeley, CA: Counterpoint, 2008.

Baxter, Charles. *The Art of Subtext: Beyond Plot.* Saint Paul: Graywolf, 2007.

Baxter, Charles. *Burning Down the House: Essays on Fiction.* Saint Paul: Graywolf, 2008.

Boswell, Robert. *The Half-Known World.* Saint Paul: Graywolf, 2008.

Brady, Catherine. *Story Logic and the Craft of Fiction.* London: Palgrave Macmillan, 2010.

Burroway, Janet. *Writing Fiction: A Guide to Narrative Craft.* Boston: Pearson, 2011.

Calvino, Italo. *Six Memos for the Next Millennium.* Translated by Geoffrey Brock. New York: HarperCollins, 2016.

Calvino, Italo. *Why Read the Classics?* Translated by Martin L. McLaughlin. Boston: Houghton Mifflin Harcourt, 2014.

Casey, Maud. *The Art of Mystery: The Search for Questions.* Saint Paul: Graywolf, 2018.

Castellani, Christopher. *The Art of Perspective: Who Tells the Story.* Saint Paul: Graywolf, 2016.

Chatman, Seymour. *Story and Discourse: Narrative Structure in Fiction and Film.* Ithaca, NY: Cornell University Press, 1980.

Dobyns, Stephen. *Best Words, Best Order: Essays on Poetry.* London: Palgrave Macmillan, 2003.

Dobyns, Stephen. *Next Word, Better Word: The Craft of Writing Poetry.* New York: St. Martin's Griffin, 2011.

Forster, E. M. *Aspects of the Novel.* Boston: Houghton Mifflin Harcourt, 1956.

Gardner, John. *The Art of Fiction: Notes on Craft for Young Writers.* New York: Vintage Books, 1991.

Glover, Douglas. *The Erotics of Restraint: Essays on Literary Form.* Windsor, Ontario: Biblioasis, 2019.

Jauss, David. *Alone with All That Could Happen: Rethinking Conventional Wisdom about the Craft of Fiction Writing.* Cincinnati: Writer's Digest Books, 2008.

Jauss, David. *On Writing Fiction: Rethinking Conventional Wisdom about the Craft.* Cincinnati: Writer's Digest Books, 2011.

Karlinsky, Simon, ed. *Anton Chekhov's Life and Thought: Selected Letters and Commentary.* Translated by Michael Henry Heim. Evanston, IL: Northwestern University Press, 1997.

Kundera, Milan. *The Art of the Novel.* Translated by Linda Asher. New York: HarperCollins, 2003.

Lerman, Liz, and John Borstel. *Liz Lerman's Critical Response Process: A Method for Getting Useful Feedback on Anything You Make, from Dance to Dessert.* Takoma Park, MD: Dance Exchange, 2003.

Livesey, Margot. *The Hidden Machinery: Essays on Writing.* Portland, OR: Tin House Books, 2017.

Lodge, David. *The Art of Fiction: Illustrated from Classic and Modern Texts*. London: Penguin Books, 1994.

Madden, David. *Revising Fiction: A Handbook for Writers*. New York: Barnes & Noble Books, 2002.

Morrison, Toni. *The Origin of Others*. Cambridge, MA: Harvard University Press, 2017.

Morrison, Toni. *Playing in the Dark: Whiteness and the Literary Imagination*. Cambridge, MA: Harvard University Press, 1993.

Morrison, Toni. *The Source of Self-Regard: Selected Essays, Speeches, and Meditations*. New York: Knopf, 2019.

Mura, David. *A Stranger's Journey: Race, Identity, and Narrative Craft in Writing*. Athens: University of Georgia Press, 2018.

Nabokov, Vladimir. *Lectures on Literature*. Edited by Fredson Bowers. New York: Harcourt, 1980.

Nabokov, Vladimir. *Lectures on Russian Literature*. Edited by Fredson Bowers. New York: Harcourt, 1981.

O'Connor, Flannery. *Mystery and Manners: Occasional Prose*. Edited by Sally and Robert Fitzgerald. New York: Farrar, Straus and Giroux, 1970.

O'Connor, Frank. *The Lonely Voice: A Study of the Short Story*. Brooklyn: Melville House, 2011.

Orner, Peter. *Am I Alone Here? Notes on Living to Read and Reading to Live*. New York: Catapult, 2016.

Prose, Francine. *Reading like a Writer: A Guide for People Who Love Books and for Those Who Want to Write Them*. New York: HarperPerennial, 2007.

Queneau, Raymond. *Exercises in Style*. Translated by Barbara Wright. New York: New Directions, 2013.

Salesses, Matthew. *Craft in the Real World: Rethinking Fiction Writing and Workshopping*. New York: Catapult, 2021.

Saunders, George. *A Swim in a Pond in the Rain: In Which Four Russians Give a Master Class on Writing, Reading, and Life*. New York: Random House, 2021.

Silber, Joan. *The Art of Time in Fiction: As Long as It Takes*. Saint Paul: Graywolf, 2009.

Spark, Debra. *And Then Something Happened: Essays on Fiction Writing*. Indianapolis: Engine Books, 2020.

Spark, Debra. *Curious Attractions: Essays on Fiction Writing*. Ann Arbor: University of Michigan Press, 2005.

Stone, Sarah, and Ron Nyren. *Deepening Fiction: A Practical Guide for Intermediate and Advanced Writers*. Boston: Pearson, 2004.

Turchi, Peter. *Maps of the Imagination: The Writer as Cartographer*. San Antonio: Trinity University Press, 2004.

Turchi, Peter. *A Muse and a Maze: Writing as Puzzle, Mystery, and Magic*. San Antonio: Trinity University Press, 2014.

Wolff, Virginia. *A Writer's Diary*. Edited by Leonard Woolf. New York: Harcourt, 2003.

Craft Essay Anthologies

Barrett, Andrea, and Peter Turchi, eds. *A Kite in the Wind: Fiction Writers on Their Craft*. San Antonio: Trinity University Press, 2011.

Baxter, Charles, and Peter Turchi, eds. *Bringing the Devil to His Knees: The Craft of Fiction and the Writing Life*. Ann Arbor: University of Michigan Press, 2001.

Gourevitch, Philip, ed. *The Paris Review Interviews, I*. New York: Picador, 2006.

Gourevitch, Philip, ed. *The Paris Review Interviews, II*. New York: Picador, 2007.

Gourevitch, Philip, ed. *The Paris Review Interviews, III*. New York: Picador, 2008.

Gourevitch, Philip, ed. *The Paris Review Interviews, IV*. New York: Picador, 2009.

Turchi, Peter, and Angela Barrett, eds. *The Story behind the Story: 26 Stories by Contemporary Writers and How They Work*. New York: W. W. Norton, 2004.

The Writer's Notebook: Craft Essays from Tin House. Portland, OR: Tin House Books, 2009.

The Writer's Notebook II: Craft Essays from Tin House. Portland, OR: Tin House Books, 2012.

Online

CRAFT, craftliterary.com

Fiction Writers Review, fictionwritersreview.com

BIBLIOGRAPHY

Akutagawa, Ryūnosuke. "In a Grove," translated by Takashi Kujima. *Rashōmon and Other Stories.* Tokyo: C. E. Tuttle, 1952.

Bell, Madison Smartt. *Narrative Design.* New York: W. W. Norton, 1997.

Castellani, Christopher. *The Art of Perspective.* Minneapolis: Graywolf, 2016.

Chakrabarti, Jai. "A Small Sacrifice for an Enormous Happiness." In *The Best American Short Stories 2017*, edited by Meg Wolitzer and Heidi Pitlor. Boston: Houghton Mifflin Harcourt, 2017.

Chekhov, Anton. Anton Chekhov to Lydia Avilova, March 19, 1892.

Chekhov, Anton. "A Doctor's Visit." In *The Lady with the Dog and Other Stories*, translated by Constance Garnett. New York: Ecco, 1984.

Chekhov, Anton. "The Lady with the Dog," translated by Ivy Litvinov. In *Anton Chekhov's Short Stories.* New York: W. W. Norton, 1979.

Chekhov, Anton. "Misery." In *The Schoolmistress and Other Stories*, translated by Constance Garnett. New York: Ecco, 1986.

Cusk, Rachel. *Outline.* London: Faber and Faber, 2014.

Dickens, Charles. *Bleak House.* London: Penguin Classics, 2003.

Doctorow, E. L. *The March.* New York: Random House, 2005.

Dubus, Andre. "The Intruder." In *Dancing after Hours.* New York: Vintage, 1996.

Eisenberg, Deborah. "Some Other, Better Otto." In *The Collected Stories of Deborah Eisenberg*. New York: Farrar, Straus and Giroux, 2010.

Ellison, Ralph. "Ralph Ellison: The Art of Fiction No. 8." Interview by Alfred Chester and Vilma Howard. *Paris Review*, no. 8 (Spring 1955).

Erpenbeck, Jenny. *Go, Went, Gone*. Translated by Susan Bernofsky. New York: New Directions, 2017.

Fitzgerald, F. Scott. *The Great Gatsby*. New York: Charles Scribner's Sons, 1925.

García Márquez, Gabriel. *One Hundred Years of Solitude*. Translated by Gregory Rabassa. New York: Harper & Row, 1970.

Guðnadóttir, Hildur. "Emmys: How 'Chernobyl' Composer Hildur Guðnadóttir Transformed Nuclear Power Plant Recordings into a Compelling Score." Interview by Jennifer Walden. *Sound and Picture*, August 26, 2019.

Guðnadóttir, Hildur. "*Joker* and *Chernobyl* Composer Hildur Guðnadóttir: 'I'm Treasure Hunting.'" Interview by Alex Godfrey. *Guardian*, December 13, 2019.

Habila, Helon. *Travelers*. New York: W. W. Norton, 2019.

Hall, Cece. *Making Waves*. Directed by Midge Costin. Ain't Heard Nothin' Yet Corp., 2019.

Hamid, Mohsin. *Exit West*. New York: Riverhead Books, 2017.

Hemingway, Ernest. "The Short Happy Life of Francis Macomber." In *The Snows of Kilimanjaro and Other Stories*. New York: Scribner's, 1927.

Hill, George Roy, dir. *Butch Cassidy and the Sundance Kid*. 1969; Los Angeles: 20th Century Fox, 2000.

Hoagland, Tony, and Kay Cosgrove. *The Art of Voice: Poetic Principles and Practice*. New York: W. W. Norton, 2019.

Homer. *The Odyssey*. Translated by Emily Wilson. New York: W. W. Norton, 2018.

Irving, John. *The World According to Garp*. New York: E. P. Dutton, 1978.

Jauss, David. "From Long Shots to X-Rays: Distance and Point of View in Fiction." In *On Writing Fiction: Rethinking Conventional Wisdom about the Craft*. Cincinnati: Writer's Digest Books, 2011.

Johnson, Adam. "Hurricanes Anonymous." *Fortune Smiles*. New York: Random House, 2015.

Levinson, Barry, dir. *Diner*. Beverly Hills: Metro-Goldwyn-Mayer, 1982.

Levitin, Daniel. "Behind the Monster Music: Why Some Tunes Scare Us." Interview by Ira Flatow. *Science Friday*, October 31, 2014.

Lincoln, Abraham. First debate with Stephen A. Douglas, at Ottawa, Illinois, August 21, 1858. mason.gmu.edu/~zschrag/hist120spring05 /lincoln_ottawa.htm.

Lincoln, Abraham. "The Gettysburg Address." Gettysburg, Pennsylvania, November 19, 1863.

Marías, Javier. *A Heart So White*. Translated by Margaret Jill Costa. New York: Vintage, 2013.

Minton Quigley, Jenny, ed. *Lolita in the Afterlife*. New York: Vintage, 2021.

Morrison, Toni. *A Mercy*. New York: Knopf, 2008.

Morrison, Toni. *Song of Solomon*. New York: Knopf, 1977.

Munro, Alice. "Royal Beatings." In *Who Do You Think You Are?* Toronto: Macmillan, 1978.

Nabokov, Vladimir. *Lolita*. Paris: Olympia, 1955.

O'Connor, Flannery. "The Nature and Aim of Fiction." In *Mystery and Manners*. New York: Farrar, Straus and Giroux, 1969.

Ogawa, Yoko. *The Memory Police*. Translated by Stephen Snyder. New York: Pantheon, 2019.

Peterson, Lisa, and Denis O'Hare. *An Iliad*. New York: Overlook, 2014.

Poe, Edgar Allan. "The Tell-Tale Heart." *Pioneer* 1, no. 1 (January 1843).

Porter, Katherine Anne. "The Jilting of Granny Weatherall." In *Flowering Judas and Other Stories*. New York: New American Library, 1972.

Porter, Katherine Anne. "Noon Wine." In *The Collected Stories of Katherine Anne Porter*. San Diego: Harcourt, 1965.

Powers, Richard. *The Overstory*. New York: W. W. Norton, 2018.

Price, S. L. "How Barry Levinson's *Diner* Changed Cinema, 30 Years Later." *Vanity Fair*, February 10, 2012.

Quirk, Tom. "The Flawed Greatness of *Huckleberry Finn*." *American Literary Realism* 45, no. 1 (Fall 2012): 38–48.

Richards, Keith. *According to the Rolling Stones*. Edited by Dora Loewenstein and Philip Dodd. San Francisco: Chronicle, 2003.

Safina, Carl. *Beyond Words: What Animals Think and Feel*. New York: Henry Holt, 2015.

Salesses, Matthew. *Craft in the Real World*. New York: Catapult, 2021.

Salinger, J. D. *The Catcher in the Rye*. New York: Little, Brown, 1951.

Salinger, J. D. "The Laughing Man." In *Nine Stories*. New York: Little, Brown, 1953.

Shepard, Jim. "Krakatau." In *Love and Hydrogen*. New York: Vintage, 2004.

Tokarczuk, Olga. *Drive Your Plow over the Bones of the Dead*. Translated by Antonia Lloyd-Jones. New York: Riverhead Books, 2019.

Tolman, Edward C. "Cognitive Maps in Rats and Men." *Psychological Review* 55, no. 4 (1948): 189–208.

Turner, Joe. "Cherry Red." By Pete Johnson and Joe Turner. Recorded December 11, 1973. Track 3 on *The Bosses: Count Basie and Joe Turner*. Pablo.

Twain, Mark. *The Adventures of Huckleberry Finn*. London: Chatto & Windus, 1884.

Twain, Mark. *The Art of Authorship: Literary Reminiscences, Methods of Work, and Advice to Young Beginners*. Edited by George Bainton. New York: D. Appleton, 1890.

Twain, Mark. *Roughing It*. Hartford: American Publishing Company, 1872.

Vanderhaeghe, Guy. "The Jimi Hendrix Experience." In *Ghost Writing: Haunted Tales by Contemporary Writers*, edited by Roger Weingarten. Chicago: Invisible Cities, 2000.

Voigt, Ellen Bryant. *The Flexible Lyric*. Athens: University of Georgia Press, 1999.

Washington Post Editors. "A Transcript of Donald Trump's Meeting with the Washington Post Editorial Board." *Washington Post*, December 2, 2021.

Whitehead, Colson. *The Underground Railroad*. New York: Doubleday, 2016.

Wills, Garry. *Lincoln at Gettysburg: The Words That Remade America*. New York: Simon & Schuster, 2007.

Wonder, Tommy, and Stephen Minch. "Getting the Mis out of Misdirection." *The Books of Wonder*, vol. 1, 9–34. Seattle: Hermetic Press, 1996.

ACKNOWLEDGMENTS

This book has its origins in conversations with students at the University of Houston and Arizona State University, and in lectures I initially prepared for residencies of the MFA Program for Writers at Warren Wilson College. All of those lectures were transformed for this book, in a few cases dramatically. Several appeared in somewhat different versions in *Fiction Writer's Review*; I'm indebted to Jeremy Chamberlin for both the opportunity and his gentle but clear-eyed editing. Thanks, too, to the Department of English at the University of Houston for funding, and to everyone at Trinity University Press.

I'm in debt to my colleagues and to the great many students who provoked discussion, listened to my earliest attempts to articulate these ideas, and made it evident when they couldn't tell what I was getting at. Special thanks to Debra Allbery, Charles Baxter, Jasmine Beach-Ferrara, Robert Boswell, Chris Castellani, Richard Schmidt, Ellen Bryant Voigt, and Ernie Wang.

Finally, thanks to Laura and Reed, for the endless support and for the music.

PETER TURCHI is the author of *Maps of the Imagination: The Writer as Cartographer* and *A Muse and a Maze: Writing as Puzzle, Mystery, and Magic*; a novel, *The Girls Next Door*; and a collection of stories, *Magician*. He is the coeditor, with Andrea Barrett, of *A Kite in the Wind: Fiction Writers on Their Craft* and *The Story behind the Story: 26 Stories by Contemporary Writers and How They Work* and, with Charles Baxter, *Bringing the Devil to His Knees: The Craft of Fiction and the Writing Life*. Turchi's stories have appeared in *Ploughshares*, *Story*, the *Alaska Quarterly Review*, *Puerto del Sol*, and the *Colorado Review*. He has received Washington College's Sophie Kerr Prize, an Illinois Arts Council Literary Award, North Carolina's Sir Walter Raleigh Award, and fellowships from the National Endowment for the Arts and the John Simon Guggenheim Memorial Foundation. He is a professor of creative writing at the University of Houston.